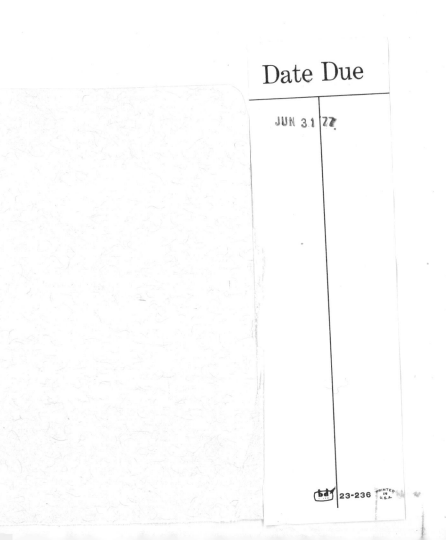

Date Due

JUN 31 77

23-236   PRINTED
IN
U.S.A.

OUT IN THE MIDDAY SUN

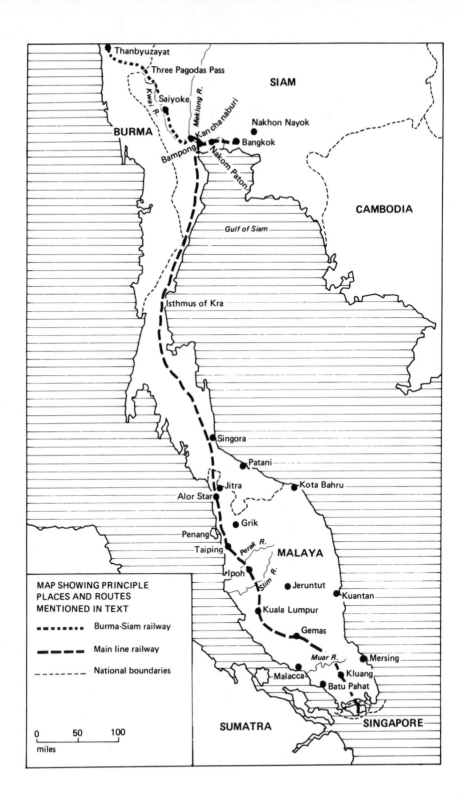

Thanbyuzayat

Three Pagodas Pass

SIAM

Saiyoke

Kwai R.

Meklong R.

BURMA

Kanchanaburi

Nakhon Nayok

Bampong

Bangkok

Nakom Paton

CAMBODIA

Gulf of Siam

Isthmus of Kra

Singora

Patani

Jitra

Kota Bahru

Alor Star

Grik

Penang

Perak R.

MALAYA

Taiping

Ipoh

Slim R.

Jeruntut

Kuantan

Kuala Lumpur

Gemas

Muar R.

Mersing

Malacca

Kluang

Batu Pahat

SUMATRA

SINGAPORE

MAP SHOWING PRINCIPLE
PLACES AND ROUTES
MENTIONED IN TEXT

••••••••• Burma-Siam railway

━ ━ ━ Main line railway

─ ─ ─ National boundaries

0   50   100

miles

Out in the Midday Sun

SINGAPORE 1941-45—THE END OF AN EMPIRE

KATE CAFFREY

STEIN AND DAY/*Publishers*/New York

First published in 1973
Copyright © 1973 Kate Caffrey Toller
Library of Congress Catalog Card No. 72-96478
All rights reserved
Printed in the United States of America
Stein and Day/Publishers/7 East 48 Street, New York, N.Y. 10017
ISBN 0-8128-1573-4

Mad dogs and Englishmen
Go out in the midday sun.
The Japanese don't care to . . .

SIR NÖEL COWARD, 1930

———

THIS BOOK IS OF COURSE FOR
C . J . B .

Contents

List of Maps

List of Illustrations

Acknowledgments

I am most grateful to the following publishers, agents, and authors for permission to quote from the books listed below in alphabetical order of authors:

AUDRIC, John: *Siam: Kingdom of the Saffron Robe,* Robert Hale and Company, London.

BARBER, Noel: *Sinister Twilight,* Collins, London.

BARCLAY, C. N.: *On Their Shoulders: British Generalship in the Lean Years 1939-1942,* Faber and Faber, London.

BATESON, Charles: *The War with Japan,* Ure Smith Publicity Limited, Sydney, Australia.

BRADDON, Russell: *The Naked Island,* The Bodley Head, London.

BURTON, Reginald: *The Road to Three Pagodas,* Macdonald and Company, London.

CAREW, Tim: *The Royal Norfolk Regiment,* Leo Cooper, London.

CHURCHILL, Winston S.: *History of the Second World War,* volumes II (*Their Finest Hour*), III (*The Grand Alliance*), IV (*The Hinge of Fate*), Cassell and Company, London, and Houghton Mifflin Company, Boston, USA.

COAST, John: *Railroad of Death,* John Coast, Esq.

COLLIER, Basil: *The War in the Far East,* William Heinemann Limited, London.

CONNELL, John: *Wavell: Supreme Commander,* Collins, London.

COWARD, Noël: *Present Indicative* and the song "Mad Dogs and Englishmen," Curtis Brown Limited, London, and Doubleday and Company Incorporated, New York, USA.

DE GUINGAND, Francis: *Generals at War,* David Higham Associates Limited, London.

GILCHRIST, Andrew: *Bangkok Top Secret,* Hutchinson, London, reprinted by permission of A. D. Peters and Company.

GORDON, Ernest: *Miracle on the River Kwai,* Collins, London.

HARRISON, Kenneth: *The Brave Japanese,* Angus and Robertson, London.

HOUGH, Richard: *The Hunting of Force Z,* Collins, London.

JAMES, David H.: *The Rise and Fall of the Japanese Empire,* George Allen and Unwin Limited, London.

LEASOR, James: *Singapore: The Battle that Changed the World,* Hodder and Stoughton, London, and Doubleday and Company Incorporated, New York, USA.

LEHMANN, John: *Armistice,* David Higham Associates Limited, London.

LORD, Walter: *Incredible Victory: The Battle of Midway,* Hamish Hamilton, London, and W. W. Norton, New York, USA.

MC CORMAC, Charles: *You'll Die in Singapore,* Robert Hale and Company, London.

MACKENZIE, Compton: *Eastern Epic,* Chatto and Windus Limited, London.

MASTERS, John: *The Road Past Mandalay,* Michael Joseph Limited, London.

MORRISON, Ian: *Malayan Postscript,* Faber and Faber, London, and Mrs Maria I. Morrison.

PEACOCK, Basil: *Prisoner on the Kwai,* Major Basil Peacock.

PETERS, G. W. N.: *The Bedfordshire and Hertfordshire Regiment,* Leo Cooper, London.

RUSSELL-ROBERTS, Lt. Col D. G.: *Spotlight on Singapore,* Lt. Col. Russell-Roberts.

SHIGEMITSU, Mamoru: *Japan and Her Destiny,* Hutchinson, London.

SPENCER CHAPMAN, F.: *The Jungle Is Neutral,* Mrs Faith Spencer Chapman and Chatto and Windus Limited, London.

SUTHERLAND, Douglas: *The Argyll and Sutherland Highlanders,* Leo Cooper, London.

SWINSON, Arthur: *Defeat in Malaya,* Ballantines Illustrated Books, Maidenhead, Berkshire.

TUCHMAN, Barbara W.: *The Zimmermann Telegram,* Constable, London, and Doubleday and Company Incorporated, New York, USA.

VAN DER POST, Laurens: *The Seed and the Sower,* The Hogarth Press, London, and William Morrow and Company Incorporated, New York, USA.

WINTON, John: *The Forgotten Fleet,* Michael Joseph Limited, London, reprinted by permission of A. D. Peters and Company.

It has proved impossible to trace the copyright-holders of the two poems "Jasper, Marble and Khaki Drill" by Reginald Levy, and "Poem after Victory" by John R. Townsend, published in the anthology *The Terrible Rain,* edited by Brian Gardner, published by Methuen and Company Limited, London. I acknowledge here my indebtedness to these two poems.

I am most grateful to the following people who supplied details concerning certain points: to Dr Alicia C. Percival for showing me family photographs and talking to me about her cousin, General Percival; to Mrs Doreen Shimeild of Potters Bar for the comment, passed on from her husband, about the prisoners who were Masons; to Mrs Helen Yexley of Winchmore Hill, formerly a WRNS officer, stationed in Colombo at the end of the war, for the facts about the news reels; to Patrick Anderson, Esq., Head of the English Department at Trent Park College of Education and formerly on the Staff of the University of Malaya, for checking my description of Singapore Island; and to Robert Druce, Esq., also of the English Department at Trent Park, for supplying the derivation of the word "doover."

I should like to thank Dr Stephen Doree of the History Department at Trent Park for reading my original manuscript and making many helpful suggestions, and Professor W. N. Medlicott, formerly Head of the History Department at my own University of Exeter, for reading the manuscript and taking so much trouble to help me in changing it from the original projected thesis into the commentary that it is now. Any faults it now has are my responsibility, not that of any people named here.

I am, of course, particularly indebted to C. J. Brereton, Esq., formerly of the 5th Battalion The Royal Norfolk Regiment, of the Officers' Battalion and H Force, whose information and assistance were essential, and who, in unwittingly prompting the writing of this commentary in the first place, caused me to find out not only the pleasures of historical research but also its therapeutic qualities. It is because I really do owe the existence of this book to him that I hope he will accept its dedication.

KATE CAFFREY
Trent Park College

When a battle is over, people talk a lot about
how the decisions were methodically reached, but actually
there's always a hell of a lot of groping around.

ADMIRAL FRANK JACK FLETCHER
United States Navy

Foreword

So far there has never been any official enquiry into the events in Malaya and Singapore of December 7, 1941 to February 15, 1942, that is to say that no Royal Commission of Enquiry was appointed,* either at the time or, as it turned out, subsequently. It appears unlikely that one will take place now, when so many of those in positions of high responsibility at the time are dead. One can therefore feel free to draw one's own conclusions from such accounts as can be found, working under none of the awe engendered by the existence of a generally accepted verdict. Since twenty-eight years to the day had passed between the first Japanese invasion of Malaya and the chance twist of conversation that prompted what is written here, starting from a point of ignorance so total as to be ludicrous, it seemed a propitious moment to try a fresh approach.

This commentary is based principally upon accounts by people who are not professional writers, and pays particular attention to the 5th Battalion The Royal Norfolk Regiment, as its initiation came from a former subaltern of that battalion. It is intended to examine the events leading to the fall of Singapore, and then to concentrate on what happened afterwards: to follow the fate of the prisoners of war, considering such questions as their accommodation, employment, activities, conditions of daily life, surroundings, linguistic development, discipline and matters of morale. I have so far failed to find an account that gives equal attention to both the campaign and its aftermath, and none, as far as I know, treats the fascinating question of language as a separate subject.

All opinions, comments, conditions of weather, and states of mind public or private, have documentary support. Unless directly quoting from one of the works consulted, the name Siam has been used for

---

* Winston S. Churchill, *The History of the Second World War*, London and New York, 1951, Vol. IV, *The Hinge of Fate*, p. 88.

Thailand throughout, principally because it was the term used by the majority of Britons at the time. (In January 1941 Churchill wanted to know why Siam was "buried under the name of Thailand." *) The American spelling of Pearl Harbor is used because it is an American possession.

* Churchill, *ibid.,* Vol. III, *The Grand Alliance,* p. 564.

PART ONE

THE LION GATE

CHAPTER I

Such Classic Ground

I

ON Wednesday January 28, 1819, Sir Stamford Raffles, accompanied by
the British Governor of Penang, Colonel Bannerman, landed on the
Island. Virtually unknown to the world at large, known to Raffles only
through his Malayan studies, and inhabited by only about a hundred
and fifty Malays and Chinese who made a modest, leisurely living from
the sea and the fertile but undeveloped land, the Island contained the
site of an ancient city whose ruins could still be seen. Quiet, green, and
undisturbed in the sun, yet within a week's sailing time of China, it
was noted as being easily accessible from Siam and at the focal point
of the Malayan Empire. Its rich potential delighted Raffles who had
been sent by the East India Company to pick a suitable site for a British
trading post that would successfully compete with the Dutch without
positively antagonising them. He wrote enthusiastically that he found
himself "in enjoyment of all the pleasure which a footing on such
classic ground must inspire." [1]

He lost no time in arranging a trading deal, signed by the Sultan
of Johore on Friday February 6 nine days after Raffles's arrival. By the
terms of this agreement Britain could build factories on the Island in
return for annual payments of five thousand dollars (Spanish) to the
Sultan and three thousand to the Temenggong, his subordinate local
chief. The arrangement paid off: within a year, Chinese-Malay immi-
gration had raised the population to ten thousand, and within five years,
when by a treaty with the Dutch Britain obtained possession of the Island
as a colony, the port was servicing well over thirty thousand tons of
shipping a year. In 1823 Raffles retired to England, and in 1825 he
bought a house in Mill Hill, where in 1826 he died the day before his
forty-fifth birthday, and was buried in Hendon churchyard, leaving
behind him a fascinating double legacy: the London Zoo, and the island
colony of Singapore whose name may be translated as The Lion Gate. [2]

The Lion House still stands in Regent's Park but Raffles's Lion Gate had a life span of one hundred and twenty-three years, two weeks, and four days from that first landing to the Sunday evening when it was formally handed over to the custody of a Japanese general. It is the step by step progress of that downfall that we are now about to chart.

2

Nobody noticed the first sign. In February 1904 the Japanese Admiral Togo made a perfectly calculated and prepared lightning attack on the Russian fleet at Port Arthur, disabling seven ships at the price of six lives and entirely reversing the balance of naval power in the Far East. The Port Arthur incident provides striking parallels with the assault at Pearl Harbor nearly thirty-eight years and two wars later.[3]

The next step was the Washington Conference of the winter of 1921-1922, which numbered among its achievements the naval treaty that established shipbuilding parity among the United States, Japan, and Britain, at the proposed ratio of five:three:five. Japan agreed to this provided that neither Britain nor the United States would build new bases or fortifications nearer Japan than Singapore and Hawaii, which with hindsight emerges as a sinister coupling. Signed on February 6, exactly one hundred and three years after the signing of Raffles's treaty, this arrangement suited the British Cabinet who on June 16, 1921, had decided to expand the military establishment of Singapore because of its advantageous geographical situation. By 1923 they had concluded that the existing port of Keppel Harbour was too exposed for the great naval base they planned to construct. A sheltered site, giving twenty-two square miles of deep sea anchorage on the Johore Strait, was selected. The harbour was to be defended by fixed guns and forts, a proposal made by the dashing Admiral Beatty which received general governmental approval.

However, two voices were raised against Beatty's suggestion. One was that of Lord Trenchard, the redoubtable head of the RAF, a deep-voiced man with piercing eyes under shaggy brows. In 1924 he had said that torpedo bombers should be used for the defence of Singapore, an idea that sounded outlandish to the navy-oriented statesmen of the time.[4] The other, even more farsighted and therefore all the more likely to be disregarded, was that of Admiral Sir Percy Scott, a small, tough, bearded gunnery expert who, as early as 1914, had held the startling opinion that submarines and aircraft would be better defensive weapons than battleships. Scott now wrote a number of letters to *The Times* pointing out that Singapore ought to be defended by a combination of submarines and aeroplanes.[5] Wedded to the concept of the Grand Fleet, a concept which in some quarters is still dying extremely hard, the Government adopted Beatty's suggestion and, after prolonged wrangling within successive administrations during which the defence programme was advanced and cut back, authorised the placement of the fifteen-inch guns facing the sea.[6] The systematic development of the naval base was not helped forward by the official view that no Far East fleet was really needed as a permanent fixture at Singapore, as the Island could be re-relieved whenever required by warships detached from the Mediterranean within seventy days. Ironically, it was to take exactly seventy days of fighting for Singapore to fall.

It is a cliché that military hierarchies tend to prepare with matchless efficiency for the last war and are likely to be fixed on one particular viewpoint. It was axiomatic that Britain, an island dependent upon the sea for its trade and safety, would regard the defence of any island in terms of sea power. The War Office and the Admiralty united in believing that Singapore could be attacked only from the sea and, happy in the knowledge that it lay three thousand miles from Japan, pinned their faith firmly to the forts, the fifteen-inch guns, and the new naval base, if the shifts of government would ever allow it to be completed. A few impressive, though isolated, demonstrations could not alter their iron purpose.

In 1928 the Staff College in India tried an interesting experiment in its annual war games, choosing the island of Salsette, north of Bombay, to simulate a Japanese attack on Singapore from the landward side. Salsette resembled Singapore closely enough in shape, size and terrain to make it a reasonable choice for this exercise but though the attack was highly successful the reports submitted about it were ignored. Every year from then on until 1939 a simulated land attack on Singapore was a war games exercise in three places: the Staff College at Quetta, the Imperial Defence College at Camberley, and the War College at Tokyo. In the first two places the maps supplied went right on dismissing the Malayan jungle as impenetrable and the lessons of the exercises went right on being disregarded. In the third place they were not. In order to justify the approved plans the British war games of 1935 included a pretence attack staged at Singapore itself using ships and aircraft. Its lack of success convinced the planners that no enemy carrier could come within a hundred miles of the Island without being

detected. This so elated the military authorities that the following year
they pulled out all the stops and organised a mass manoeuvre with a
hundred aircraft taking part. An anti-aircraft battery set up its single
gun outside the Raffles Hotel. Passing Europeans cast casual glances
at it as they hurried by on their way to the hotel cabaret, but Japanese
reporters crowded around to watch the whole operation and were rewarded by the officers of Malaya Command with outline drawings of
the naval base and its defences. This might have made the Chief Staff
Officer stop and think; only that spring he had been on the China coast
observing Japanese combined operations, and had noted that they were
using equipment far in advance of anything the British had at the time.
He suggested that the defence of Singapore imperatively required plenty
of modern aircraft, but by now the War Office was inured to tuning
itself out like a hearing-aid whenever anyone struck up this old and
irritating song. The Chief Staff Officer, appointed to Malaya only that
year, was a thin, delicate looking, bucktoothed Lieutenant-Colonel called
Arthur Ernest Percival.[7]

Percival's commander was Major-General W. G. S. Dobbie, a quiet
and thoughtful man who believed in the power of prayer even after
his experiences as GOC * Malaya, and in 1937 he was apparently dealt
the joker—the perfect card. He was asked to review the defences of
Malaya from the Japanese standpoint. Aided by clear, painstaking
reports from Percival, and reminded that the fleet would take seventy
days to get there, Dobbie concluded that it was possible for the Japanese
to land in Malaya during the northeast monsoon (October to March),
that such landings would be helped by bad visibility making air reconnaissance difficult, that the Japanese would first set up air bases in Siam,
and that the most likely landing places were Singora, Patani and Kota
Bahru. The following year he lobbed in another comment, that the
Malayan jungle was not impassable. He had mapped out a programme
that the Japanese were going to follow precisely, and the War Office
paid no attention either to that or to his accompanying requests for
reinforcements, apart from grudgingly sending along an extra sixty
thousand pounds which was spent on machine-gun emplacements on the
southern shore of the Island.[8]

All this time the construction of the naval base had been jolting
along in fits and starts, reclaiming eight million cubic feet of swamp
and excavating a further six million cubic feet in a levelling process that
changed the course of a river and created space for what in the end

* General Officer Commanding.

amounted to a small town. There were dry docks and graving docks, one of which could comfortably have held the *Queen Mary*. All of them were bordered by a spiky fringe of enormous cranes, including one that could lift a gun turret out in one piece. A floating dock big enough for sixty thousand people to stand in it had been towed all the way from England at a cost of a quarter of a million pounds, ten thousand pounds of which was the charge for passing the Suez Canal. There were underground stores, bombproof and specially ventilated, to be crammed with munitions of all kinds and enough food to victual the Royal Navy for three months, machine and repair shops, oil tanks that could hold a million gallons (enough to refuel every ship in the Royal Navy in one operation), living accommodation for thousands, some of it barrack blocks for the twelve thousand Asians who would work there, and provision for churches, cinemas, shops, and seventeen football fields.[9]

At the same time there were hundreds of Japanese throughout Malaya and Johore and on the Island, working as fishermen gaining a precise knowledge of the coasts, as village shopkeepers with a useful line in developing films, as barbers who indulged in ostensibly artless gossip, and as cycle repairers who knew where every bicycle in the neighbourhood was to be found. Going for picnics they amused themselves by timing and observing the aircraft coming in and out, particularly the Catalina flying boats, and they amused the European residents by watching the construction of troop fortifications, taking turns at a telescope. They liked making trips up-country to photograph game, becoming well acquainted with jungle tracks as they did so. Those who worked on Japanese-owned estates unobtrusively collected stockpiles of bricks, girders, and tree-trunks, and placed them, carefully concealed, near many of the two hundred and fifty bridges on the main trunk road running down the Malay Peninsula from the Siamese border to Singapore. None of the European civilians gave a thought to any of this; it did not occur to them to be suspicious.[10] No navy or army in the world was fit to be mentioned in the same breath as the British Army and the Royal Navy, and as for the air force, it was widely believed that slant-eyed people could never become efficient fliers. In any case, look at the mess the Japanese were making of the "China Incident."

This persistent underestimation of the Japanese achievement in China was one of the more serious mistakes made by the United States as well as by Britain. As the China Incident dragged on, it looked as though Japan had bitten off considerably more than she would ever be able to chew. Yet Japan had gained control of most of the Chinese coastline and the principal Chinese railways, had occupied the industrial coastal and riverside areas and all the main cities, and had compelled the Chinese to rely upon their two long overland routes, the so-called Red Road to Russia and the still partially incomplete Burma Road that was to cast a long shadow before the end. The Japanese had done a good deal of bombing and had also set up an alternative Chinese government that functioned fitfully but with more apparent calm than the factions that gathered around Chiang Kai-Shek, well known to the western powers, and Chou En-Lai, of whom no one outside China seemed to have heard. Certainly at this stage no one would have put his money on Chou En-Lai as the eventual winner.

But probably the biggest mistake the western powers made was forgetting, or overlooking, the fact that Japan had had over four years of combat experience in China, experience that neither American nor British forces had had. Western spokesmen habitually dismissed Japan as economically or diplomatically weak; either viewpoint led them to assume a parallel military inferiority. Oscillating between exaggerated fears of the Yellow Peril, with which they more or less impartially blanketed all the Oriental peoples, and the racial prejudice of pink against yellow which produced contempt, the westerners never reached anything approaching an accurate assessment of the Japanese potential. The most cordial treatment Japan received from outside during the nineteen-thirties came from Germany, and it was hardly to be supposed that Hitler, obsessed by his dreams of Aryan supremacy and racial purity, thought of Japan as anything more than a string of postcard islands inhabited by little yellow men whose hearts were in the right place and who, under suitable German guidance, might be trusted up to a point to keep all the other little yellow men quietly out of Germany's way in her triumphant march to world leadership. They would, the Germans thought, make good slave-masters when the time came.[11]

As far as all this went, the reactions of America and Britain were similar, though naturally America kept a steadier eye on the possible menace presented by Japan than Britain did. Right up to the outbreak of war in 1939, the British Government observed no sign of open Japanese hostility, resting comfortably on the fact that Japan was the natural preoccupation of the United States and that America could never sit back and watch a Japanese assault on any of the European settlements in the Far East without doing something about it.

Britain's attention was focused, first, last, and all the time, on

Germany. While the Government still made bold flourishes for the newspapers and the electorate about the sacredness of Empire, it realised well enough that Britain could not protect her interests and possessions in the Yellow Sea. The furthest place she could expect to defend if open conflict broke out between Britain and Japan would be Singapore. There were, of course, no official doubts whatsoever on this score. It appeared utterly unlikely that Japan would (or could) take on war commitments beyond China, and even if she did, it was quite fantastic to imagine her provocatively tweaking the lion's tail. Singapore, everyone knew, was an acknowledged fortress, situated as far from Japan as Southampton from New York, sea communications would be the easiest thing in the world to cut, and, after all, with Pearl Harbor conveniently placed as it was, the American fleet had only to sail out, find the Japanese fleet, such as it was, and sink it. To armchair strategists on both sides of the Atlantic (some of them in influential jobs) the idea of the Japanese fleet seemed as laughable as the idea of the Swiss Navy.

Amid thunders of newspaper applause the Naval Base was opened officially on February 15, 1938 and the illusion of Fortress Singapore was more strongly believed than ever. The Naval Base itself, and the whole Island, Raffles's Lion Gate, had precisely four years to go before the last hopes and illusions came tumbling down like the walls of Jericho.

3

The Island is predominantly green. All the books agree about that. But what is apparently impossible is to find out its exact dimensions. Nearly every writer mentions some figures, no two sets are the same. Its width varies from 28 to 13 miles, its length from 13 to 7. One book, the stately *Encyclopedia Britannica,* austerely opts for an area of 209.6. Is all this disparity a sign that still, after all that has happened, people are not really bothering? The simplest way, if the least original, is to say that the Island is a little bigger all round than the Isle of Wight * and somewhat the same shape, though considerably lower in contour. Several rivers cut into the Island's territory, and mangrove swamps divide the Island into three parts. The only steep coast is on the south-west, around the area of Pasir Panjang. Elsewhere the swampy coastline squelches

---

* For the benefit of the American reader, The Isle of Wight, about similar in size to Martha's Vineyard, lies just off the south coast of England. In shape it is not unlike Santa Rosa, off the California coast.

down to the blue sea scattered with little islands and, along the whole
north coast, to the Strait of Johore, bridged by the Causeway, eleven
hundred and fifty-five yards long and sixteen yards wide, carrying a
road, a railway, and water-pipes.

All agree that the Island is beautiful, in a mixed-up, picturesque
way. The Singapore River is crammed with sampans, the centre of
Singapore has some large Occidental buildings such as Robinson's store,
the Raffles Hotel, and the Cathedral, built—apparently out of icing
sugar—by the side of the smooth green spread of the cricket field,
known as the padang. Robinson's was always the European rendezvous
for coffee, and the hotel was cherished rather for its Somerset Maugham
associations than for the distinction of its décor. The crowded streets
of the centre, full of arcaded shops and houses in yellow or blue-white
stucco ornamented with red Chinese lettering, "grow wonderfully seedy
and dishevelled in decay." Further out, broad grass-lined avenues lead
past white government buildings to the genteel, immaculate suburbs,
brilliant, like the parks, with the tropical blooms of bougainvillea,
calla lilies and frangipani.[12]

The traffic policemen wear little wings, so that they are spared the
exertion of having to stand with arms outstretched in the heat, and the
taxi drivers have been succinctly described as "all Moslems so they are
not afraid to die." [13] Visitors notice the early mornings when the breeze
off the ocean crackles in the stiff palm trees, the refreshing early evenings when birds settle to sleep on the telephone wires, wing to wing
for miles; [14] they also notice the visual excitement of the place, the
travelogue conventions of washing hung on bamboo poles across narrow
streets, the bedlam of traffic scattering fowls and children and rickshaws, the pavements where fish dries amid incredible smells and clouds
of flies. The airless heat before the rainstorms that split the sky apart,
as Sir Noël Coward found, produces rain like a steel curtain, recognisable as rain only because "it couldn't possibly be anything else,"
then abruptly stopping to reveal a relaxing sea and an apologetic sky
of amazing freshness.[15] Mr Patrick Anderson compared the town with
a painting by Dufy, saying that the light is intense but frivolous, "which,
with the fierce materialism of commercial interests, reinforces the idea
that Singapore is a bulging, glittering purse, carelessly dangled from
the belt of Asia."

If the town is like a Dufy, says Mr Anderson, the rest of the
Island is like a Gauguin. Among the swamps and the coconut groves,
the rubber plantations and the patches of jungly scrub looking like

damp tufted wool, are areas of earth "scooped out into red laterite bluffs by Army engineers and left to erode miserably," and the two great reservoirs, which look like beautiful natural lakes.[16] Here and there are native villages, known as kampongs, and airfields scraped and drained (sometimes imperfectly) out of the swamp and the earth. Chopped out of the north coast to the east of the Causeway is the Naval Base, and, at the north-eastern tip of the Island, stand the great solid blocks of Changi Barracks, facing their vast asphalt Gun Park and their equally vast padang, and the somewhat Bastille-like mass of Changi Jail. On the south-east edge of the town is Keppel Harbour, the port of Singapore, surrounded by its customs sheds, fuel tanks, offices, stores, huge warehouses known locally as go-downs, all pervaded by the distinctive smell of Singapore, and swarming with crowds made up mainly of Tamil labourers.

Malaya itself is the southern part of the Malay Peninsula, the pear-drop shape swelling out from the slender stem of the Isthmus of Kra. About four hundred miles long from the Siamese frontier, in width it varies from fifty or sixty miles to two hundred or two hundred and fifty: again the books do not agree. It is largely composed of granite mountains that fall to the coastal plains out of which great limestone bluffs abruptly appear, and the coasts themselves consist of mangrove swamps and picturesque sandy beaches fringed with palms. The narrower and swampier east coast is less hospitable than the west, so it is the west side that has better roads, the main railway, and more people.

Three-quarters of Malaya is tropical forest. Scorched by the sun, drenched by the rain, the decay of growth is swift and so is the re-growth. The jungle, which at midday has the atmosphere of the Orchid House at Kew,[17] is a thick blend of vegetation on the grandest scale: enormous trees, clumps of bamboo, tall palms, huge ferns, tangling creepers some flowering and some growing like octopus tentacles as big as hawsers, banana trees with leaves six feet long, other tropical fruit including mangosteens, rambutans covered with red spines, jackfruit like prize marrows, coconuts. There are great drifts of orchids in all colours, soft mosses, clusters of giant fungi.

Most of the time the whole place is eerily silent except for the buzz of millions of insects. Across it spreads a network of streams and creeks, and another of paths and tracks, both making travel quite possible if one knows them. Journalists, bemused like all Europeans by the strangeness of this immense greenhouse, tended to make much of the wild life that they never saw, tossing out phrases like "crocodile-infested" and "man-eating," but the sad truth is that the most that was ever seen by newsmen and troops alike was an occasional glimpse of a peacock in a glade, a lizard on a tree, a few monkeys swinging or scampering across a path. Not a trace of the splendid leopard or elephant or tiger. And as for the other conventional idea of snakes in the greenery (or curled in the rafters or waiting for you in the bath), that proved to be equally without foundation.[18]

Apart from the tropical forest, there were rubber plantations that gave wide stretches of country the strong smell of latex and formed a dreary element in the scenery. It is interesting to know that Sir Compton Mackenzie considered rubber groves the most depressing form of vegetation and that, according to him, troops who had to spend much time among those hot, damp, dark and rigidly regular acres of trees often fell victim to a mild depressive illness they called rubberitis.[19] Mr S. J. Perelman's reaction on seeing a rubber plantation was that no one whose name was not Harvey Firestone could feel excited at the prospect of all those millions of future hot water bottles.[20] Few observers have a good word for the rubber trees that were imported into Malaya from Brazil by way of Kew Gardens in the last quarter of the nineteenth century.

There are also tin mines in Malaya, especially near Kuantan on the east coast; nearly half the tin in the world comes from there. The other notable marks of mankind to be found in the thirties were the scattered airfields which were to prove a particularly fatal element in the campaign, and the few large settlements created by the earlier Empire-builders who with true Victorian exuberance blended in their construction an unconquerable determination to recreate a mixture of Liverpool, Tunbridge Wells and Surbiton with a soaring capacity for imaginative flights that led them (for example) to make the railway station at Kuala Lumpur look like a demented mosque.[21]

The climate of Malaya is hot, humid, and enervating. For such a large area (about the size of England and Wales) the population is small, estimated in 1938 to number about five and a quarter million, of which over four million were Chinese and Malay and three-quarters of a million were Indian. There were fewer than thirty thousand Europeans and just on eight thousand Japanese. Singapore accounted for nearly six hundred thousand altogether, of whom eight thousand were Europeans. This meant that throughout the whole of Malaya one person in one hundred and seventy was European; in Singapore, the ratio was one in seventy. There had been peace in Malaya for over a century, the British having bought their way in instead of taking it by force of arms.

Perhaps it was this that influenced the British there to think of it as a territory that would never have to be fought over; it did not seem like an eastern Gibraltar. In any case, life for the British in Malaya was good: easy, protected, with plenty of jam today and (apparently) a large supply steadily rolling in for tomorrow. The rumours of wars were a long way off. No one was going to fight over Malaya. There was no fuss, no worry; small quantities of equipment kept coming in, nothing big or panic-making; the Naval Base was there, the fifteen-inch guns were there. Few people knew what Dobbie had said or that in February 1939 the Chiefs of Staff admitted that it was not possible to state definitely how soon "after Japanese intervention" a fleet could be sent to the Far East, nor what it would consist of when it got there.[22] What this cautious statement implies, whether deliberately or not, was that any fleet sent to the Far East would comprise whatever was left over from the Atlantic and the Mediterranean that could be scraped together and sent within the seventy days.

Brigadier C. N. Barclay comments on the fact that even after war had broken out in Europe the European residents of Malaya seemed to be mentally sitting in a corner with their eyes shut and their fingers in their ears, waiting for it to go away. Anyone who hinted at the possibility of war with Japan was called an alarmist. Anyone who suggested defence exercises which might mean a few minor inconveniences was deeply resented. The rubber plantations were sacred, so realistic training was out of the question. In cultivated areas, troops were told to keep to the roads, though in actual fighting conditions no enemy was going to be equally obliging. The building of defensive works and weapon ranges was objected to as damaging, troublesome and costly, and the employment of civilian labour for military purposes was resisted for an astoundingly long time. The pattern of life with its regular office hours, golf, cricket and racing, "bands on the club lawn" and what Brigadier Barclay charitably describes as "the somewhat petty social life" went on "with the Japanese at the gates." [23]

4

But they were not at the gates yet. Logically, Japan seemed the proper country to be the centre of power in Asia—at any rate to the Japanese, who pointed to their history and culture as the best in the Far East, and in the thirties they added economic pressure. The world depression had reduced foreign markets, nations had raised tariff barriers; Russia and China loomed more hostile; Germany and Italy were beginning to spread their conquests further. Japan saw a real need to extend Japanese influence and vital resources in trade and living space by diplomatic and military action: the Cabinet statement of August 11, 1936 spoke of the need "to advance and develop the Empire towards the South Seas." [24] On November 25, the German-Japanese Anti-Comintern Pact was signed and a week later the Tokyo Asahi newspaper warned shrewdly: "if Japan made an enemy out of England which holds much latent power in the Far East . . . England, France, America and Russia would cooperate." [25] Europe, however, was occupying England's attention just then and it was America that was jolted to attention first, seven months later, when the "China Incident" began.

All the conventional moves of the period were then made. The League of Nations formally declared Japan the aggressor; President Franklin Roosevelt proposed a conference in Brussels to mediate between China and Japan; Secretary of State Cordell Hull said that America was divided between her two traditional and conflicting viewpoints regarding foreign affairs: wanting to stay out and feeling she ought to go in. Meanwhile the China Incident dragged on and after a while the focus settled back on Germany.

At intervals the Government of Australia, who after all were a good deal closer to a possible Japanese threat than any other Allied powers and had become understandably jumpy, tried nervously to protest. The British Government met them with soothing words, hopefully repeating the old bromides about their Far Eastern strength and Japan's crippling commitments, in all of which they seemed able to believe in spite of certain individuals' recurring doubts. Indeed, many of the professional soldiers in India and Malaya felt (with some justification) that the pact signed between Stalin and Hitler in the summer of 1939 had alarmed the Japanese and taken the pressure off a little in the Far East.

In Singapore, the normal round of peace time Army life was easy and pleasant. One regimental HQ was at Tyersal Park, three miles from the town centre, and Captain (as he then was) Denis Russell-Roberts lived agreeably in the Goodwood Park Hotel opposite the Tanglin Club, which he would see in a very different light two and a half years later.[26] RAF Sergeant (as he then was) Charles McCormac said that life was particularly comfortable at Seletar, which had its own golf course and yacht club, a private swimming pool, and private taxis that cost about a pound for an all-day hire.[27]

The principal British civilian in Malaya was not only disinclined to dwell upon Japan's possible aggression but positively discouraged from doing so by the fantastic complexity of his job. Sir Thomas Shenton Whitelegge Thomas, GMCG, OBE, Governor of the Straits Settlements, presided over a governing body that might have to deal with ten others before any measure could be taken to affect Malaya as a whole. The eleven pieces into which Malaya was administratively divided varied greatly in size and in character. They ranged from the comparatively densely populated and westernized small area of Penang to the one hundred and sixty mile long and mostly undeveloped state of Trengganu which had no railway lines and only one main north–south road—the northern part surfaced but ferrying two rivers on its way to the capital, and the southern part poor, hardly more than a track in places, with lots of ferries and one spot where it crossed a beach passable only at low tide.[28]

Government officials' home leave was postponed on the outbreak of war and this meant that the normal tours of duty, four or five years, were extended to six or seven without a break by the time war came to the Far East.[29] Sir Shenton Thomas had been appointed in 1934 and was overdue for home leave. Son of a Cambridge vicar, he had now almost reached the retirement age. A thick-set, amiable man, he suffered from overheat and overweight and hoped vaguely that events in his locality would not prevent him from retiring comfortably as soon as he decently could.[30] He was going to be disappointed.

5

When the field gray tide of German troops and armour rolled across the Polish frontiers on September 1, 1939 and the second instalment of the Great War opened in Europe, official British opinion regarding the Far East as summed up by the First Lord of the Admiralty took the line that Australia and New Zealand were safe from invasion as long as the Royal Navy was undefeated and Singapore inviolate. This was a reassuring prediction as the world knew the Royal Navy was invincible, and Singapore could hold out all right, adequately garrisoned and supplied with six months' food and ammunition. Even if one allowed oneself a moment of cautious reflection it still appeared true that Singapore could hold out until the Italian fleet had been "liquidated" and the Mediterranean made safe.[31] (There must be no chance for a

Goeben * episode in this war as there had been in the other.) Japan, too, when all was said and done, would have to take on an impossible task if she wished to attack Singapore. She would have to send the invasion force, which could not include fewer than sixty thousand troops, over three thousand miles of ocean. Even if by some miracle they managed to reach the Island, there were the fifteen-inch guns, there was the garrison, there was the bristling fortress, reinforced that August by the Sikhs and the Argylls, and also a vastly superior fleet speeding to the relief. The besiegers' situation could only be seen, inevitably as death and taxes, as increasingly desolate.

Unfortunately, Mr Churchill's optimistic picture was based on two false assumptions: that there would be an adequate garrison on the Island, and that a relieving fleet would be so powerful that it could sweep effortlessly from the seas any hostile opposition that a foolhardy enemy might send out against it. The Admiralty's declared policy was that a fleet would be sent to Singapore when it totalled a minimum of seven capital ships and a carrier, ten cruisers, and a couple of dozen destroyers, and this could be assembled and ready, they said, by the early spring of 1942. They also said that a smaller fleet than this would be strategically unsound.[32] Whether or not they thought that a fleet of the size they proposed would be strong enough to deal with anything the Japanese could bring out against it they did not say.

The Chiefs of Staff in London meanwhile agreed that the minimum number of modern aircraft required for the defence of Malaya was three hundred and thirty-six.[33]

Throughout the changes of Japanese government during the late thirties and the variety of their approaches to the United States, Cordell Hull remained relatively unmoved: to him all Japanese statesmen were much the same and he was not prepared to make concessions favouring one above another.[34] The Japanese were divided among themselves too, their governments splitting between the moderates and the extremists and all of them splitting between the Army and Navy, between whom inter-service rivalry was intense. In June 1940 these disparate elements crystallized into a newly constituted government headed by the pliant Prince Konoye and including the militant General Tojo as Minister of War and the untried Yosuke Matsuoka as Foreign Minister. Matsuoka, described as "garrulous, unprincipled and conceited," believed that

---

* *Goeben* was the German battleship that was mistakenly allowed to escape into the Black Sea in World War I, forming a perpetual threat thereafter to the British fleet.

Germany and her satellite Italy would beat Britain. All Japan needed to do was sound friendly, thereby being rewarded with good conduct prizes in the Far East to the point where Japan could overshadow Australia and New Zealand and give India to the Russians to keep them happy.[35] There was some justification for his beliefs at this point as Germany was now at the height of her achievement: her victorious troops spread from the north of Norway to the Pyrenees, and Spain was sympathetic to her cause so there would be no trouble there. All that opposed her was Britain, that flippant, out-of-date power with not enough sense to know defeat when it stared her in the face.

The fall of France gave Japan a perfect opening to isolate China and make threatening noises at the British. On June 20, the Pétain Government agreed to let Japan make a "military mission" into Indo-China. By September Japan had completely overrun the province of Tonking. The border had been closed between China and Hong Kong, where the British had destroyed road and rail bridges and sent away women and children, and the Japanese had gathered about five thousand troops on the frontier line. Japan now had a big naval base seven hundred and fifty miles from Singapore and airfields within three hundred miles of the Malayan coast at Kota Bahru. One main prop of the British argument against the likelihood of Japanese attack was swept away.[36]

In Churchill's first message to Roosevelt as Prime Minister he said Britain looked to America to keep the Japanese quiet in the Pacific and that Roosevelt could use Singapore "in any way convenient," but in reply Roosevelt simply pointed to the imposing presence of the United States Fleet at Pearl Harbor.[37] America had already cut oil supplies to Japan, which helped to provoke the Japanese policy statement of July 27 which made three aims clear: to hold firm against American pressure, to prevent aid to China, and to wring vital materials out of the Dutch East Indies. This led to a stronger statement on September 4:

Japan's Sphere of Living for the construction of a Greater East Asia New Order will comprise: the former German islands under mandate, French Indo-China and Pacific Islands, Thailand, British Malaya, British Borneo, Dutch East Indies, Burma, Australia, New Zealand, India etc. with Japan, Manchuria and China as the backbone.[38]

In the American quarterly *Foreign Affairs* of July 1940 appeared a comment that looked prescient enough nineteen months later: "Suppose, for instance, that the British lose Singapore. This would all but wreck American conceptions of Pacific strategy . . . Singapore under friendly British rule is almost as important as Pearl Harbor." [39]

6

Japan got nowhere at all in her efforts to gain vital raw materials, and the Allied powers came more and more to accept the idea that she might be rash enough to try force. In August 1940 Churchill told the Prime Ministers of Australia and New Zealand that he did not think this would happen unless Germany successfully invaded Britain, but if Japan attacked, her first objective would probably be the Dutch East Indies. Singapore would of course be defended, and if attacked, which was unlikely, it "ought to stand a long siege." The Eastern Mediterranean Fleet was about to be reinforced and could at any time be sent through the Canal to the Indian Ocean "or to relieve Singapore"; Britain should base on Ceylon a battle cruiser and a fast aircraft carrier.[40] He told the Admiralty that if Japan declared war the *Hood* should be sent to Singapore with three eight-inch gun cruisers, two ships of the *Ramillies* class, and twelve long-radius destroyers.[41]

The warning note Churchill proposed at the Atlantic Charter Conference, telling Japan to stop or she would regret it, suited Roosevelt but horrified Cordell Hull, who watered it down into an orthodox statement that America would take all the necessary steps to safeguard American rights and interests. It was in August too that the Chiefs of Staff in London, who had said that a minimum of eighteen battalions would be needed for the defence of Malaya, said that Hong Kong was an outpost of "no vital importance" and warned against reinforcing it.

In September Japan signed the Tripartite Pact in which she agreed with Germany and Italy to assist one another against any attack including that by any power not as yet involved in the war. This dismayed many Japanese, including the Emperor and Admiral Yamamoto, who called Matsuoka's policy "outrageous" and said that Russia might "stab Japan in the back." The Emperor pointed out that in the war games postulating encounters between the Japanese and American fleets the Japanese always lost.[42] Churchill, still stressing the power of the Royal Navy, reminded General Ismay that the danger from Japan was no worse, an assault on Singapore was remote, Pearl Harbor was a deterrent and the Japanese were unlikely to gamble on anything so foolish. Singapore must be defended by a strong local garrison and the general potential of sea power, but the idea of trying to defend the Malay Peninsula "cannot be entertained": a single division could "make no impression upon such a task." He preferred the Australian Brigade to go to India rather than to Malaya because India was better for Middle East training and there was no need to keep the Seventh Australian Division out of the Middle East.[43] On September 15 he told the First Lord that he doubted whether Naval Intelligence was right about their Japanese figures—they usually exaggerated Japanese strength and efficiency.[44] By October he thought the Japanese danger seemed less: they had not attacked in the summer when Britain was weakest so it was unlikely now when Britain was obviously stronger and had not been invaded.[45]

After a quarter of a century these Minutes have an air of whistling in the dark. Of course at the time there was no way of knowing that events would develop as they did, tangling plans and priorities so that the whole Far Eastern question was pushed further and further down the list, below the invasion threat to Britain, the Battle of the Atlantic, the shifts of emphasis in the North African Desert campaign, the Mediterranean clashes, the build-up of supplies to Russia, and the distant goal, from which Churchill never for long averted his gaze, of the eventual liberation of Europe and, above all, of France. Compared with these needs clamouring for a share of the Allies' stretched resources, the far-off mutterings in the Orient frequently went unheard. Besides (they repeated it like an incantation), the Far East had the big guns, the vast Naval Base, the huge prestige, the powerful fortress in the sun. Who would dare attack it?

7

On October 4, 1940 Churchill asked Roosevelt if he would like to send an American naval squadron, the bigger the better, on a friendly visit to Singapore. It would be welcome, and the top brass concerned could discuss naval and military problems in Malaya and the Philippines and they might invite the Dutch to join in.[46] Nothing came of this. Towards the end of the month Churchill was still demurring about Australian and Indian troops for Malaya, preferring them to be sent to the Middle East where the need was positive. The Chiefs of Staff threw in a request for two hundred more aircraft and eight more battalions for Singapore and were told that Commonwealth commitments made both impossible.

About twenty-three airfields had now been completed in Malaya, fifteen of them grass surfaced, which was not the most suitable thing for rainy tropics, and the more northerly ones lacking camouflage so that they stood out vividly against the surrounding jungle when viewed from the air. The ground to air radio was out of date, limited in range and liable to break down with maddening frequency. There was not enough anti-aircraft fire power, and communication between airfields was shaky and inadequate.[47] A split had developed in inter-service relationships—this showed even in the situations of their HQ, miles apart on the Island—and each was quick to blame the other two. The RAF said Malaya could be invaded from the north; the Army said (officially) that it could not and that in any case the RAF had built the airfields where the Army could not properly defend them; the Navy said that the attack could only come from the sea. All three Services united only in execrating the civil administration, which thought the rubber plantations were sacred and was sticky about releasing civilian labour to work on military jobs.

In an attempt to heal the breach, a new Commander-in-Chief Far East was appointed in October: Air Chief Marshal Sir Robert Brooke-Popham, former Governor of Kenya, now sixty-two. A tall, lanky man with a tawny moustache, a high voice, and a bashful manner, he was noted as the first man to fire a gun from a plane—in 1913. The appointment was popular until it dawned on the press that it did not apply to the Navy. "Brookham" would be in charge of the Army and RAF only. The Navy still had its own C-in-C, and, what was more, it controlled the Intelligence Service. Brooke-Popham did the best he could by setting up his own HQ at the Naval Base, but this put him fifteen miles away from the other two HQ and exasperated [48] them even more.

Churchill was still saying hopefully that the Japanese Navy was unlikely to go far from its home bases while superior battle fleets lay at Singapore and Pearl Harbor, and the "strict defensive" was the Far East policy.[49] Then early in December he suddenly noticed that Japan was moving up on Saigon and other naval and air bases within much easier striking distance of Singapore and the Dutch East Indies and heard that Japan was preparing "five good divisions" for a possible overseas expeditionary force. Nothing in the Far East could deal with that if it developed.[50] He still maintained that it would "ruin the Mediterranean situation" to send a naval squadron to Singapore but promised to build up Middle East forces "in a fluid condition" to send east if need be. If Japan attacked, he was sure that the United States would come into the war and "put the naval boot very much on the other leg." [51] Singapore begged for more aircraft but he said that flying boats could not be spared "to be about idle there on the remote chance" of a Japanese attack.[52]

Meanwhile the Japanese sent a military mission to Germany to study the technique of war as shown by the world's specialists in this art. The Japanese took their goods where they found them, borrowing and assimilating ideas freely, such as the importance of the air arm, the effect of propaganda, the need to co-ordinate the Services and the blessings of mechanisation. They also used foreign equipment, putting British, Swiss and American parts into their aircraft and trying them out in tactical flights evolved from the Chinese experiences.[53]

The leader of this mission was a fifty-five year old doctor's son who liked gardening and fishing, a solidly built, highly strung, thoughtful and brilliant professional soldier called Tomoyuki Yamashita. He was a lieutenant-general and his staff considered him the finest in the army.[54] He was going to capture the Lion Gate in fourteen months' time.

8

The groundwork began on January 1, 1941, the year that would turn the hinge. An unpretentious wooden barrack block in Formosa, known as the Taiwan Army Research Section or Number 52 Unit, housed Colonel Tsuji, confident, pushing, and capable, and his ten assistants. They drew up reports from embassy staffs, agents and sympathisers, pestered specialists, studied diet and hygiene, sanitation and medical care, clothes, transport and communications, all in terms of Malaya and Singapore. They turned themselves into the most knowledgeable group on earth when it came to tropical jungle warfare, finding out all about marching in unaccustomed heat, preserving weapons and vehicles in wet forests and sea water, living off the country, making a sound psychological approach to victory and finally administering occupied territory. They came up with the conclusions that Singapore's back door was unguarded, that the RAF was far weaker than the papers made out, that the British Army in Malaya had a top strength of eighty thousand, and that each Japanese division engaged should take with it an engineer regiment to repair all or any of the two hundred and fifty bridges on the road from Siam to Singapore.[55]

In that same January (when Dr Philip Bloom in Singapore delivered the Russell-Roberts' baby daughter [56]), the question of Hong Kong came up again. Churchill went full stretch on this one, minuting bluntly that there was not the slightest chance of holding or relieving it and that it would be "most unwise" to increase the inevitable losses there. In fact, he said, the garrison ought to be reduced "to a symbolic scale." Japan would "think long" before declaring war on the British Empire, and whether there were six battalions at Hong Kong, or two, it would make no difference to the choice.[57] On St Valentine's Day Brooke-Popham said that Hong Kong could defend itself for four months, that Singapore could hold out even if Johore went (Johore?) and that the Japanese planes were inferior to the Buffalo.[58] Just how inferior it is hard to determine, for the Buffalo fighters were as inadequate as the Vindicators, whose wing fabric peeled off in dives and had to be repaired with hospital adhesive tape, according to the American Marines who flew them.[59]

In March, Matsuoka visited Berlin, where Ribbentrop told him that Russia, with a hundred and fifty German divisions to the west of their frontiers, would never dare to strike at Japan if Japan attacked Singapore as they ought to do.[60] Hitler himself reinforced this, saying that the seizure of Singapore would mean a decisive success affecting the entire conduct of war of the Tripartite powers. Ribbentrop also gave Matsuoka a hint about the coming attack on Russia, but it did not appear to sink in as on April 13 Matsuoka signed the Neutrality Pact with Russia, both sides pledging neutrality in case of war with either by others.[61]

By then the new General Officer Commanding Malaya had been appointed and given three days' notice to fly out to the Island. He was Lieutenant-General Arthur Ernest Percival, CB, DSO*, OBE, MC, formerly General Dobbie's Chief of Staff.

Of all the individual characters concerned in the Singapore campaign General Percival seems the most controversial, perhaps the most puzzling. Some observers found him colourless, good on paper but timid in practice, personally brave but lacking dynamic leadership. Some criticised him for going by the book and hesitating to take command decisions. Some said that he was not the sort of general the troops got to know, not the star quality kind that made legends like Mont-

gomery or Vian or Tedder. One look at his photograph makes it clear
that he was not the dashing type. He had the Percival face (it goes
back astonishingly unaltered through generations in family portraits),[62]
but in his case the face was tragic, somehow, its future defeat built in.
There can be no doubt that he was a kindly, considerate man, a man
of honour, one who would not ask others to do things he would not do
himself. Equally there can be no doubt that when he attended the big
reunions after the war he was warmly greeted by the men he had led
into captivity.[63] And considering the bed of nails he took over in
Malaya Command, it remains highly debatable whether Montgomery
or anyone else could have made the answer come out differently.

Percival's start in his new Command was not smooth. The flying
boat he was supposed to travel by broke down and it took five weeks
to repair it. On arrival in Malaya he found no military aircraft available for his use, so he made his tours of inspection in civilian planes.
He saw the badly sited airfields, showing up boldly, he saw that the
promised aircraft had not arrived, he saw that the defence works
Dobbie had proposed from Percival's own reports four years earlier
were still on paper. He also saw that there were no tanks from one end
of Malaya to the other.

The work that Colonel Tsuji's team was doing in Formosa was
part of the grand design. Japan might not have to strike, the moderates
hoped, but they agreed with the militants that everything had to be
ready in case. Japan should be able to move before the north-east monsoon and the winter gales broke over the Pacific, but it would be helpful if she could wait until winter began to spread its iron crust over
Russia. It would also be good if she could achieve all her objectives
before the Manchurian frontier felt the spring thaw.

The whole plan hinged completely upon supplies. It would be short-
sighted in the extreme to open a full scale conflict without making
sure of the vital materials—oil, tin, rubber—that South-East Asia contained in abundance. Working backwards from the oilfields of Sumatra
and Java, the plan called for defeat of the Americans in the Philippines
and of the British in Malaya in order to avoid flank attacks on a direct
push for the Dutch East Indies, and in order to win Malaya and the
Philippines the British and American fleets and air forces must be put
out of action. So the final design shaped itself into a complex but
logical sequence, further influenced by the need to go on fighting China
(which reduced the Japanese troops available for action elsewhere),
the necessity to take the oilfields undamaged which made surprise

essential, and the state of the weather which ruled the timing. The job was, therefore, in step by step order, to set up bases in Siam and Indo-China, to attack Malaya while knocking out the American fleet at Pearl Harbor, to deal with the British fleet if any, to occupy Malaya, the Philippines, Hong Kong, and the Dutch East Indies, and at last to take over Burma and the Andaman and Nicobar Islands.

The first of these steps had already been taken. The weather placed the next move at early December. It should take fifty days for the Philippines, a hundred for Malaya, a hundred and fifty for the Dutch East Indies.[64] If this splendid programme worked out it might well persuade the Western powers, already up to their necks in Europe and the Mediterranean, to recognise Japan as the leading nation of the East and not put themselves to the trouble and cost of laboriously reconquering remote territories scattered over a huge, unwieldy area and inhabited by Asiatics.[65] That would settle everything beautifully. The Japanese would have their living space, resources, and prestige, the Europeans would go away, and all would be well.

9

In Malaya everything went on as before. The stores bulged with food and medical supplies, drink flowed in the clubs, salmon and strawberries came in fresh every day, orchids and roses filled bowls in shady rooms, there was dancing every evening and the streets were brightly lit.[66] Captain Russell-Roberts moved with his Sikhs from Ipoh to Kuantan, where they made camp in a rubber plantation so they could not be seen from above. The Captain's bedroom had a tree growing through it, which was most attractive.[67]

In Hong Kong a new commander came in, Major-General C. M. Maltby, relieving Major-General A. E. Grasett who went back to his native Canada and persuaded the Canadian and British top brass to allow two more battalions to come to Hong Kong "to enable longer resistance." [68] Far East Air HQ received "accurate and illuminating" reports from Chunking on a Japanese Zero shot down over China, and pigeonholed them.[69] The American magazine *Life* carried an article showing how the Japanese could attack the fleet at Pearl Harbor and invade down the west coast of Malaya, and a CBS broadcast by Mr Cecil Brown warned the British against the ostrich attitude of their

citizens in that region. Later the British War Office withdrew his cre-
dentials, saying that his comments were bad for morale.[70]

A big detachment of Australian troops arrived in Singapore on
August 15, 1941, among them a young gunner named Russell Braddon,
who lost no time in noticing the gulf between the Army and the
Navy: "about such nautical matters as coming down a gangway, the
Army becomes deeply perplexed: but, given a lorry, it knows exactly
what to do." Overloaded with heavy clothes and equipment, the Australians filed ashore in the stifling heat and were driven to Neesoon
Barracks, where they arrived in a fierce downpour of lukewarm rain.
In the morning their greatcoats were replaced by "slickers," crescent-
shaped waterproofs that let in all the rain and kept them sweating like
pigs: "a completely useless garment." They were also warned about the
risks of contacting hookworm and tinea, and were issued with sheets,
this last such an unusual thing that the officer in charge was known as
"What, sheets for the gunners" for the remainder of his career. A week
later they went up to Tampin near Malacca, a hundred and fifty miles
away, and began training. They had "cool, airy, wooden huts" to
live in, and liked that, but made the unpleasant discovery that the owners of the rubber plantations levied a fine of five pounds for damage to
any of their trees.[71]

One detail is worth recording as incongruous in the extreme. The
British residents in Malaya and Singapore had always been great sup-
porters of the Empire; to them it was logical for the map of the world
to show its big splashes of red: there ought to be even more of them.
The Empire was splendid, linked in its brotherhood. The sun never set
on it, it put to shame the second-class Europeans and even more the
renegade colonials, particularly the United States. Many of these residents had a plainly hostile attitude towards America, the classic stand
of critical disapproval mixed with envy of the rebel son who had not
only dared to cut the umbilical cord and go off on his own but who
had made good and now was making a spectacle of himself swaggering
about the place and whistling cheerfully because he could come home
and buy half the street. America didn't know its place. But the Empire,
ah, that was a different matter.

And when the Australian troops spilled out into Singapore the
British residents cut them dead. They looked down their noses at the
boys from down under, or ignored them completely. They had them
turned away from their clubs and so drove them to the only restaurants
that would serve them, which were on Lavender Street, the local red

light district. Much later, when the fortunes of war had altered everything, they said in a pained way that it had been hard to get together
when the Australians were always hanging about in the houses of ill
fame.[72]

Another arrival in Singapore that month was the new Chief Engineer, Brigadier Ivan Simson, a good-looking, forceful professional aged
fifty-two. He had not been driven to Lavender Street but went practically
everywhere else, on fact-finding expeditions all over Malaya that totalled six thousand miles. The facts he found were what Percival had
found: the lack of defences, the blithe unawareness, the happy apathy.
He was very much shocked and angry, which had consequences in the
coming months.[73]

That month, too, Captain David James, who had lived in Japan and
who spoke Japanese, and who was now sixty, went to Sarawak to look
at the military situation there. He reacted very much as Simson did, and
got into trouble for it.[74]

No one connected these events at the time specifically with the Atlantic Charter conference which was then taking place. Churchill met
Roosevelt at Placentia Bay in Newfoundland and photographs were
taken showing the two of them at the morning service on the crowded
ship's quarterdeck, joining in the hymn "For those in peril on the sea."
But there was a link for all that. The ship was the *Prince of Wales*.[75]

10

September: the war was two years old, yet its shadow had not obviously fallen across Malaya. One isolated voice spoke, that of a British
businessman called Becker who said that if it came to the crunch Siam
would side with the Japanese. No one listened. He went right on saying it, everyone went on not listening, until eventually some of his drift
penetrated to his seniors, who reprimanded him and arranged for his
recall to England. He was thus spared from taking part in the events
he had partially foretold. In time he became a captain in the British
Intelligence Corps, particularly consulted (ironically enough) on Siamese affairs.[76]

Percival worriedly counted his forces. He had thirty-one battalions
in three divisions, two reserve brigade groups, two fortress brigades
and a detached battalion; he asked altogether for forty-eight battalions
in five divisions, one independent brigade and two detached battalions.

While waiting for London's reply, he worked out his strategy for the forces that he had. The Island must have its garrison. He planned for one division to defend southern Malaya and provided for a smallish reserve force. That left a corps of two divisions to meet any attack on the north Malayan frontier. The corps commander, Lieutenant-General Sir Lewis Heath, would have to break up one division to defend the scattered airfields and use his other division to bar the main route to the south. The best places for the Japanese to land would be Singora and Patani, the best place to stop them would be on the Patani road at a good defensive position called The Ledge. The trouble was that The Ledge was over the frontier in Siam, and everybody had been warned not to violate Siamese neutrality. A plan was drawn up, none the less, under the code name Matador, which was to be used if possible; if not, Heath's men would have to stand at Jitra, protecting the airfield of Alor Star.[77]

Another report from Chungking came in on another shot down Zero, and this was pigeonholed as the first had been.[78] Grasett wrung an agreement from Canada to send two battalions to Hong Kong (the official history calls the deterrent potential of two battalions "an egregious absurdity"), and the choice fell on the Royal Rifles of Canada and the Winnipeg Grenadiers, both of which had been on garrison duty and had no tactical training.

Meanwhile, the Japanese went on systematically with their own preparations. Their consulate in Honolulu was asked for periodic reports on American warships at Pearl Harbor, which the planners in Tokyo had divided into five sections for easy reference. They particularly wanted to know whenever two or more tied up at the same wharf. Five days later, on September 29, they set up codes for all this, which put the early stages of their attack project into gear. By October 20 the whole thing was worked out in detail and agreed.[79]

That was four days after Tojo became Prime Minister, retaining at the same time the post of Minister of War. He had been needling away all along that the talks with the United States should stop and the war should start. Now, with the programme set and the starting date fixed for early December, it was of course more sensible to keep the talks going, however deadlocked they became, so that America would suspect nothing. Admiral Nomura was doing the Japanese talking in Washington: they liked him there, but draft and counter-draft came and went and no agreement seemed in sight. Japan, like Percival, had assessed the available forces. After allowing for home defence and the fighting in China, Manchuria, and Korea, the Japanese could use what was left: eleven Army divisions, a strong carrier fleet, a couple of dozen long-range submarines, five hundred Navy aircraft and seven hundred Army aircraft. It did not look all that much to take on two big powers.

If the Japanese High Command spoke on October 20, so did the Admiralty in London. For weeks now they had been arguing with Churchill about the composition of the Far East fleet. Churchill wanted to send at least one modern battleship, and he was backed up in this view by his Foreign Secretary, Mr Anthony Eden as he then was. The Admiralty, on the other hand, preferred to keep the more modern ships to take on the Germans rather than the Japanese. However Churchill rejected as "unsound" their opinion that the speed of one of these ships was "inadequate to run down a Japanese eight-inch gun cruiser." In the end the Admiralty gave in and agreed to send the *Prince of Wales,* the *Repulse,* and the carrier *Indomitable* to Singapore. The first two were to go to Cape Town where the carrier would join them. The Commander-in-Chief of this fleet was, as expected, Acting Admiral Sir Tom Phillips, then fifty-three, a small, irascible man with a pale, set face, sharp eyes, and a strong will, whose hobby was repairing watches and who was reputed to have great obstinacy and no sense of humour. Phillips wasted no time, travelling up to Glasgow by train and taking command on October 25, when he hoisted his flag on the *Prince of Wales* and sailed down the Clyde, escorted by the destroyers *Electra* and *Express,* in chilly, drizzling weather just as the day grew dark.

As soon as the composition of the Far East fleet was announced, protests poured in from the various commanders in the Home Fleet at the folly of removing the *Prince of Wales* from the area while the enemy battleships *Tirpitz, Admiral Scheer, Scharnhorst* and *Gneisenau* still had to be dealt with. These protests made no difference to the course of events, but a core of bitterness remained which those events did little to remove. Even non-naval men were stirred to demur: Captain (now Sir) Andrew Gilchrist considered the project "a hazardous political gimmick rather than a considered warlike opinion." There was, of course, a particularly hard mishap to come: the *Indomitable* ran aground on a sandbank in the West Indies while working-up, when Phillips was nine days out of the Clyde, and the damage would delay her too long for the rendezvous at the Cape. The rest of the fleet, known as Force Z, had to go on without the carrier. No one at this stage seems to have realised quite how vital the carriers were to be.[80]

Two other sets of people sailed that month, both on October 27: the 53rd Brigade, of which more later, and the 5th Bedfordshires. The Bedfordshires sailed with the 4th Norfolks on the SS *Reina del Pacifico* for the Middle East—at least, that was their ultimate destination as far as they knew. They headed out across the Atlantic where on November 4 the United States Navy took over escort duty, and at Halifax they transferred to the USS *West Point* on which they sailed for the Cape. The regimental transport had gone on another ship and they never saw it again.[81] They were part of an Army group known as the 18th Division, and they were not going to end up in North Africa.

II

Unlike investigations into other episodes of the Second World War, a feeling of almost preordained doom associates itself with the Singapore campaign. The person who comes to it fresh, with many years intervening between the event itself and the present day, finds a disquieting atmosphere of fatality emanating from the available books and reports, and, what is perhaps worse, a kind of symbolic writing-off, once the disaster had taken place, as though that was that, it could not now be helped, and the less said the better.

The story of the action leading to the fall of Singapore on February 15, 1942 is practically a classic of misunderstanding, error and default on the one side and, on the other, opportunism so brilliant that its beneficiaries themselves were stunned by it. Over and above the deeply felt disappointment of the British military authorities, the appalled realisation that a vital base was lost and that Australia would now be aware of the Yellow Peril breathing down her neck as never before, was the shocking humiliation of knowing the whole world, and in particular those parts of it Whitehall still obstinately regarded as the "lesser breeds without the Law," had been able to witness the complete débâcle. Possibly this is the key to why so many chroniclers have treated the aftermath of the surrender as something to be swept hastily under the carpet.

On many occasions in many wars it has been found that a specific danger has been present for years, has been clearly identified and recognised, and has been left neglected until a bold adversary has seized his moment and done exactly what has been warned of for so long. In 1913, American Secretary of the Navy Josephus Daniels complained that "his admirals 'sat up nights thinking how Japan was planning to make war

on America and steal a march on us by taking the Philippine Islands
and going on to Hawaii.' As this was a blueprint of Pearl Harbor
twenty-eight years in advance, these admirals of an earlier generation
at least were wide awake." [82]

People were not wide awake in November 1941: American Admiral
Ernest J. King was quoted then as saying that "an unwarranted feeling
of immunity from attack" seemed to have "pervaded all ranks at Pearl
Harbor, both Army and Navy." [83] He could have said the same of
Singapore, which was "stiff with troops," tested its sirens punctually
every Saturday morning, looked into the sky and saw planes flying con-
fidently in the blue, and observed at night the big arcs of the searchlights sweeping over the water. There were more troops coming, people
said; everything was just as it should be. There were always a few
doubters, but nobody paid any attention to them.[84]

There certainly were troops coming. On November 2 the Chief of
the Japanese General Staff received three men who had reported for
briefing. Their jobs were impressive. Lieutenant-General Homma would
attack the Philippines, Lieutenant-General Imamura would attack the
Dutch East Indies, and Lieutenant-General Yamashita would attack
Malaya and Singapore. He was offered five divisions to do it with. He
replied calmly: "No—four will be enough." [85]

CHAPTER II

Outbreak

I

ONE of the most sacrosanct places in Japan is the Imperial Shrine at Ise, which contains the three Sacred Treasures: the Mirror, the Jewel, the Sword. It is possible to look at the war which Japan now recklessly began in terms of these treasures: the mirror in which they saw their greatness reflected, the jewel of the prize, the sword with which they intended to carve it out and defend it against all comers. Described, accurately, as "an obedient nation of heroes," well trained, indoctrinated, backed by ably planned offensives and led by admirably competent executives, they set in motion the actions that truly made it a world war.[1] It is interesting that the Imperial Shrine is the headquarters of the Kamikaze—the Divine Wind belief.

The opening move started on November 26 at Tankan Bay in the Kurile Islands, where a few fishermen's huts and a tiny radio station alongside the small concrete pier witnessed, through the sea-mist, the departure of the attack fleet. Three submarines led off. Two hundred miles behind them came a light cruiser leading nine destroyers. Then the Striking Force itself, Vice-Admiral Chuichi Nagumo's twenty-eight ships, stole out into the fog, got into formation, and headed off at the dignified speed of thirteen knots.[2] The destroyers had names like *Valley Wind* and *Mist of Flowers;* the big carriers were called *Red Castle, Increased Joy, Green Dragon* and *Flying Dragon, Happy Crane* and *Soaring Crane.*[3] Between them they carried four hundred and fifty aircraft whose pilots averaged eight hundred hours.

These aircraft were to spring the trap on the American Fleet at Pearl Harbor. Admiral Nagumo had doubts about the success of his mission; he hoped for an order that would force him to turn back,[4] but instead, on Tuesday, December 2, came the code message "Climb Mount Niitaka." This meant Go ahead as planned: Pearl Harbor was to be attacked early on Sunday morning, a choice dictated by the reports

of Japanese agents that American battleships always stayed in harbour
on Sundays. On the Saturday evening Nagumo hoisted on his flagship,
the *Red Castle (Akagi)*, the flag flown at Tsushima by Admiral Togo
(it was historically very fitting), and ordered course south towards
Oahu as the sun went down and the sea swelled higher. At the same
time other groups of Japanese transports were approaching their individual target areas, notably sixteen off Singora and Patani in the Gulf
of Siam, three off Kota Bahru to the south, and seven others beyond
Singora to the north.[5] General Dobbie had been perfectly right.

2

On Sunday November 16 the Japanese Consul-General, Ken Tsurumi,
went down to Keppel Harbour to see the Japanese liner *Asama Maru*
leave Singapore. On board were about four hundred and fifty Japanese
men, women and children from all parts of Malaya—fishermen, geisha
girls, barbers, iron and tin miners, planters, bankers, businessmen and
consular officials. Only ninety of these were travelling first class. They
left behind at least two thousand Japanese in the eleven states, but it
was still a significant exodus and somebody ought to have remarked
on it.[6] On the same day the clipper from Manila brought in two American Brigadier-Generals, Robert L. Maxwell and Raymond A. Wheeler,
to confer with Brooke-Popham, while up in Hong Kong the two Canadian battalions landed, with neither carriers nor lorries, bringing the
total garrison strength to twelve thousand men, five old planes, a destroyer, eight motor torpedo boats and "a few old gunboats."[7] In Cape
Town the *Prince of Wales* arrived to find a plane waiting to fly Admiral Phillips up to Pretoria to confer with Field-Marshal Smuts.[8]

Two days later the *Prince of Wales* sailed again, and Smuts sent
his opinion to Churchill. It was uncompromising. The sagacious old
soldier thought it foolish to divide British and American sea power
between Singapore and Hawaii, saying that the two fleets separately
were inferior to the Japanese Navy, and warning Churchill that if the
Japanese were "really nippy" (a nice pun under the circumstances) they
would be able to give the Allies "a first-class disaster."[9] On the same
day, in Kuala Lumpur, Sir Shenton Thomas, speaking at a budget meeting of the Federal Council, said that Malaya had become very strong
and that the Mother Country, by which he meant England, had also

become very strong and had promised all the help Malaya would need in time of war.[10]

The troops stationed in Malaya were enjoying themselves quite well on the whole. There was plenty of sport, the men were "magnificently healthy," and, partly because of this and partly through their innate irreverence for military spit and polish, much of what they had to do seemed a huge joke. There were surprise visits from the top brass, for which a routine had been worked out that was worthy of St Trinian's: the usual "scruffy guard" would be signalled to disappear, his place being swiftly taken by a "Special Glittering Guard" who stood by for such emergencies. One day Brooke-Popham himself came up to inspect Mr Braddon's camp at Tampin. Going along the lines, he asked the men what they had done in civilian life; he was met by a tissue of un-blushing lies as a solicitor said he had been a plumber, a carpenter said he had trained choir boys (and gave Brooke-Popham "a very lewd look"), "a hardened journalist" said, fluttering his eyelashes, that he had been a ballet dancer, and Mr Braddon himself said "mortician" (which Brooke-Popham, poor chap, said was "very interesting"). Apart from the visits, and the sports, and the drill, the troops saw films, went taxi-dancing, and made friends with the swarms of Malay children who followed them about, cadged their cigarettes, offered them their sisters, and called every Australian they met "Joe."

The troops knew perfectly well that the local population, who did all kinds of chores for them and came to the camps as traders, could see for themselves what equipment they had, could count them on pa-rade, check their ration figures when delivering the vegetables, count them by their laundry or by looking at the vehicles in the car park. They could even count their mortars in the rubber or their bombs which were perpetually being moved to drier ground; and could report any or all of this to whom it might concern.[11]

Captain James left Sarawak for Singapore on Thursday November 20 in disgrace. He had spent nearly three months there, looking at the defences, which he said were "farcical." Between Kuching and Brunei, three hundred and fifty miles apart, all communication was by water.[12] The defence plans would have been uproariously funny if the situation had not been so serious. It seemed, thought Captain James, as though the Japanese were expected to arrive in a fleet of junks and land in sampans, armed with swords and bows and arrows. To oppose this medieval force was one almost as medieval: it was thought that three companies of infantry, a few squads of volunteers without rifles, some head-hunters, and "blow-pipes, parangs and fixed bayonets" would be sufficient to deal with the enemy. Wire ropes raised across wooden trestles would immobilize landing strips; the Royal Artillery would open rapid fire (with what?) on the opposing task force; the Royal Engineers would "scamper about touching-off explosives" (lovely phrase) to blow up the refining equipment and pumping plant; and (the crowning touch) the Officer Commanding the Miri detachment would blow up the underwater pipe-lines by pressing an electric plunger "concealed under his bed." The Officer Commanding at Seria would do the same—Seria was thirty-two miles away across a wide river that had no* bridge.[13]

The whole thing took a more serious turn on October 19 when a Japanese naval plane made an hour's reconnaissance over Kuching and this was promptly reported. Malaya Command replied after an interval that it was "unlikely" the aircraft was Japanese; later still that no British or Dutch planes had been over Kuching, which Kuching knew; later again, that no American planes had been over either so the aircraft reported must have been Japanese; "in future," concluded the message stiffly, "send this type of information *immediately*." [14]

For commenting on all this and warning the local government that the Japanese could easily capture Sarawak,[15] Captain James was rebuked and recalled by Malaya Command with orders to delete these damaging remarks from his report.[16] In spite of protests from Sarawak where the Government agreed with him, Captain James was ordered back and told on arrival in Singapore that General Percival was "very angry with him." A week later Percival visited Kuching and worked out a fresh defence plan whereby the full Punjabi force was to move inside a three and a half mile perimeter and hold the airfield at all costs, a modern version, reflected Captain James, of the laager method used in 1906 against the Zulus armed with assegais and knobkerries (he could have referred it further back, to the covered wagon days); and was "blown sky high" later.[17]

But throughout these weeks Brooke-Popham was preoccupied with the vexed question of Operation Matador, which hung upon the relationship with Siam.

3

Siam at that time had two rival leaders. One was the Prime Minister and near dictator, Colonel Pibul, otherwise known as Plaek Pibulasong-gram (Siamese names are incredibly complicated), and his Foreign Minister, Mr Pridi, or Nai Luang Pradit Manudhorn, a self-made liberal with a French law degree, formerly a professor of law in Bangkok.[18] Mr Pridi, a calm, slow-spoken, stocky man with a friendly manner and great natural dignity (no one ever thought of slapping him on the back, according to Captain Gilchrist), was of left wing views and had a fine reputation. Colonel Pibul was of right wing views but hoped to keep out of trouble for as long as possible.[19]

The difficulty was this. Japan realised as clearly as anybody else did that bases within easy striking distance of the British possessions were essential, and the obvious places to control were French Indo-China or Siam or both.[20] France had seized Indo-China, today called North and South Vietnam, Laos and Cambodia, in the middle of the nineteenth century, and Siam resented this. Siam also resented the French seizure of other bits of Siam in 1893 and 1907. It was the bait of "the lost provinces" that Japan used to gain Siam's support, a tactic which recalls the help offered to Mexico to recover her "lost territories" which helped bring America into the war in 1917. In 1940 and 1941, however, France, defeated in Europe, was weak enough to tempt Siam into a war. It was not much of a war—the French managed to sink a "large Siamese warship"—but it was enough for Japan to come in as mediator and put Siam under an obligation by awarding her some of the lost territory but not all, at a conference in Tokyo on May 9, 1941.[21] The French, who had feared worse terms and therefore hastened to accept, found themselves trapped in any case, for the Japanese now had their pretext, saying that they "found it necessary" to send troops into Indo-China to "help in maintaining order." Japan now had the necessary use of main air and naval bases in Indo-China and an excuse for infiltrating into Siam, and were far better off than if they had had to make a straight fight for Bangkok. All this time the British and Americans believed that Siam was the primary objective and they encouraged her not to give in to Japanese aggression.[22]

The encouragement had to remain chiefly verbal. Britain had no spare supplies, and America had taken back fourteen modern fighter planes in protest against Siam's opposition to the French. Britain did eventually "scrape up a few bits" and sent the Siamese Air Force some aviation fuel, but Colonel Pibul did not feel any more eager to commit himself.[23] He went on with his loudly vaunted cultural development programme which (among other things) persuaded all the more prominent Siamese to wear hats and gloves in the western manner, neither of which suited the charming Siamese appearance.[24] Mr Pridi, viewing all these incidents with grim realism, held doggedly on to his office in spite of hints and threats, and also clung to his beliefs. In due course he was able to develop a considerable secret service known as the Free Siamese Movement in which the British took part.[25]

This explains why the British authorities were so anxious not to upset Siam. It was so likely that the Japanese would try landings at Singora and Patani that it was only a matter of common sense to have troops positioned to bar the way; yet the British Minister in Bangkok, Sir Josiah Crosby, sent messages imploring Brooke-Popham not to jeopardize Siam's favourable reactions to Britain by sending soldiers across the border. In the end Brooke-Popham was left in the impossible position of being able to give the order for Matador only if his men had thirty-six hours to get ready and could move twenty-four hours before the enemy came ashore. The most slow-witted person on earth would know that sixty minutes', let alone sixty hours', warning, was beyond the scope of the wildest dream.[26]

Matador bedevilled all plans and hung like a cloud over the heads of all concerned before it was finally scrapped or, more accurately, allowed to lapse into oblivion. Sir Compton Mackenzie describes it as a cloud-cuckoo-land operation, which under its peculiar circumstances it certainly was.[27] Another complicating factor was the information given to the troops in defence lectures. Intelligence officers solemnly told them that the Japanese were all small, shortsighted, frightened of the dark, equipped with rifles dating from the Old West, guns left over from the war of 1905, and aircraft made from old kettles and kitchen utensils, which, of course, slant-eyed people were unable to fly.[28] They were (the lecturers went on) inexpert at night-fighting, addicted to stereotyped methods and plans, had very little artillery and fewer automatic weapons than the British, and even if they could fly their obsolete planes they were too myopic to be able to dive-bomb.[29]

The reality was rather different. In November 1941 the Japanese had an army over a million strong, organised in about ninety divisions, of which fifty-one were on active service. The navy, recently modernised, had six fleet and four light carriers, thirty-nine cruisers (eighteen of which had eight-inch guns), a hundred destroyers, sixty-three submarines, and eleven battleships including the 63,700-ton *Yamato,* laid down in 1937 and just completed. The army and navy air forces together had five thousand first-line aircraft and six thousand pilots, the élite of whom were the carrier pilots. They flew the single-seater Mitsubishi fighter known as the Zeke if it flew from a carrier, the Zero if it was land-based. Light, fast and superbly manoeuvrable, the Zero, flown with flair and dedication, could outdo anything else in the air.[30] Japan was as ready as she would ever be for a short war. Some of her leaders had doubts about the wisdom of getting involved in a long one. Admiral Yamamoto, who had been blooded at Tsushima, told Prince Konoye: "If I am told to fight regardless of the consequences, I shall run wild for the first six months or a year, but I have utterly no confidence for the second and third years of the fighting." [31]

There were no doubts at all about the opening stages. On November 15, Tokyo told their Honolulu Consulate that relations with the United States were highly critical and asked for the harbour reports which arrived twice a week to be sent, from then on, at irregular times. The Americans observed messages going back and forth between Tokyo and all sorts of places in the East, but thought they must be routine and did not even pass the word to their own people in Hawaii.[32] In Washington the talks went grinding on. On November 20 Admiral Nomura was authorised to propose an agreement, known as Plan B, which would prohibit any advance in the Pacific by both powers, excluding Indo-China from which Japan would withdraw by stages into the north, after making an interim agreement to withdraw completely from Indo-China as soon as the China Incident reached peace "or other equitable settlement." America was to advance no obstacles against whatever "equitable settlement" was reached. America should also lift her trade embargo against Japan, and help Japan to obtain such supplies as she required from the Dutch East Indies.

Cordell Hull then opened a fresh series of meetings with the British and Chinese ambassadors and the Australian and Dutch ministers, showing them the draft of a modus vivendi proposal whereby America and Japan would promise not to cross any frontier unless attacked, Japan would withdraw from southern Indo-China and reduce her forces in northern Indo-China to 25,000. America would make a new trade agreement which would allow Japan (among other things) oil for civilian use, and would invite the other interested governments to make similar concessions. America would also provide facilities for a peace con-

ference in the Philippines if asked, and not oppose any negotiated settlement between Japan and China. If this plan was agreed, it should
remain in force for three months, subject to extension. The ministers,
leaving the State Department cheerfully on November 23, told reporters
that there was "no fear of anything and no cause for alarm."

Next day Roosevelt sent copies of Plan B and the modus vivendi
proposals to Churchill privately, saying that he thought the American
plan a fair one, but that Japanese internal politics would decide any
yea or nay and he was not hopeful. Meanwhile the Dutch approved the
modus vivendi, the Chinese had doubts, and the British and Australians
stalled, saying they were still awaiting instructions. In the early hours
of November 26, as Admiral Nagumo's fleet was beginning to move,
Hull received a firm "no" from China, lukewarm consent from Australia
and the Dutch government in exile, and, from Churchill, a message
expressing British unwillingness for Japan to be appeased at the ex-
pense of China. He said Britain did not want to fight Japan and he
trusted Roosevelt and the State Department to conduct all negotiations
in their own way.

Faced with this disappointing response, which convinced him that
the other four powers did not realise the importance and value of the
modus vivendi, Hull told Roosevelt that he thought it best to drop all
interim schemes. Instead he drew up a ten-point programme for what
he hoped would be a final settlement, leaving out the part about America not interfering in any peace settlement in China—he had never liked
that, as it implied condoning Japan's past aggression—and stating un-
equivocally that Japan should withdraw all her troops from Indo-China
and from China as well.[33]

The Japanese at a conference of government and military leaders
decided that the United States was displaying an unrelenting attitude
and that war was inevitable, but that the talks must go on as long as
possible, for it was not yet the first week of December.

All this time a prolonged wrangle had been going on in London
following the decision of November 1 to replace Brooke-Popham. Back
in September Churchill had sent the Chancellor of the Duchy of Lan-
caster, Mr Alfred Duff Cooper, to Singapore to study the ways in which
all the British authorities in the Far East consulted one another, and
to report on how to make them more effective. In Malaya alone, as we
know, there were eleven separate governmental bodies, and relations between the three armed Services were strained and bitter. Duff Cooper, in
the awkward position of a civilian advising the military and an out-

sider advising the residents, got on the wrong side of both. He had certainly found plenty of wastage in communication: for example, two officials, one working for the Ministry of Economic Warfare and the other for the Ministry of Information, each with his own staff, were doing exactly the same job, living in the same house and sharing all their knowledge as each piece came in. Both were excluded from receiving any naval information, as this was in the hands of an officer who wanted to stop everybody, especially the Americans, from getting any knowledge at all, according to Duff Cooper's report.[34] An impatient, quick-tempered man, Duff Cooper took an instant dislike to Brooke-Popham and pestered Whitehall to withdraw him, which they agreed to do, but then hesitated as somebody voiced doubts about horses in midstream. Their hesitation went on just long enough to save Brooke-Popham, if that is the way to put it when he was expected to defend Malaya with about two-thirds of the forces required and without proper air cover.[35]

On November 21 Brooke-Popham asked the Chiefs of Staff in London to tell him under what circumstances Matador could be allowed. They took four days to reply, and when they did it was to say discouragingly that they could not commit themselves in advance, but that he would receive a decision within thirty-six hours of a firm report that the enemy was moving. It is as well to remember at this point that the Japanese could start landing an expeditionary force at Singora within thirty-three hours of leaving Saigon.[36] Matador was therefore a dead duck. Brooke-Popham, however, clung to it stubbornly. On November 29 the Indian troops at Jitra were placed in the second degree of readiness, which meant that they were under six hours' notice to start Matador. It also meant that work on the neglected defences of the Jitra position went on more slowly than before.[37]

All the troops in Malaya noticed the shortage of ammunition. At Tampin there was "not even enough ammunition for issue to guards on sentry duty at bomb dumps," nothing but three-inch mortars for the artillery, and no automatic weapons at all, yet every day the manoeuvres went on with truckloads of equipment and every man wearing a tin hat and a gas mask. At least there was transport.[38] The two Canadian battalions sent to Hong Kong landed there on November 16 and found that their transport had been sent to Australia by mistake.[39] The citizens of Singapore might think there were plenty of planes, but the men training up-country saw very few. The books available show as little agreement about the number of aircraft the Allies actually had in Malaya as they do about the dimensions of the Island. Was the correct figure for front-line aircraft 164? 158? 144? It seems that there were 88 in reserve, 21 of them temporarily in the repair shops.[40] Whatever the true figures were, they were not enough.

4

A few people were now getting ready to push the button for some sort of action. On November 27 the United States Chief of Naval Operations, Admiral Harold R. Stark, sent to Hawaii and the Philippines a "war warning" to expect an aggressive Japanese move in the next few days, probably against the Philippines, Siam, Kra or possibly Borneo. Next day Admiral Husband E. Kimmel who had become Commander-in-Chief Pacific Fleet over the heads of thirty-two other admirals placed his command at the lowest degree of combat readiness. A stream of messages flowed into Honolulu, reporting Japanese troop and fleet movements, almost all southward.

The Indians up at Jitra still stood in readiness for Matador, though readiness is perhaps a misleading word for troops recruited during a rapid expansion, short of experienced officers and NCOs and not trained as a fighting team, who had arrived in Malaya piecemeal and who had been told that the Japanese preferred to advance along main roads.[41]

The Australians were told that the Japanese would use gas and liked setting off firecrackers to frighten their enemies. (In practice, commented Mr Braddon ruefully, they worked "on the old-fashioned principle that mortar bombs are better." As the men in all their heavy equipment ran up and down the roads, sweat pouring off them, one Australian prophesied: "We probably won't be able to do the Japs much harm, but at least the (blanks) 'll have to chase us all the way to Singapore before they catch us." [42]

A Reuter dispatch on Monday December 1 reported that the opinion in Singapore was that the Japanese were apparently preparing to back down.[43] It is difficult to know what this was based on, as on Tuesday the Japanese Imperial Conference, with the Emperor present, formally ratified the decision of November 27, and it was then that the message was sent to Admiral Nagumo: "Niitaka Yama nobore" (Climb Mount Niitaka).[44] As he read the signal with its fatal three words he knew there was no turning back now.

That same day the Far East fleet, having made the crossing of the

Indian Ocean in ten days, reached the Island.[45] "Soon after 2 pm," said
The Times, "large numbers of warships were seen steaming in single
line through waters some miles away from Singapore harbour, silhouetted against a background of blue sky and green islands." [46] Crowds
lined the shore to watch the ships come in, and those who were there
witnessed something historic: "the last occasion," in the words of Mr
Richard Hough, "when the influence of the armoured capital ship, as
a representation of authority and power, was demonstrated without
qualification or compromise."

The reception committee on the quay included Brooke-Popham,
Percival, Duff Cooper and Shenton Thomas. It also included Admiral
Phillips, looking "grey with weariness," who had flown from Colombo
in a flying boat to confer with the officials of Singapore, leaving the
fleet under the command of Captain William Tennant of the *Repulse.*
Captain Tennant was surprised that the RAF had not escorted the battle
fleet in.[47] He and Phillips were concerned and alarmed when they
realised just how inadequate the RAF in Malaya was. Air Vice-Marshal
Pulford explained to them that he had forty-three Buffalo planes fit for
service and these had given endless trouble, requiring twenty-seven
modifications before they were reasonably safe or ready for battle, yet
still taking half an hour to climb to 25,000 feet.[48] These were the
planes that the hapless Brooke-Popham had described as "quite good
enough for Malaya."

The less knowledgeable beholders of the fleet's arrival were more
interested in the "glamour ship," *Prince of Wales;* indeed so much more
attention was paid to her than to *Repulse* that Tennant's crew sar-
donically referred to their own ship as HMS *Anonymous.* The *Singapore Free Press* of Wednesday December 3 complained that many journalists, especially Australians, were not invited to watch the fleet come
in, thereby losing good propaganda value. A Japanese reconnaissance
plane saw the battleships in the Naval Base that day and identified them
correctly by their gun sitings, finding the report confirmed by British
newspapers which had, of course, splashed the story all over their front
pages.[49]

On Thursday Phillips flew to Manila, using one of the three aircraft in Singapore that could make such a trip, to confer with the
United States commanders in the Philippines.[50] They agreed that what
they needed was a strong battle fleet at Singapore or perhaps Manila
and a strong cruiser force in the triangle of sea between Sourabaya,
Borneo and Port Darwin, but as things were at present they must all

manage with what they had. Admiral Hart agreed that if war broke out
the American destroyer flotilla at Balikpapan should move up to Singapore.[51]

Three other incidents took place on that Thursday. *The Times*
correspondents on the Island sent London a dispatch saying that the
arrival of the fleet was likely to make the Japanese concentrate on con-
trolling Siam by peaceful means; they estimated the Japanese troops in
Indo-China at "perhaps 60,000." [52] Brigadier Simson, having found that
soldiers training in Malaya had little idea of how to deal with enemy
tanks and knowing that pamphlets explaining this had been sent out
from the War Office months before, found the pamphlets, tied in bundles, stored tidily in cupboards at HQ, undisturbed, undistributed and
apparently unknown. He rushed off to Percival and asked permission to
draw up and distribute a "new condensed leaflet." Percival agreed,
though he did not think the Japanese would use tanks.[53] The reader
may wonder why the original ones could not be given out then, for no
one on the Island knew just how late in the day it was.

Yamashita's men knew. Colonel Tsuji looked at the gold and silver
waves of Samah harbour, at the deep red sun and "the moon like a
tray," as the twenty ships of the convoy formed up and the naval es-
corts took station on either side and the force that was going to invade
Malaya started moving. "This was surely the starting point," wrote
Colonel Tsuji, "which would determine the destiny of the nation for
the next century." [54]

5

At a cocktail party in Bangkok on Friday December 5 the Siamese
Foreign Minister, Nai Direck Jaiyanama, asked Captain Gilchrist how
far the friends of Britain could rely on her to protect them. He received the stock answer: Britain had stood alone so long that resources
were stretched to the limit, but war production was going ahead by
leaps and bounds and Britain always won the last battle. Also one must
never forget the presence of the Far East fleet. The Minister replied:
"It's a question of *confidence.* If you leave us out on our own, exposed
like this, you just can't expect us to behave like Greece and die to the
last man." The Minister also promised: "We shall resist." [55]

That day the Chiefs of Staff told Brooke-Popham that he could put
Matador into operation with no reference to Whitehall if he thought
the Japanese had entered Siam or were about to land on the coast of

Kra. A secret agent's report had convinced Brooke-Popham that some Siamese government members had asked the Japanese to send an expeditionary force for Kota Bahru as though to Kra, tempting the British over the frontier, so that Siam could then openly ask for Japanese help. This trap Brooke-Popham was determined to avoid.[56]

At that moment he was without both the fleet commanders, and indeed without one of the big ships. Admiral Phillips was still in Manila and Captain Tennant had taken *Repulse* over to Darwin on a short trip to reassure the Australians. Something came in that day, however: a squadron of Beauforts, built in Australia, the first planes to come to Malaya from the Commonwealth. Brooke-Popham and Air Vice-Marshal Pulford watched them come in.

Back in England the Prime Minister left to spend the weekend at

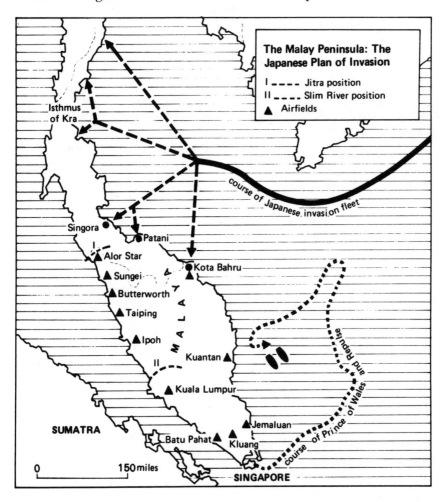

The Malay Peninsula: The Japanese Plan of Invasion

I ---- Jitra position
II ---- Slim River position
▲ Airfields

Isthmus of Kra

course of Japanese invasion fleet

Singora
Patani
Alor Star
Sungei
Butterworth
Taiping
Kota Bahru
Ipoh
Kuantan
MALAYA
Kuala Lumpur
course of Prince of Wales and Repulse
SUMATRA
Jemaluan
Batu Pahat
Kluang
0   150 miles
SINGAPORE

Chequers and Mr A. V. Alexander made a speech at Bristol in which he referred to the Far East: "The threat has not abated and the aggression may be imminent." [57] In the south Atlantic the troopships carrying the 18th Division made their landfall off the South African coast and docked in Cape Town next day. It was that next day, Saturday December 6, that everything really started moving.[58]

6

The Intelligence people reported to Brooke-Popham that Japanese convoys had left Saigon and that transports escorted by warships were heading towards the Gulf of Siam. They also said that the Siamese frontier guards were setting up road blocks on all the roads leading south from Singora and Patani. All forces were promptly ordered to "the highest degree of readiness"; in the case of the Indian troops in the north this meant being put on thirty minutes' notice to start Matador, so hour after hour in drenching rain they stood by, one battalion up on the frontier, two in camp with their trucks loaded ready and three beside the trains that were waiting to move them forward.[59] Phillips was recalled from Manila and Tennant told to bring *Repulse* quickly back from Darwin. He did so, and the elderly ship responded very well, cutting across the calm sea at twenty-seven knots, while Yamashita's convoy, observed by a British plane at about half-past one, had the good luck to run into thick weather as it rounded Cambodia Point and was lost to view.[60]

Brooke-Popham, still uncertain about Matador, got a telegram from Sir Josiah Crosby in Bangkok imploring him not to risk losing Siam's good opinion by sending troops over the border. He reasoned that if the convoys were making for Singora and Patani, the Matador chance was lost and if not it would put him in the wrong. On the other hand, if the Japanese meant to keep him guessing for a couple of days, Matador might be right. He finally decided to wait for a dawn reconnaissance and told Heath so.[61] Meanwhile a large number of Australian troops went down into Singapore to hold a grand ceremonial parade, marching and countermarching with "their impressive armour" throughout the afternoon.[62]

Mr Braddon spent that same afternoon playing rugger against an Army Service Corps team who fed them handsomely and then wiped them out on the field. After the game they showered and dressed, then went into Malacca to amuse themselves, eating, dancing or going to the cinema. At about half-past ten they were called urgently back to camp and instantly jumped to the conclusion that the war had started. They commandeered any kind of transport they could lay their hands on, cars, trucks, rickshaws, and set off in pitch darkness to cover the fifteen miles back to Tampin. It was then past midnight. No one there seemed to know anything, so they all sat on the beds cleaning their rifles. The NCO came in and issued each man with five rounds of ammunition. An Australian called Johnny Iceton said, "It bloody well *must* be war." [63]

At dawn next morning a Catalina was sent out to see what it could find, and failed to return. The weather over the Gulf remained thick so further reconnaissance was impossible.[64] Brooke-Popham and Percival, in consultation, decided not to order Matador that day, but having told Heath this they added that he had better be ready to move on Matador at first light on the Sunday.[65]

Like the Battle of Midway, which was complicated by being fought backwards and forwards across the International Date Line, the order of events of December 7-8 is equally complicated by the time factor. Dawn on Sunday at Pearl Harbor was shortly after midnight on Monday morning in Malaya. The simplest way seems to be to follow the main trends of events separately, bearing in mind that the opening shots of the Far East war were fired at Kota Bahru (frequently misspelt as Bharu), which means Newcastle.

The weekend of December 7-8 in the key places followed a pattern of largely unapprehensive calm suddenly jolted into horrified awareness. Sunday in Singapore, the last day of peace there, opened with a sharp rebuke on the telephone from Brooke-Popham to Mr James Glover, editor of the *Malaya Tribune,* because the headlines that morning read: "27 Japanese transports sighted off Cambodia Point." Brooke-Popham said it was most improper to print such alarmist words. The Reverend Jack Bennitt overslept and was late for early service. Brigadier Simson spent most of the day at Fort Canning, organising the distribution of his anti-tank leaflets. Many English residents met as usual for drinks at the Sea View Hotel, where they listened to the Palm Court kind of music dispensed by the orchestra and joined in the singing of "There'll Always Be an England." People ate the customary curry tiffin, went swimming, went to the pictures or visited friends; the long sunshiny day passed in utter, ordinary calm.[66]

With the coming of darkness, the ships in the Gulf came into their final positions. Sixteen transports stood off the Siamese coast preparing to land the first wave of the Japanese 5th Division at Singora and Patani. Three transports approached Kota Bahru with part of the Japanese 18th Division, known as the Chrysanthemum Division and considered their finest except for the Imperial Guards.[67] Seven other transports covered the rear of the convoy, north of Singora, to put ashore a regiment of the 5th Division who would capture the airfields. Standing by at battle stations were 170 bombers and 150 fighters with 36 reconnaissance aircraft whose task was to cover the landings, occupy the captured airfields as soon as possible and make air raids down the Malay Peninsula as far as the Island itself.

By ten that night (ten past four in the morning at Hawaii) the Japanese were ready to start putting ashore more than twelve thousand men, all intensively trained in jungle fighting, and all except the Imperial Guards experienced in combat. They also had some seven thousand vehicles, ninety medium and a hundred light tanks, and boundless confidence.[68] The heavy rain had stopped, the wind had died down, and the moon was shining on the beaches at Kota Bahru. Heath's Indians, holding a line of fortified pillboxes, opened fire on the Japanese landing craft, which came steadily on, and by one in the morning, after about an hour of fighting, the Japanese assault wave was established on its beachhead and the pillboxes were silenced.[69]

At Singora the water was choppy, the splash of the waves drowning the noise of the engines, and about a third of the troops fell out of the boats before they could jump. Here the landing was unopposed, the defence trenches empty, and as the Japanese moved into the town they found the street lamps shining on deserted streets. A staff officer ran straight to the Japanese Consulate, where he found the Consul, Mr Katsuno, asleep; roused with some difficulty, he simply murmured: "Ah! the Japanese Army!"

An RAF operations officer on duty in Singapore answered the telephone and heard a voice in Kota Bahru say: "Someone's opened fire." "Who? us or the Japs?" he asked. The voice replied that it was us—no, it wasn't, it was the Japanese, and went on to ask whether to bomb the troop transports or the escorting cruisers. "Go for the transports, you bloody fools," roared the officer impatiently. It was too late either way: the Japanese had landed.[70]

At a quarter past one Percival rang up Sir Shenton Thomas and got him out of bed. To Percival's report of the Kota Bahru landings Thomas answered: "Well, I suppose you'll shove the little men off." Thomas then rang police HQ and told them to start rounding up all the Japanese men on the Island, rang Stanley Jones, the Colonial Secretary, and told him to stand by, woke the servants and ordered coffee, woke Lady Thomas and told her what was happening, rang other key officials, then dressed. He and his wife went out on to the upstairs balcony of Government House and sat drinking their coffee overlooking a great vista of Singapore brilliantly lit by moonlight and its own street lighting. Lady Thomas went back to bed and the Governor paced the garden, thinking. At just on four o'clock Pulford telephoned to say that enemy aircraft were approaching the Island and were then twenty-five miles away.[71]

The air raid sirens started up with their spine-chilling wail and woke Mr Ian Morrison, who looked through the window and saw all the street lamps shining and searchlight beams sweeping the sky. Flashes and bangs, explosions of guns from the dock area and the centre of town, and the steady drone of bombers could be heard. One or two cars with dimmed headlights sped through the streets, which were otherwise deserted; then shouts were heard, the voices of ARP * wardens, and people began to appear.[72]

Mr Glover, awakened by the sirens as Mr Morrison had been, flung on his clothes, got out his car, and drove to the *Tribune* offices. By the time he reached the waterfront, it was crowded with people, mostly Chinese and Malay, who apparently thought the whole thing was a practice alert, as did some officials who ought to have known better. One Englishwoman blown out of bed by the blast of a bomb telephoned the police who told her not to worry, it was only a practice.[73] Mr Morrison noticed the searchlights going out one by one, and the night grew quiet again. Eventually the all clear sounded and the first streaks of dawn revealed the damage. Sixty-one people had been killed and a hundred and thirty-three injured. Most of the bombs had fallen in Chinatown, but one had caught Robinson's restaurant and one had registered a near miss at police HQ, where the Inspector-General, Mr Dickinson, finally came off duty at about seven in the morning.

Air attacks had broken out all over. Timed to coincide as closely as possible with one another, they had come at breakfast time on Guam in clear weather; at noon on Wake Island where thirty-six bombers flew in under cover of a rain squall; at nine-thirty over Lingayen Gulf in the Philippines; at breakfast time in Hong Kong, where the raid cost the garrison all five of its aircraft.[74] At Wake Island, where there was no warning because there was no radar, seven of their twelve outdated

* Air Raid Precautions.

Wildcats, landed only four days earlier, were destroyed on the ground. The white Pan American clipper floating on the calm lagoon was riddled with bullets but was able to take off during the afternoon, overloaded with civilian personnel, and make the thousand-mile flight to Midway.[75]

The garrison in the Philippines had leapt to battle stations as soon as the famous signal was received from Hawaii: "Air raid Pearl Harbor —this is no drill." Indeed it was not, but if it had been there would have been plenty of red faces and a flood of irate questions afterwards. The sequence of disregarded or delayed messages held their pattern steadily to the final moment of truth and even beyond it. The news that the Japanese ultimatum was due to be presented in Washington at one in the afternoon (8 am Pearl Harbor) came in at ten and was not sent out until General Marshall came into his office at a quarter past eleven. It alerted (or was intended to alert) the Philippines, San Francisco, Panama, and Honolulu. Atmospherics interfered with the Army radio in Honolulu so the message was sent through commercial channels, not even marked urgent, and reached Hawaii twenty-two minutes before Captain Fuchida led the first attack wave down for the strike. The message, true to the tradition of lovely old silent films, was given for delivery to a boy on a bicycle. On his way to HQ, he realised he was going to be delayed—the bombs spoke louder than the paper in his pocket. He was four and a half hours late handing the message in, and the decode took place at 2.58 pm, precisely seven hours and three minutes after the news it carried became academic. By that time 2,403 people were dead and 1,178 injured, six ships were sunk and twelve damaged, and a half a million dollars' worth of damage had been done in Hawaii. The Japanese casualties were less than a hundred, they had lost twenty-nine aircraft and all five of their midget submarines.[76]

They had lost more than this, however. They had made the strike, created the full surprise, taken the offensive boldly and carefully, but they had not caught the American carriers, nor destroyed the repair shops and maintenance yards and the big, vital fuel dumps. The American Navy would live to fight another day. The Japanese had brought America with her bottomless resources into the war, and brought her in united. Overnight the isolationist voice was dead. The "obedient nation of heroes" had cast the dice, but the winning number had not, in fact, come up.

7

It did not look like this at first, but if there was any doubt, it was not in Winston Churchill's mind that night. Three hours after the raid at Pearl Harbor he heard the news of America's entry into the war and realised at once that, no matter how long it lasted or how it ended, Britain was on the winning side, that Hitler and Mussolini faced certain defeat and that the Japanese would be "ground to powder." Too happy at that moment to worry about anything, he went to bed in a mood of soaring euphoria, secure in the knowledge that Britain would be safe and victorious, and slept "the sleep of the saved and thankful."

(He had, however, made the prophetic comment which appears on the very same page of his book: "I expected terrible forfeits in the East; but all this would be merely a passing phase." How terrible they were to prove and how long the phase would take to pass were about to be emphatically demonstrated.) [77]

Next morning Churchill's formal and courteously worded declaration of war was presented to the Japanese Government. By that time matters in Malaya had already shown the shape of things to come concerning the biggest British forfeit of all.

CHAPTER III

The Push from the North

I

WHEN the air raid started on Singapore there was only dance music on the radio.[1] That same day, in Calcutta, General Wavell made a speech as part of a National Defence and Savings Week in which he said that he had been impressed, on a recent visit to Burma and Malaya, by the strength of the defences that any attackers were likely to meet, and that these defences, land, sea, and air, were being reinforced all the time.[2] In Bangkok the Siamese Cabinet was summoned to discuss the Japanese request for free passage for their troops through Siamese territory. As Churchill knew, they wanted access to Singora and Patani, and he sent the Siamese Cabinet a message saying "Don't give in," but Pibul was careful not to be available and therefore no orders went out. Eventually there was some resistance to both Japanese and British crossing the borders, but not much. Pibul ordered a cease-fire very quickly, particularly against the Japanese, which, coupled with his absence from the Cabinet meeting, supports the theory that he was collaborating. Captain Gilchrist did not think the British ought to have required him to order complete resistance, as all Siam could have done would have been to delay the Japanese for a couple of hours, no more.[3]

Early on Monday morning, December 8, while the bomb-rubble was being cleared in Raffles Place, the long process of recrimination began, starting with acid questions as to why the ARP posts were not manned on the Island in spite of Flight Sergeant Webb's signal from his Catalina that he had sighted a Japanese fleet off Kelantan.[4] There had been no blackout, no alert in advance to the civilian population. That same morning the war correspondents were summoned to a press conference by the Army Public Relations Unit. The landings at Singora, Patani and Kota Bahru were announced. One communiqué used the phrase "mopping-up" which led everybody to assume that the landings could not amount to much and were being dealt with satisfactorily. Reports

67

were coming in of air raids on Manila and the assault at Pearl Harbor.[5] The Japanese had destroyed a hundred American aircraft and damaged air bases in the Philippines at a cost of seven planes.

Admiral Hart was at Manila Bay with two cruisers, four destroyers and all his submarines; his third cruiser with five destroyers was at Tarakan and the other four were on passage from Balikpapan to Singapore as arranged. This created the paradoxical situation that the American forces in the west Pacific, where invasion was hourly expected, were much weaker than in the central Pacific, where no attack was likely.[6] But at Pearl Harbor the decoded messages, looked at in sequence, leave no doubt about the eventual attack there. The trouble was that they came in among a mass of other material, not all officers had had access to all the relevant dispatches that poured in, and in any case each was usually read while the officer delivering it stood waiting to take it back to be destroyed at once. There was also inter-service jealousy just as there was in Singapore, which made for faulty liaison, and Washington was not helpful, for while the service chiefs there believed war was certain (as Kimmel and Short did in Honolulu) they expected the Japanese to go for Siam, the Dutch East Indies, Malaya, and possibly Wake, Guam, and the Philippines. The sudden flood of reports showing Japanese convoys moving south made Pearl Harbor seem still more secure; they forgot that battles are won by surprise.[7]

Listening to the official reports at the press conference, Mr Morrison was aware of the relief that everyone present felt at the end of the period of uncertainty and strange unreality. "We all agreed [it seems strange to recall now] that no war could possibly have begun in a more auspicious way." The European residents of the Island shared these feelings, drinking toasts to their new allies and reading the communiqués, which told them that all the Japanese surface craft at Kota Bahru were "retiring at high speed" (as indeed they might, having landed their troops) and that the "few troops left on the beach" were being "heavily machine-gunned." It gave no hint of the many enemy soldiers who had successfully left the beaches for their initial advance inland.

Two Orders of the Day had by now been posted, one in Malaya, the other in Japan. The Japanese Order said: "Patiently have we waited and long have we endured in the hope that our Government might retrieve the situation in peace. But our adversaries, showing not the least spirit of conciliation, have unduly delayed a settlement, and in the meantime they have intensified economic and political pressure to compel our Empire to submission." The other, printed in Chinese, Malay and English, stated: "We are ready: we have plenty of warning and our preparations have been made and tested. . . . We are confident. Our defences are strong and our weapons efficient. . . . We do not at this moment forget the years of patience and forbearance. We have borne with dignity and discipline the petty insults and insolences inflicted on us by the Japanese in the Far East." [8]

This Order had been drafted six months previously. Its comforting claims had not been true then, and were not true now. It came from London, where, presumably, it appeared to be true. A great many people in Singapore thought that it was. A few knew better, including the assistant editor of the *Tribune,* Mr George Hammonds, who had toured Malaya and the Island often enough, and recently enough, to know that there were very few defences, none at all on the north coast of the Island, and not one tank in the whole of Singapore.[9]

Another person who knew something about the state of the defences, Captain James, reported for duty as ordered by Malaya Command at the Australian HQ in Johore Bahru.[10] Far away at Cape Town the officers and men of the 18th Division, quartered on board their American troopships and still bound for the Middle East, noticed the change of attitude of the American officers and ratings on realising that Pearl Harbor had put them all metaphorically as well as literally in the same boat.[11]

Fourteen hundred miles north of Singapore the British forces in Hong Kong moved into their defensive positions. Known nicely as the Gindrinkers Line, these positions amounted to a sequence of delaying posts three miles north of the city. Maltby expected to hold them for a week or ten days. The line had a string of names evocative of an adventure story: Gindrinkers Bay, Golden Hill, Smugglers Ridge, Tide Cove, Port Shelter,[12] and Maltby directed operations from his HQ known as the Battle Box, approached down a hundred and two steps in thirteen flights, and built four years earlier. All day forward patrols carried out planned bits of demolition, fired across the water at columns of Japanese infantry, and, as night fell, discovered that the Japanese were "making the most of the bright moonlight by which our intelligence supposed they would be bewildered." [13]

Captain Russell-Roberts at Kuantan, listening to the broadcast from Singapore early on Monday morning, was horribly alarmed to hear that some of the bombs dropped during the night had contained gas. This was denied later, after the "shattering news" of Pearl Harbor was announced, but it gave the Captain a bad fright worrying about the safety of his wife and baby daughter. Altogether it was "a black and miserable Monday." The rain poured down, drenching all the men to the skin, and the news from the north was bad: the Japanese at Kota Bahru had fought their way ashore, almost wiping out the Dogra battalion on the beaches. More enemy troopships had been sighted in the China Sea and the northern airfields had been fired on.

A Garhwali battalion assigned to defend eleven miles of beach between the Kuantan and Balok rivers had three companies up and one in reserve and two ancient eighteen-pounder guns among its unimpressive equipment, and was expected to prepare concrete pillboxes, barbed wire entanglements, and to lay mines. Two and a half Sikh companies were manning the river defences on the Kuantan and the Soi, including a ferry crossing and the road approach from Pekan, leaving no reserve at all to defend the Pahang River twenty-two miles to the south.

During the afternoon the Captain's men were moved out to defend the airfield which had twenty-six planes (ten new Australian Hudsons, ten old Blenheims from Burma and half a dozen Swordfish and Wildebeestes which flew at one-third of the Zero speed), but no new fighters and no anti-aircraft guns, while the ground staff had come up only the Thursday before from the Island. The Captain, last away, soon reached his HQ among the rubber trees six miles from Kuantan and one mile from the airfield which they had been told to defend to the last round and to the last man as that was the whole reason for their being there.[14] Brigadier Painter was naturally worried. The airfield was badly sited, and he had only two battalions, and two howitzers, though sixteen field guns came up later. By four in the afternoon Pulford had decided to withdraw all serviceable aircraft left at Kota Bahru to Kuantan. The ground staff set fire to the buildings, but did not destroy the bombs or fuel dumps or put the runways out of action.[15]

All this time the various corps HQ all over Malaya were ringing up Malaya Command at Fort Canning to ask for precise orders. "Even then," wrote Mr Bateson, "Malaya Command creaked rustily into action." [16] Brigadier Barclay noted that Percival's force was some seventeen infantry battalions short of his requirements, that he had not one single armoured fighting vehicle, and that most units were short of modern equipment, experienced officers, and trained specialists, and that he had been told above all to protect the airfields. In view of all these factors, said Barclay, Percival could not "locate his troops to the best advantage militarily" so that he had "wide dispersion of Army formations and a deployment which was militarily unsound." [17]

At eleven-thirty that morning Percival issued orders to cancel all thought of Matador and take up defence positions astride the roads coming south from the frontier. At the same time he sent "mobile columns" into Siam to "disrupt and delay" the Japanese advance. These orders took two hours to get through and it was two o'clock in the afternoon when Lieutenant-Colonel Moorhead's scouts reached the padlocked frontier gate on the Patani road and smashed it open. The Japanese had had "a flying start" of ten invaluable hours. The Indians, weary and lowered in morale after three days of standing by in pouring rain, came up to their assigned positions at Jitra to find the gun pits and trenches brimming with water and the wire that should have been strung and the mines that should have been laid still packed for the mythical Matador move.

Moorhead's HQ at Kroh did not seem to realise the need for speed. In any case his troops had to clear road blocks at every bend—and there were many—while two companies cut through thick jungle on either flank to drive off snipers. By dusk they had penetrated only three miles inside Siam. That evening the Japanese marched unopposed into Bangkok.[18]

That evening, too, there was hardly a light to be seen in Singapore. The Chinese ARP wardens, anxious to appear keen after yesterday, pounced on anyone lighting a cigarette in the street, checked car lights if they were even moderately bright, and shouted frenziedly up at windows showing the slightest chink of light. A good deal of arguing went on about the non-provision of shelters.[19] The official answer was that the Island was too low-lying and too riddled with swamps for shelters to be safe. Recently a big underground car park has been built in Raffles Place.[20]

One event that was going to raise questions to which there could be no right answers had already begun. At half past five that day the two big battleships left Singapore. They went out very quietly, *Repulse* leading, then allowing *Prince of Wales* to go ahead. Silhouetted black against the red sunset they slid up the strait with hardly anyone watching from the shore. Pulford had promised a reconnaissance but had said that fighter protection was most unlikely, and, as the ships passed the signal station at Changi, he confirmed that it was impossible. Admiral Phillips shrugged his shoulders and said: "Well, we must go on without it." As the ships moved northwards up the east coast of Malaya he sent a signal saying that he hoped to surprise enemy transports next day and was sure every man would give a good account of himself. His words were more prophetic than he knew: "We are looking for trouble. No doubt we shall find it." [21]

2

The *Guardian* leader on Tuesday December 9 opened with a well-judged reference to the Japanese "apparatus of surprise," which, "stretched across the Pacific," was "immense." Regarding the Gulf of Siam, it said that "at present . . . we must suppose that Japan holds sea supremacy in these waters."

At first light the Hudsons were sent from Kuantan to bomb the Japanese at Kota Bahru, and lost five aircraft doing so. The Japanese replied with a raid lasting an hour and a half carried out by two flights of twenty-seven planes each. The Sultan of Kelantan then left Kota Bahru and Brigadier Key, who had skilfully disengaged his troops during the black drenching night through marshy and leech-infested country, found himself obliged to draw back still further. His brigade was reached by a single-track railway only, there were no roads across his line of communications, bombing raids were constant and accurate and he was in danger of being cut off.

It was also clear by now that the main Japanese attack was going for the west coast.[22] They had moved in weaving prongs of assault over the Siamese border, where all resistance on the part of the Siamese collapsed suddenly that afternoon, and were aiming at Alor Star, Kroh, and Grik.[23] To stop these troops Moorhead's men had been sent forward to The Ledge, but they moved with as much difficulty on Tuesday as they had on Monday and were still twenty miles short of The Ledge by dark.[24] Pulford in the meantime faced the fact that all three of his airfields in northeast Malaya (Kota Bahru, Machang and Gong Kedah), which Key had been told, like Painter further south, to defend to the last round and the last man, had become useless to him. Kuantan was now virtually a forward landing field. Furthermore, over half his air force had been lost in less than two days. He ordered all the remaining aircraft in the eastern sector back to Singapore.[25] Captain Russell-Roberts was not going to see another British plane for seven weeks.[26]

At Jitra the defence went on, with "tired, soaked, dispirited troops" working "knee deep in mud." [27] They were not the only ones. Down at Mersing the Australians, hastily sent over from Tampin, were toiling up and down a hill of red clay cut into terraces by open-cast mining, carrying ten thousand mortar bombs up a mile-long slope turned by the rain into "an orange ribbon of grease." When at last they finished the job they were set to dig slit trenches and gun pits, lay signal wires and clear fire lanes, and take bearings, which was impossible as the ore deposits in the rocks made every compass reading come out different.[28]

In Singapore Mr Glover dug a trench shelter in his garden and fixed up an emergency printing plant in his compound. Mr B. C. J. Buckeridge of the Fire Service persuaded a Swiss importer to let him have helmets for his men, for in spite of repeated requisition orders none had arrived. The helmets looked just like German ones, but he knew it was not their appearance that mattered.[29] Captain James was sent up into the rubber north of Kota Tinggi to work at battle HQ of the 8th Division.[30] Out in the Pacific the islands of Wake and Guam suffered air raids all day.

All day, too, the battleships steamed north, veiled in mist and warm rain that blotted out visibility. The clouds moved low most of the time and made a welcome screen. Close to one o'clock a Catalina appeared out of the fog, came in "brave and low" over the *Prince of Wales,* and signalled: "Japanese making landing north of Singora," the news they had hoped for. Both ships went on, prepared to make their turn at dusk for the run to the coast and the Japanese transports.

The weather had been ideal all day, but about five o'clock it abruptly changed. The clouds lifted, the mist melted, the sea lay clear and sharp under a golden sunset sky that cast long beams across the water. In the distance three aircraft hung above the horizon. Now that there was no doubt he had been spotted, Admiral Phillips decided to go back to Singapore. At half past six, he detached the old escort destroyer *Tenedos,* due to be sent back any way because of her limited range, asking her to send a message at eight next morning requesting all available destroyers to be sent out to meet him. He stayed on course until dark, after which he planned to turn as though for the coast but in reality draw away to the south. He passed on this information to *Repulse* at eight in the evening.[31]

If Phillips had kept on heading north for "a few more minutes" he would have come within striking distance of four Japanese heavy cruisers which he could certainly have outfought, but this is not what happened. He turned as planned while all the time the aircraft of Admiral Matsunaga's force at Saigon searched energetically for him. At midnight a message from Singapore told Phillips that the Japanese were landing at Kuantan. This was, so to speak, on his route south; he could be off Kuantan by dawn, and smash the transports there comfortably enough. The two ships steamed on through the night under cloud that had thickened again. At twenty past two in the morning a Japanese submarine found them.[32]

As a footnote to the day, during that same night the Japanese at Hong Kong advanced upon the Gindrinkers Line. The spearhead of the attack was an infantry regiment, the 228th, dashingly led by Colonel Teihichi Doi whose cheerful disregard of regimental boundaries caused some offended muttering. All was forgiven, however, when within three hours his men had brilliantly captured the Shing Mun redoubt, the key to the whole line. Within forty-eight hours the defenders had withdrawn from the positions Maltby had hoped to hold for a week and a half, and had fallen back upon the city.[33]

3

Wednesday morning, December 10, saw further air attacks at Wake Island and the Philippines, and the invasion start in Luzon. It also saw the assault on Guam—twenty-five minutes of fighting and all was over: the Japanese had conquered their first enemy territory.[34]

The so-called invasion at Kuantan has never been satisfactorily explained. Shots were certainly fired on the beaches. Bits of boats and floating logs and planks are said to have been found. Some writers thought it was a deliberate feint to lure Phillips to his doom, but this is not consistent with Matsunaga's frantic attempts to find him. Mr Morrison thought that goats wandering on the beach touched off land mines: this sometimes happened. In fact, for several days the newspapers reported either no change in the Kuantan area or no enemy progress at Kuanfan.[35] Whatever the truth is, it is clear that Phillips believed the Japanese were landing at Kuantan and he took his force there to bring its decisive weight into whatever conflict might be raging. He stood off Kuantan at eight in the morning, a clear day dawning mauve and grey, brightening as "a huge red sun rose slowly out of the sea behind them." On the palm-fringed silvery brown sands, as the destroyer *Express* signalled, all was "as quiet as a wet Sunday afternoon." At eight-thirty *Tenedos,* far to the south with her message duly sent, signalled that she was under bomb attack (she managed to escape unhurt); so Phillips instantly set course for the Island at best possible speed. By now the sun was well up and the day growing hot; the sky was deep blue above the calm water.[36]

Matsunaga's ninety-five search aircraft took off from Saigon between half past seven and half past nine, flying at their most economical height, with "the leanest setting of their mixture controls" to save fuel, and the crews carrying lunch of rice cake spread with bean paste, and thermos flasks of coffee syrup. They had been on the hunt for seventy-two hours with only the briefest rest periods, but they were still alert and determined. By eleven o'clock they were on course for base after the sweep, when Ensign Hoashi in a reconnaissance plane sighted the two battleships. Within eight minutes nine bombers appeared, in close formation, and accurately bombed *Repulse,* scoring one direct hit that damaged the catapult aircraft and started a fire which the crew got under control in ten minutes.[37]

The torpedo planes, which should have come in on the tail of the bombers, were late, arriving at half past eleven and diving twelve minutes later while the bugles sounded the alarm on the two big ships. *Prince of Wales* took a torpedo astern that jammed the port propeller, put the rudder out of action, holed the hull and made the ship list thirteen degrees at once as she steamed helplessly in a fixed circle. The out of control balls went up and she signalled an enquiry to *Repulse,* which replied: "Have avoided nineteen torpedoes till now, thanks to Providence." [38] Captain Tennant, watching for RAF planes to come to his assistance, learnt with horror that no message had been sent to summon them; he promptly ordered one, giving details, but the next wave of bombers came in before it could be sent. At twenty past twelve *Repulse* took the first hit, and five minutes later, in spite of Tennant's expert manoeuvering and the valiant way the old ship answered the helm, four more torpedoes struck, their "trails speeding like ruled white lines on the blue sea." Seven minutes later, *Repulse* went down. Tennant had not attempted to leave his ship, but fortunately he was picked up by some of his crew on a Carley float.[39]

All this time Ensign Hoashi, circling over the scene of battle and excitedly giving a kind of running commentary to bring in the rest of the attack planes, had observed the way in which one squadron had split up, diving in from all directions upon *Repulse.* He now saw that three aircraft had gone for the *Prince of Wales,* which, down to fifteen knots speed and with only a few guns still firing, was trapped in her circle and could not get out. A neat row of nine bombers, like the one that had opened the assault, came over; the three torpedoes had of course hit the ship and the last nine bombs were so much trimming. The crew had ten minutes in which to abandon ship and they did so in disorder.

At twenty past one the ship foundered, just as Flight-Lieutenant T. A. Vigors led in his flight of five Buffalo planes from Kallang. They had scrambled in eleven minutes after the attack signal came in at Singapore at four minutes past twelve, and had pounded along as fast as they could go, making the trip in an hour. Vigors circled the scene, seeing that the destroyers *Essex*, *Electra*, and *Vampire* were picking up the 2,081 survivors. Admiral Phillips was not among them. He went down with his ship, and 839 other men went down with him. His legacy was a lasting argument about his failure, or possibly refusal, to call for fighter cover and to keep his HQ informed when he changed course. The kindest, and perhaps the correct, explanation is that in December 1941 all the British commanders overestimated the battleship and underestimated the Japanese air power, and clung to the sacred precept of radio silence.[40]

The news reached Singapore that evening. It had not been the best of days up to then. Duff Cooper, in a move announced only two days before and certain to exacerbate feelings on the Island still further, had been appointed Resident Cabinet Minister for Far Eastern Affairs with orders to form a War Council and report direct to the War Cabinet in London. Duff Cooper had held his first War Council that day and had widened the breach between himself and Brooke-Popham and the Governor. Duff Cooper had said the War Council was there to wage war; the Governor did not want to have to consult Duff Cooper on every small point; Brooke-Popham said he took his orders from the Chiefs of Staff in London. The meeting developed into what Mr Barber later described as "unseemly wrangling." [41]

In addition, the news from the north was not good. The Indians moving towards The Ledge had got within six miles of it in lorries, the nearest place, in fact, where motor transport could turn, and then had gone a mile further on foot, when they met the leading enemy tanks which had already covered seventy-five miles from Patani.[42] The Japanese attacked repeatedly, with such deadly effect upon the men opposing them that Moorhead had to fall back to one defensive position after another, none of them satisfactory.[43]

The chain of command was complicated—from Singapore Brooke-Popham and/or Percival passed their orders to Heath at Kuala Lumpur, Heath sent them forward to Murray-Lyon at Kroh who signalled up to Moorhead. Throughout the campaign communications were maddeningly unreliable and choked with protocol to an astonishing degree. Mr Leasor refers to an urgent telephone conversation between Percival and Brooke-Popham that was interrupted by the operator saying: "Your three minutes have expired, sir," and cutting the connexion.[44] The combined effect of Brooke-Popham's vacillations over Matador, the uncertain quality of communication, the slowness of Moorhead's advance to the vital Ledge which he never did reach, and an apparently general failure to grasp the importance of speed, was that time was lost that could never be retrieved. The pattern of withdrawal crystallized into standard practice.

By Wednesday night, with the Far East war sixty-six hours old, Murray-Lyon's two brigades were standing across the road and railway at Jitra in waterlogged ground and the Japanese were fast approaching. Outposts tried to hold them off at forward positions but were soon overrun with heavy losses in men, guns, and vehicles. Murray-Lyon's reserve troops, coming up as fast as they could in answer to his signals, were split up as soon as they arrived to make good the gaps in the other brigades, leaving him with no reserves to fall back on when the Japanese came on again in the morning.[45]

That evening in Singapore Mr Morrison went for a walk round Chinatown and found crowds of Chinese digging trenches and making shelters of sorts on every open piece of ground, watched by more crowds of old men, women and children. The children were having a lot of fun playing among the diggings. There was a wonderful atmosphere of helpfulness and friendly co-operation.[46] (In contrast to the acrimonious War Council.) Tennis players at the Cricket Club had their showers and came into the bar for drinks as music played on the radio. There was the usual dancing at the Raffles Hotel. The club radio music suddenly stopped and everyone fell silent as the announcement came over that the two battleships had been sunk. One man dropped his glass. Horrified conversation babbled out. When the news got to the hotel, the veranda cleared "as though the last waltz had just been played." At the hospital, a doctor suggested to Mrs Dickinson, just coming off the day shift, that she had better stay to meet the casualties that might be arriving soon.[47]

In England, where it was early morning, Churchill was awakened to the worst shock he had yet received during the war. Bitterly distressed, within two days he was estimating to the Foreign Secretary that the Japanese could attack where they liked. He considered the area so enormous, however, that "the use of their power could only be partial and limited"—he could equally well have said the same about the British—and predicted that the likeliest attack would fall on the Philippine Islands, Singapore, and the Burma Road.[48]

Churchill, who signed his war telegrams to Roosevelt as "Former Naval Person," had, of course, a special feeling about the Royal Navy. It may be possible, though at this stage unprofitable, to speculate how much the loss of the two big ships had blunted his sensibilities towards the perils menacing Singapore and how far it influenced the decision to divert the reinforcements to Malaya. He certainly cabled a warning not to let troops required for the "ultimate defence" of the Island to be used up or cut off in Malaya, as nothing compared in importance with "the fortress." [49] This cable was sent on December 15: the words "ultimate defence," used so soon, have an ominous ring. Churchill persisted (naturally) in thinking in terms of Fortress Singapore, as a properly fortified stronghold that could be fought for, point by point, acre by acre, perhaps even room by room like Stalingrad, swallowing up armies of thousands over a period of months. Not for five more weeks would he realise the truth.

4

The Jitra position had been designed to protect the airfield of Alor Star, a place hallowed in the memory of those who involved themselves with the early years of flying, for many celebrated fliers had staged there, including Amy Johnson.[50] A regiment of Gurkhas being retired down the Gurun road on Wednesday evening passed Alor Star, where the hangars and fuel tanks were on fire. It had been evacuated that morning without a word. When the Japanese came to the attack again on Thursday morning, Murray-Lyon ordered the Punjabis nearest to them to fall back slowly to allow the longest possible time for the stubbornly continuing defence work still grinding on in the rain at Jitra.[51] By now the situation in north Malaya showed two parallel developments, one on the Singora road running south through Jitra, Alor Star and Gurun, the other on the Patani road running south-west to Betong and Kroh, both roads meeting at Sungei Patani just above Penang. On both roads the Japanese attacked hard, pushing on with infantry, taking sudden bursts with tanks through driving rainstorms with visibility down to twenty yards, sending small parties of soldiers round on the flanks to cut off, or threaten to cut off, the soaked and weary opposition. Much gallantry was shown, but inexorably the Japanese moved forward as the 11th Indian Division in its separated units, taking heavy losses, fell slowly back, nearer and nearer to Butterworth and the island of Penang.[52]

At one point the Japanese found an abandoned armoured car in which they picked up a blood-soaked map marked with coloured pencils showing all the British defensive positions before Jitra. Armed with this gift they were able to move decisively and precisely, so that, prepared to lose a thousand men over Jitra, they lost, in fact, twenty-seven.

On Thursday December 11 came the first major air raid on Penang. Twenty-seven bombers in perfect formation dive-bombed in groups of three while thousands stood in the streets and watched. They did not watch long. Most of the bombs exploded in the thickly populated native section of Georgetown, and the planes followed this up by screeching down low and machine-gunning the streets. The whole thing lasted nearly two hours. Many fires blazed up, hundreds of people were killed and injured, all the essential services broke down. The fire station took a direct hit, and many people rushed for the hills on the mainland while the shopkeepers hurriedly boarded up their shops as the looting began. No one appeared available to work the ferries, fight the fires, search for victims, clear up the débris or bury the dead: there was indescribable confusion.[53]

Over the water where the ships had gone down the day before the Japanese dropped flowers. They reported this in a broadcast: "To the souls of the departed heroes of the British Navy who fought to the last, sleep in peace—this was the tender sentiment of the Wild Eagles who were strong in battle." [54]

No tender sentiment was aroused by Duff Cooper's broadcast in which he tried to make light of the disaster, saying that this was not the first time in their long history that the British had met with calamity and surmounted it; Britain had other battleships and was building more; Malaya stood now only where she stood a month ago; these were great days when safety hardly seemed honourable and danger was glorious.[55] These lofty phrases only served to rub salt in the wound.

The guns and bombs went on crashing away at Hong Kong and Heath travelled to Singapore by train from Kuala Lumpur to discuss with HQ the possibility of pulling the forces left in the Kota Bahru area back to Kuala Lipis, an enormous leap south almost to the level of Kuantan.[56] There, after two nights in the plantation, Captain Russell-

Roberts and his men were moved still further into the rubber and away from their seventy transport vehicles. It was too muddy and wet to bivouac, and in any case they were deprived of their tents, so they built makeshift huts where the Captain went round all day armed with a flit-gun against the swarms of mosquitoes infesting the place. They stayed there for the rest of the month. No more was heard about defending the airfield to the last round and the last man.[57]

It was Murray-Lyon's turn now to receive this bold directive. He had asked permission to withdraw his tired soldiers to Gurun, thirty miles south of Jitra, where a natural defensive position could be found, though of course it was so far unprepared. He was rung up by Percival and told to hold Jitra "to the last round and the last man." Percival had issued an Order of the Day that called upon everyone "in this hour of trial" to "stand fast come what may," as the Empire was watching and Britain's reputation and holdings in the Far East were "at stake." Murray-Lyon's men did their best, but it was not enough to stop the Japanese, and when at last they were allowed to fall back it proved to be a much harder business than it would have been if permitted earlier.[58]

While Murray-Lyon wrestled with his difficulties at Jitra, over on Wake Island came the one good action of the day in terms of results. At five on Thursday morning Rear-Admiral Kajioka's small invasion fleet, rolling heavily in the trade wind, opened its bombardment. The garrison of 522 men, most of them marines, promptly replied to such good effect that Kajioka lost 500 men, two destroyers, and much face, and withdrew, vengefully promising to try again. He did so less than two weeks later.[59]

<h1 style="text-align:center">5</h1>

The Japanese armour with its headlights blazing charged straight down the trunk road during the night,[60] and the ragged opposition, misled by inaccurate reports, pulled back two miles at one place without consulting anyone, committed all the troops at another in a mistimed counter-attack, and left a gap half a mile wide at another by Friday midday.[61] In the afternoon a complex manoeuvre brought chaos because one flank waited on the other, so that the eventual move was made at the cost of one company which never got its orders. The unfortunate Murray-Lyon, hearing rumours of some kind of disaster in the rear and reports of a fresh attack up front which turned out to be groundless, also having news of Moorhead's backing up on the Patani road, asked again to be allowed to withdraw to Gurun. Heath supported this request and finally Percival gave permission, saying that Murray-Lyon had only one Japanese division against him and that he must hold north Kedah, but it was best to dispose his forces in depth and he could fall back at his own discretion.

Thankfully Murray-Lyon gave his orders and the whole of his force started down the one road in bad weather. It was a wretched retreat. Some units never got their orders, many were separated, some went by the coast and some across country,[62] and by the end of Saturday, after a week of war during which many of the men had had no sleep and many had not eaten for thirty-six hours, the 11th Indian Division, drenched, mud-stained and exhausted, assembled as "a shadow of itself," some sections having lost more men in that last withdrawal than in the fighting that went before it. The Japanese found fifty field guns and fifty heavy machine guns left at Jitra, three hundred vehicles, three months' provisions and enough ammunition for a division. At Alor Star the bridges had not been properly blown and were repaired in an hour, and the airfield, taken over by two Japanese squadrons, was found rapidly operational, with bombs piled at the perimeter and a thousand drums of high-octane fuel, both of which happy finds were quickly put to use against the retreating forces. In one hut the Japanese even found bowls of soup on the table.

Over on the Patani road Moorhead received an order from Murray-Lyon. It had been brought 113 miles through the wet night by a motor-cycle dispatch rider, and it said that Moorhead could withdraw upon Kroh, but once there he must hold to the last round and the last man.[63]

6

The Times of Friday December 12 reported: "In the Kuantan area the troops hold their original front." [64] The *Guardian* of the same day said: "There is no report of further attempts to land in the Kuantan area, nor were enemy ships seen in that direction by air reconnaissance during yesterday. . . . Our troops still hold the original front." [65]

And Churchill telegraphed Wavell to say that the British 18th Division, now rounding South Africa, were being diverted to Bombay. Wavell might find some use for them.[66]

CHAPTER IV

Straight Down the Middle

I

THE survivors from the battleships were each given a present of six dollars and eighty cents by the Sultan of Johore. This was then about forty-seven shillings, now £2.35 or $5.64. The marines from *Prince of Wales* were formed into A Company, the marines from *Repulse* into B Company, and both were attached to the Argyll and Sutherland Highlanders—a move that resulted in their being called (unofficially) the Plymouth Argylls.[1]

The Times of Saturday December 13 contained an assessment of Japanese naval strength. The Japanese, it said, had 12 battleships (one sunk and one crippled), 12 heavy cruisers, 20 light cruisers, 120 odd destroyers (presumably they meant about 120), and 80-90 submarines. As the reader looks at this list he can hardly fail to notice the one great omission: where is there mention of the core of the fleet, the carriers? There was also an article on north Malaya that stated that the geography of the country to the west of Kota Bahru "would render a land invasion driving south towards Kuala Lumpur and thence to Singapore almost impossible."[2]

Whoever wrote that article was not on the road from Alor Star that morning, where Murray-Lyon and his Officer of Sappers stood on the south bank of the Sungei Kedah in watery sunlight and waited while the last troops crossed before ordering both the road and rail bridges to be blown. The Japanese were hard behind them—two motorcyclists "roared down the road" but were "soon despatched"—and the road bridge quickly went up. The railway bridge was tougher, and did not fall, though it was damaged; at that moment an armoured train came steaming down the line from the north, jumped the gap, and went right on southwards out of sight. Fresh explosives were rapidly laid and touched off, and the bridge went just as the van of the Japanese infantry came in view. The Gurkhas held them off while in the pouring

83

rain the straggling retreat continued down the one jammed road. By
that night they had reached the chosen defensive position three miles
north of Gurun, occupying a stretch two miles wide between jungle
hills and straddling the road and the railway. It took the Japanese
barely thirty hours to repair the Sungei Kedah bridge and hurry off in
pursuit. During that night the weary remnants of the 11th Division
had to make a start on the digging and wiring that nobody had so
far managed to do.[3]

That day the British residents of Penang were told to prepare for
evacuation. There is some doubt about just whose order this was. Mr
Barber says it was the military commander in Penang; Mr Morrison
said it was either Malaya Command or the local military, but both
agree that the civil government had nothing to do with it. Whoever
was responsible, the effect was calamitous. The streets of Penang had
been plastered with copies of the Order of the Day ("We are ready;
our preparations have been made and tested; our defences are strong
and our weapons efficient; we are confident"), and, with the war only
a week old, the "invincible tuan" was getting ready to go. Mr Morrison
found it acutely distressing and embarrassing to see the reaction of the
native population: the British "had ratted," had "thought of saving
no skins but their own," leaving the natives to face the Japanese "as if
they didn't give a damn what happened to them," and without a word
"had suddenly legged it as hard as they could." Of course the British
had been given secret orders, had been told not to say a word on
grounds of security as this was a military operation, and of course they
had obeyed. The evacuation took two days and as the first train loads
came in to Singapore the rumours and counter-rumours on which the
Europeans there were living multiplied hugely.[4]

2

Sunday December 14 opened the second week of the war, a week in
which a great deal of care and thought and the most high-powered
levels of signalling staff and equipment were used in a "scrupulous yet
utterly indecisive" series of telegrams between London, Delhi and Rangoon, trying to work out satisfactorily the correct constitutional relations
between the Governor of Burma and the Commander-in-Chief India.[5]
"Our troops have retired to prepared positions" became, and remained
for the next two weeks, the "daily dirge" on the radio.[6]

The war correspondents set up a routine for getting reports from the front. They made their rear HQ in one of the many big empty houses with beautiful gardens some forty or fifty miles behind the action: the house-owners, government officials or planters, had left for the south and the deserted buildings were used by the armed forces as well as by the journalists. The Public Relations Unit gave them four staff cars, an army truck and a dispatch-rider, and every day they toured the front, or as near to it as they could get, visiting the various HQ and returning in the evening to write up their reports, which were then sent to Singapore to be censored and sent out. The news in Singapore was always two days old, sometimes even older, and the correspondents preferred to be closer to the focus of events. Their cars were obvious bomber targets and they drove about keeping a lookout for planes all the time. When they caught sight of one they would stop the car, scramble out, and fling themselves flat in the rubber until the enemy had flown past. Mr Morrison makes it clear that the word "front" is misleading: in Malaya there was never a front as such, but forward outposts in the jungle. The only time a true front existed was when the two sides faced each other across the Strait of Johore.[7]

Only two British regiments were stationed in north Malaya at the outbreak, the East Surreys and the Leicesters, and both were so badly cut up in the opening engagement that their survivors were regrouped into one unit known as The British Battalion. Mr Morrison thought highly of it: it was not usually headline material but it "stuck gamely and cheerfully to what was a heartbreakingly discouraging task." [8]

The only British troops in Malaya who had really had some training were the Argylls, who were stationed at Port Dickson at the outbreak and were sent up to the Grik road, south of Kroh, to hold the Japanese aiming in the direction of Ipoh.[9] The Argylls had worked out the same type of encircling and outflanking tactics as the Japanese had, and were very good at it, fighting "like tigers"; but there were not enough of them to make the final difference.[10] Their OC, Colonel Ian Stewart, had some months before the war made them march from Mersing to Singapore, about a hundred miles, which they did in six days; on arrival, all the drivers who had brought down the Bren guns and supplies had to march an equal distance round the Island. A tall, lean, blue-eyed man of great ability and much personal charm, Stewart was promoted to brigadier soon after the fighting started.[11]

At about three o'clock on that Sunday afternoon the Japanese came straight down the road to attack the Gurun position, and fighting went on for a couple of hours, while Heath, who had come up from Kuala Lumpur, conferred with Murray-Lyon at his HQ south of Gurun and Moorhead's men retired as ordered upon Kroh. Heath agreed to let Murray-Lyon take his tattered battalions back to the Perak river, a frighteningly long leap of retreat of sixty miles, but asked him to hold them on the way at the Muda river in order to cover the Penang approaches while the town completed its evacuation and scorched earth policy. Checking by telephone with Percival, Heath obtained agreement as far as the Muda but was told that Murray-Lyon must not go back from there without Percival's permission.

The Japanese attacked again during the night, again straight down the road, got through the Punjabi outposts, through some of the British Battalion positions, took one regimental and one brigade HQ at the cost of every man there, and smashed a gap clean through the centre. Murray-Lyon wasted no time but decided to withdraw behind the Muda river that night, permission or no permission.[12]

Down in Singapore the air raids had stopped for the time being, and there was little or nothing in the way of hard news coming in, so that most people kept going on rumour. Mr Hammonds was able to follow the Japanese rate of advance more reliably than most by watching the advertisements of the Hong Kong and Shanghai Bank: these gave daily lists of "branches closed until further notice." Otherwise there were few signs of menace.

The parties and dances went on, there was plenty of food (the hotels kept two meatless days a week but poultry and game did not count), and there was plenty of petrol, for everyone could draw the extra allowance for civil defence workers, and many Europeans had two cars so they drew petrol for both and used it for one. Schools and churches prepared nativity plays and carol services, wives mixed the Christmas pudding, and the hot monsoon rains poured down. There was one reminder of the war, however, that grew more insistent as the days went by: the trains from the north bringing in, not just civilians leaving their estates, or British from Penang, but the wounded soldiers from the areas where the fighting was going on.[13]

A sense of crazy unreality was beginning to percolate every aspect of life from the outposts to the Island. This was going to increase steadily as the weeks went by, but it was already showing.

Mr Morrison and his fellow reporters went to the Majestic Hotel at Ipoh for lunch and found it almost deserted. There had been two air raids that morning and the hotel staff had bolted, leaving as self-appointed manager a drunken middle-aged Scotsman, who was wandering round with a loaded shotgun. He was a planter on his way south with his Eurasian mistress, Rose, who was completely devoted to him and who talked to the journalists about her childhood in Siam and her cleverness in outwitting the Chinese traders who tried to cheat her. Their car stood outside, crammed with belongings. The reporters helped themselves to drinks from the bar and food from the kitchen, while the radio played loud dance music through the empty rooms. It was like a scene from a film, one of those attractively tarnished pieces of seedy heroics and fading gangsters characteristic of Hollywood's best period.[14]

3

On Monday December 15, with two months of Raffles's Lion Gate still to run, Far East HQ agreed that control of Burma air forces should be transferred to India, subject to three conditions. First: until the RAF Singapore had been strongly reinforced Burma's air resources could be called on to attack Japanese shipping in the Gulf and Japanese troops on the Isthmus and near Bangkok. Second: India or Burma Air HQ should take over plans of operations for the RAF bomber squadrons in China. Third: they should do this for the American bombers in China as well. It sounded all right, but Singapore had no idea how low the India-Burma air resources were, and nobody told Wavell anything about it, or his Air Staff either, until the conclusive signal came in at Delhi.

Percival was taking another look at his troop dispositions, and finding the choice of strategy neither simple nor attractive. One Japanese division was coming down the trunk road south of Alor Star. Another was coming down the trunk road to threaten Kroh and Grik. A third was coming across country from Kota Bahru. All three were moving south at a surprisingly steady rate, and as the peninsula narrowed the lines of advance would begin to converge. To meet them Percival had what was left of the 11th Indian Division, badly mauled and depleted from the havoc of the first week, the Australians under the command of Lieutenant-General Henry Gordon Bennett in Johore (Mr Braddon's unit on the mud near Mersing among them), the Sikhs and Gurkhas behind Kuantan (Captain Russell-Roberts's party in the rubber trees included), and the Island garrison. He had been told to defend the airfields no matter what. But the airfields were widely separated, hard to reach and easy to lose, and there were not nearly enough aircraft left to provide cover.

Percival knew by now that the 18th British Division was on its way, but they could not arrive for almost a month and the troops he had would have to hold till then. There was no point in dwelling on the additional facts that the 18th Division was new and young, untrained for jungle warfare, and due to arrive in Singapore from a very long sea voyage so that they would still be soft. The plan Percival worked out was for all his available soldiers in north Malaya to get behind some natural obstacle that could bring the tanks to a halt and regroup there. It was most prudent, he thought, to select the Perak river where the road and railway cross it at Kuala Kangsar, north-west of Ipoh, and due south of Grik.[15] It was well placed to meet a frontal assault but (like all the chosen defensive positions) not proof against the infiltration of small groups round the flanks, something that the Japanese were particularly good at. It also meant losing Penang, but the enemy was uncomfortably close to Penang any way and the Europeans had left.

On Tuesday December 16 the *Guardian* leader, headed simply "Singapore," and sober and sensible in tone, made special reference to the airfields of Malaya. "We have no clear idea here of how many there are of these airfields or where they are placed." Singapore must be kept in "active use." The headlines of the main news column read: [16]

ENEMY GAINS GROUND IN NORTH MALAYA
BURMESE AIR BASE LOST
THE SIEGE OF HONG KONG BEGINS
AMERICANS BOMB 2 TRANSPORTS
SITUATION WORSENED

The Times reported "activity in Kelantan" and that the enemy had gained ground in "the north-west province of Kedah," going on to say that fighting continued "south of Kedah." A look at the map would show that this meant the Japanese had gone beyond Penang.[17] The papers still kept pretty quiet about Penang: the *Straits Times* that day grumbled that it was getting more information about distant wars than about what was going on "on our own borders." But Singapore soon knew that Penang was in enemy hands. Not only were the refugees coming into the Island, but the Japanese were broadcasting in English from the Penang radio station ("Hello, Singapore, this is Penang calling—how do you like our bombings?"). Mr Morrison was appalled to find that the radio station had been left intact. It was so obviously one of the principal objectives to prevent the enemy from seizing, and "two minutes with a sledge-hammer and all that delicate machinery would be comparatively unserviceable." [18]

Communiqués were sent out saying that a complete scorched earth policy had been carried out in Penang, and it is true that stocks of oil and petrol were burnt, ammunition blown up, the power station put out of action and the civil airport partially destroyed, but the Japanese found many ships, barges, junks and yachts untouched in the harbour. *The Times* did not get the report of the evacuation until December 20, at least five days after it happened, and it quoted Mr F. D. Bisseker, described as "a senior unofficial member of the Legislative Council," who said that Penang had been "bombed into impotency." The civil population, he said, had "evaporated in the most amazing manner," there was looting, pollution, "complete disruption," dirt, stink, débris, rats, blood, "innumerable horrors which cannot be mentioned." [19]

The slow pull back towards the Perak river ground on. In Singapore the signal advising C-in-C India of Duff Cooper's appointment was somewhat belatedly sent, and the composition and terms of reference of the War Council made public. There were seven members besides Duff Cooper: the Governor, the C-in-C Far East, the Naval Commodore, the Air Officer Commanding, the General Officer Commanding, the Director of Propaganda, and the OC Australian Troops, when in Singapore. Their task was to relieve of extra responsibility the C-in-Cs and HM Representatives in the Far East, and to give "broad political guidance."

The Times leader of Wednesday December 17 pointed out that the Singapore defence plans had been based on assumptions of naval superiority and at least air equality, "neither of which at present exists," and that the danger was not the capture of Singapore "which is strong enough to withstand far greater forces than the Japanese are yet able to deploy against it" but that its effectiveness as "a naval base and great commercial port" might be comparatively neutralized.[20] The legend of the fortress was as strong as ever.

On Thursday December 18 two things happened that showed variants on the shape of things to come. The first was the arrival of twenty-two men at Tavoy on the coast of Burma. Led by Captain N. F. Nicholson they had got away from Bangkok some days previously and had made a most uncomfortable journey up a river and over the hills.

Plagued by colic and leeches, they arrived in ragged clothes and with ragged beards and went on to Rangoon, arriving four days later at ten in the morning just in time for the first air raid, described by Captain Nicholson as a "filthy mess." The party travelled out of Bangkok to the west until they reached the river at an old walled town called Kanchanaburi. The river was the Kwai.[21]

The other happening was that the Japanese chose that night to launch their full assault on the island of Hong Kong. The tide was favourable and the night dark, as the moon was not due to rise before midnight. Thick smoke from a blazing paint factory and burning oil tanks screened their approach still better, and this was added to a little later when a rubber factory caught fire. The Japanese pushed ashore with full determination and were met by a stubborn and gallant defence fighting bitterly and disjointedly in small detachments. The week-long process of surrounding and overrunning these, piece by piece, had begun: it was going to finish on Christmas Day.[22]

4

Now a great fuss broke out on the Island about the digging of trenches on the sports grounds to prevent enemy aircraft from landing there. It was difficult for the municipal engineers to rustle up enough labour to dig them but, having done this, and having started to dig straight trenches six feet wide and three feet deep, somebody said straight ones were air raid traps when it came to machine-gunning and the trenches must be staggered. When the job was well under way, somebody else asked what was going to be done about the piles of earth excavated from the trenches, as soft earth was ideal for parachutists to drop on and it must all be carted away. Right on the heels of this last objection came the public health authority, stating that trenches in low ground bred mosquitoes and that they must all be filled in. They finally compromised by filling them half in, a typical kind of Singapore solution at that period. Down at the docks shiploads of essential supplies for the troops stood waiting to be unloaded and important stocks of rubber stood waiting to be loaded while the civil authorities wrangled with their opposite numbers in London about rates of pay for the dock labourers.[23]

A man called John Brown in Grimsby wrote to *The Times* that air support was vital to protect fleets. *The Times* published his letter on Friday December 19, along with one from Lord Strabolgi saying that Britain should have at least one carrier in the Far East.[24] In the *Guardian* the lead story was a despatch from Libya and the Malaya news took second lead, but there was a powerful Low cartoon called "the lesson that must be learnt" showing the supreme importance of airfield defences and referring to Kota Bahru. There was a description by one of the Singapore radio commentators of a visit to Army HQ in the north where the general—presumably Heath—had not slept for three days but was "unperturbed," dealing with telephones, orderlies, despatches, interviews and conferences "with no more excitement than and as politely as if he had been planning a cocktail party instead of war." [25]

The Japanese who had landed at Kota Bahru had by now pushed down the coast as far as Kuala Trengganu and were clearly headed for Kuantan. Over 160 miles of territory the local administration had broken down, numbers of armed Japanese were at large in it and most bridges, ferries and telephone wires were intact, as well as the roads such as they were: to the south of Kuantan ran a hundred miles of jungle with no road leading south beyond Pekan at the mouth of the Pahang river. The only way out was the 100-mile Jeruntut road, which could be cut at any point, and its two ferries, one at each end, were easy to put out of action. By now a few reinforcements from the north had got as far as Kuantan where they were welcome, bringing a few armoured cars commanded by Lieutenant Tovey, who had made some very useful reconnaissance patrols in Trengganu.[26]

By dawn on Sunday December 21 the Japanese had driven a wedge between Maltby's two brigades in the dripping tangled hills of Hong Kong. The way Far East events were going provoked Sir Compton Mackenzie to say that the troops in Malaya, Hong Kong and (later) Burma were "expended like instalments of hire-purchase to keep an Empire." [27]

On Sunday, Pibul's government in Siam signed in Bangkok a complete pact of defensive and offensive alliance with Japan, to take effect at once, by which Siam would help Japan by all political, military and economic means in her power.[28] This was going to come in useful later when the Japanese had over eighty thousand prisoners of war in Malaya to dispose of, feed, secure and employ. On the same day the Japanese Imperial Guards saw their first action. Yamashita's forces were always strung out, but were so competently organised that he was able to bring fresh small units through to the head of his columns all the time, which kept up the momentum of attack and caused the British and Indians to believe they were up against a legend.[29]

5

Wavell spent the fourth week of December, third week of the war, preoccupied with the question of the Burma defences, in the course of which he had a meeting with Chiang Kai-Shek. The second, and fatal, attack on Wake Island took place, beginning before dawn on Tuesday December 23, and taking that day to complete. Admiral Kajioka made no mistake this time, arriving with two carriers, the *Green Dragon* and the *Flying Dragon* (*Soryu* and *Hiryu*), and at the day's end accepted the surrender of all three islands that formed the group, along with 470 servicemen and 1,146 civilians, who became prisoners. Fifty-two American soldiers and marines and seventy civilians had died that day, and the Japanese had lost 820 dead and 333 wounded.[30] On the same day the Japanese began to test for themselves the "farcical defences" of Sarawak, defended by "that expendable battalion" of Punjabis under Lieutenant-Colonel C. M. Lane, which took heavy losses and fought with immense tenacity and valour until the few that were left were taken prisoner fourteen weeks later.[31] *The Times* said that it had been "authoritatively stated in London" that a complete scorched earth policy had been carried out in Penang,[32] while the *Guardian* printed the menacing headline: "Hong Kong Still Holds Out."[33] By nightfall the Japanese had nine battalions ashore on Hong Kong island, and the end was drawing very near.

The Australian Associated Press received a report from Singapore that all over Malaya people were wanting to know why, after two years of assurances that the defences were impregnable, strategic defensive areas had already been lost and Singapore itself had been put on the defensive. The man in the street was beginning to realise that the enemy had again been underestimated. Concerning the raids on Penang, people were asking why the defences had been constructed in the first place if it was not intended to use them.[34] Someone who might be able to supply answers to questions of this sort arrived in Malaya that day: Lieutenant-General Sir Henry Pownall, KCB, KBE, DSO, MC, who had come to take over from Brooke-Popham. Whitehall had agreed to change horses after all.

Much of the responsibility for the changeover rests with Duff Cooper. It is true that Brooke-Popham was due to be replaced and that Pownall was designated his successor even before the Far East war started but, as has been seen, Whitehall had been hesitant. The Chiefs of Staff had told Churchill that the three commanders of the military services in Malaya controlled operations, and that Brooke-Popham had no power to intervene, and this information was passed on to Duff Cooper, who pressed his views that Brooke-Popham ought to be re-called, views he transmitted to Churchill through the War Cabinet secretary. This method worked: at all events, it was after receiving these messages from Duff Cooper that Brooke-Popham's recall was hurried through and Pownall was asked to leave for Malaya as soon as he could be ready.[35]

Churchill himself was by now at the White House, having made the eight-day crossing of the Atlantic in the new battleship *Duke of York,* which was still working-up, and flying in to Washington from Hampton Roads on the evening of December 22. In the course of the talks with Roosevelt, Churchill reaffirmed Britain's war policy, which was to defeat Germany first and then turn its full attention upon Japan. It was by now obvious that the Philippines could not be held, so the Allies must at all costs hang on to Burma and Australia. At the same time they must hold the line Malaya-Sumatra-Java and the rest of the Indonesian archipelago, to protect the air bases (there might have sounded a hollow laugh from north Malaya at this point), the naval bases, and the lines of communication between the Far East and India, the Middle East, and Britain. After long talks, and voicing many doubts, Britain agreed to General Marshall's proposal for a unified overall command in the Far East. The plan was announced almost two weeks after Churchill's arrival in the United States.

Another change of command took place on December 24, when Brigadier A. C. M. Paris took over from Murray-Lyon, whose men took this as a direct admission of failure. The 11th Indian Division had a high opinion of Murray-Lyon, whom they had known for a year, and they had liked his Divisional symbol, an eleven-spoked wheel, "intended to symbolise the wheels of the 11th Division revolving towards Singora." [36]

It seems incongruous to mention it, but that day was, of course,

Christmas Eve. Greetings were sent to all ranks of the troops in be-
leaguered Hong Kong, from the Governor, Sir Mark Young, "in pride
and admiration," exhorting them to "fight on, hold fast for King and
Empire," and from Fortress HQ, which was briefer:

> Christmas greetings to all. Let this day be historical in the grand
> annals of our Empire. The order of the day is Hold Fast.[37]

It is one thing to say it and another to do it, and for those tired men
worn with fatigue, reduced by heavy losses—one battalion down to
175 out of their original 800, and the other, almost as badly depleted,
with its back to the sea, and all of them short of water—the end came
quickly. At a quarter past three in the afternoon of Christmas Day
Maltby told the Governor that any further resistance was impossible,
and that evening in the Peninsula Hotel in Kowloon Sir Mark Young
formally surrendered the Crown Colony, unconditionally, to General
Sakai.[38] "It had taken Japan eighteen days," wrote Mr Bateson, "to
conquer her first defended British territory." The British had lost 955
killed and 659 wounded and missing; the Japanese had lost 675 killed
and 2,079 wounded.[39] "Sir Mark Young," said the *Guardian,* "stayed at
the Peninsula Hotel overnight under the protection of Japanese
troops." [40]

6

Christmas Day brought no joy in Malaya. Half the tin mines and one
rubber tree in every six were in enemy hands. The big ships were at
the bottom of the sea. The aircraft strength was halved. Dissension and
squabbling rent the War Council, fussy protocol strangled civil and
military co-operation. The Australians at the Bukit Langkap mine had
just finished undoing all the work of the first frantic days and gone
back on orders to Mersing, where they ate a large Christmas dinner and
next day underwent an air raid by twenty-seven persistent bombers.[41] In
Washington the Allied summit meeting agreed on the formation of Far
East Command, known as ABDACOM *—the ABDA powers being
American, British, Dutch and Australian—and named as Supreme Commander General Sir Archibald Wavell, of all British generals the one
with the highest reputation at this stage in the war but one, as Mr Swinson pointed out, who "had an unlucky streak in action and often seemed

* Australian, British, Dutch Allied Command.

to arrive on the scene when the situation was desperate." [42] Pownall was to be Chief of Staff, and the naval, air and land forces were to be under the command of Admiral Hart of America, Sir Richard Peirse of Britain with the American Major-General Lewis H. Brereton as his deputy, and the Dutch Lieutenant-General H. ter Poorten. Chiang Kai-Shek of course remained Supremo of all forces in China.

ABDACOM was an attractive concept, and it set the pattern for all the invaluable mixed commands that were to follow and make such a difference to the rest of the war, but it ran into difficulties at once. Wavell, expected to co-ordinate forces of mixed troops scattered all over an enormous area in comparatively small groups with widely separated bases, quickly found that some of them were not in direct touch with his Java HQ; the Burma forces, for example, could communicate with him only through Delhi. The march of events also proved too fast for such a patchy organisation and ABDACOM began to fall to pieces even as it was being put together. The assorted commanders were in the position of people hastily trying to plug a leak in one place while water poured out of holes in half a dozen others.

Having accomplished the recall of Brooke-Popham, Duff Cooper now increased the pressure to oust Sir Shenton Thomas. In an off the record talk with Mr Dickinson, Inspector-General of Police, Duff Cooper asked for his reactions if Whitehall could be persuaded to recall the Governor. Dickinson, startled by this surprising and indiscreet question, replied that it would be a tremendous blow to morale as the Governor represented the King and had established good relations with the various native leaders. Duff Cooper then put forward the idea of recalling Sir Shenton Thomas's Colonial Secretary, Stanley W. Jones, CMG, appointed in 1939. Jones was conscientious and reliable, but brusque, impatient and high-handed in manner so that he frequently antagonised the people he had dealings with. Dickinson did not always approve of Jones's manner, but he did not think it a good idea to have him withdrawn. After this talk, which took place over a whisky and soda on the veranda on a hot sticky evening, Duff Cooper wrote to Churchill that some senior civilian officials were not coping very well and that changes might be necessary, but he did not mention specific names.[43]

Another meeting took place on the evening of Boxing Day, the day on which Hart left for Java and Pownall took over officially from Brooke-Popham. At half past eleven that night Brigadier Simson, tired and grubby from his journey from Heath's HQ to Singapore, presented himself at Flagstaff House to speak to General Percival. The General invited him in, gave him a whisky and soda, and sat listening while Simson poured out an impassioned plea to set up defences along the north shore of the Island. He said he had plenty of equipment, mines, wire, tank blocks, underwater obstacles, searchlights, and plenty of native labour. He talked on and on, it was nearly one o'clock in the morning, both men were tired, and Simson felt he was making no impression. Finally he asked why the General would not agree. Percival said he thought the construction of this kind of defence work would be bad for morale. Simson, surprised and horrified, stood up to go; but not before making one final remark: "Sir, it's going to be much worse for morale if the Japanese start running all over the Island." [44]

Simson had just come down from the north, where the Japanese were continuing to set the pace. They were free of excessive administration, simply organised, lightly equipped and "ignoring, almost recklessly, normal security precautions." Driving down the roads to the south, moving small groups in boats down the streams and rivers to get behind the British outposts, they kept the British "constantly looking over their shoulders." Whenever the vanguard showed signs of flagging, fresh troops were leap-frogged through them to keep up the momentum of advance so that the British were "hustled out of one defence line after another."

The British had an elaborate administration, held cautiously to the book of rules and were loaded with masses of cumbersome equipment. The Indians at Jitra had been pushed back by "only the advance guard of the Japanese 5th Division." The withdrawals often started before a serious attack developed; the British command "failed to think and act aggressively" and usually did not stop to find out the strength of any infiltration, let alone make positive counter-attacks, organise ambushes or set up patrols in reply. Right from the start the Japanese therefore "gained a moral ascendancy that was never shaken." [45] An additional complication was the wretched communications which broke down time and again so that orders failed to reach their destination, and were any way being constantly changed. The Perak river position was a case in point. It was not a particularly good position as the river did not run at right angles to the road, but Yamashita expected it to be defended in some strength. He ordered a regiment of the Imperial Guards to make a hook movement upon Ipoh, and on Boxing Day, much to their surprise, they went across the river unopposed. At the same time Yamashita, bothered by a narrow pass that a determined adversary could hold for weeks, told the commander of the 5th Division, the rather fragile-looking Lieutenant-General Takuro Matsui, to drive from Ipoh straight for Kuala Lumpur.

Yamashita disapproved of letting the British get away during the night retreats. He was emphatic about this: "I don't just want them pushed back, I want them destroyed." [46] The drive began and by the end of the day on Saturday December 27 the British were out of Ipoh. Presumably the Scotsman from the hotel had gone ahead of them. On the same day, in the Philippines, Manila was declared an open city, and General Jonathan Wainwright was ordered to defend Bataan, where his men were about to experience the same ordeal, of forever looking over their shoulders for the enemy, with which the British in Malaya were now only too familiar.

Over in the Kuantan sector a message came for Brigadier Painter on the newly completed telephone line from Kuala Lumpur to say that he was to regard the beaches as the outpost line and get everything, including all his guns and vehicles, behind the river. Painter, acutely conscious of his instructions to defend the airfield at all costs—the project to which all his plans and work had been devoted—and uneasily aware of the enemy moving steadily towards him, objected, saying that the beaches were unsuitable as an outpost line.[47] Garhwali patrols on forays up into Trengganu had met Japanese troops in lorries feeling their way forward.

On the morning of December 28 he put these views and the facts before Major-General Barstow, who had come up by car to see for himself. Barstow agreed that Painter was right and went back to report to Percival. By that time the British on the west coast were falling back upon Kampar, with the enemy in tanks and lorries and on bicycles coming straight down like a running tide behind them. The Argylls and Punjabis gallantly held the rearguard; at Dipang, above Kampar, Colonel Selby's Gurkhas had established a bridgehead and the Argylls came through it, led by Stewart whom Mr Morrison had interviewed. As Stewart met Selby over the bridge he said: "I've come to hand over this business to you. It's a running concern." [48]

CHAPTER V

In and Out the Windows

I

THE crucial year was coming to its close. The Japanese Army was advancing down both coasts in Malaya, driving the dwindling British air forces back from one airfield after another, often causing them to quit before a particular base was seriously threatened. All the forward airfields went in the early days. They were sometimes abandoned in such confusion that large stockpiles of fuel and ammunition together with quantities of road metal were left for the enemy to find. They made good use of such bonuses, speedily repairing runways and fuelling planes so that within hours the airfields were working to capacity and the retreating Birtish were harried even further.

The Japanese infantry stood up in light easy clothes and carried the barest minimum of accoutrement, whereas the British, in the vivid description of Colonel Spencer Chapman, were "equipped like Christmas trees with heavy boots, web equipment, packs, haversacks, water bottles, ground sheets and even greatcoats and respirators so that they could hardly walk, much less fight." [1] The key difference, however, was in morale: the British were falling back and they knew it, the Japanese were advancing at a great rate and they knew that, too. The attackers came cheerfully on, elated by success, and the defenders dropped stolidly back, puzzled by the way in which they reached one supposedly defensive position only to find that there was no time to prepare it before they were off again to trudge away to another.

One small, isolated action on Sunday December 28, three weeks from the outbreak, showed what might have been done. A group known as the Perak Flotilla, consisting of the twenty-three-year-old destroyer *Scout* and a few light craft with fifty Australians organised by the Royal Navy, code name Roseforce, went up to disrupt Japanese lines of communication west of the Perak river, where they landed successfully near Trong and were able to ambush and put out of action lorries and staff cars on the coast road. This action had little or no effect on the outcome of the campaign as a whole, but several dozen Roseforces might well have turned the course of events.[2] No one else attempted anything like it.

Barstow, having returned to HQ, rang up Painter on Monday evening to say that he had explained Painter's views to Percival and that fresh orders were on the way. These stated that it was vital to keep the brigade and its "valuable equipment" intact "for fighting elsewhere"; the principal responsibility of the CO was to hold the airfield "for a few extra days," not to "jeopardise his force." Painter, now forced to do his homework all over again, started making plans that night and continued at a staff conference in the morning that was interrupted by air attacks. The Japanese planes went for everything including the ferry, where they severed a cable. Painter's sappers repaired this, splitting the ferry in two for safety, and during that Tuesday night all the guns and vehicles were shipped over to the slightly more sheltered south side of the river.[3]

On that same Tuesday the Bedfordshires landed in Bombay, where they were able to spend "three useful weeks getting fit and trained." [4] Wavell at Meerut spent "a long happy day" pig-sticking and came back in the evening to find a telegram from Churchill appointing him Supreme Commander of ABDACOM. He commented: "I've heard of having to hold the baby but this is twins." [5]

Up in the north the British were standing at Kampar. This was the best position that they had so far found: a four-mile semicircle with an open field of fire over a tin mining area, astride the trunk road, and flanked by ranges of hills up to four thousand feet high, covered with jungle. Behind them was a big rubber estate. There was a side road that looped round the hills to the west and the enemy might come by that, or take troops in boats to the mouth of the Perak river and cut the line there, in which case the craft left behind at Penang would come in useful. Brigadier Paris dispersed his forces to guard against the varied possibilities and throughout December 30 little probing moves were made and held.[6]

Down in Singapore Duff Cooper presided at a meeting of the War Council which assembled minus the Governor. Sir Shenton Thomas was making a tour up-country, and Jones stood in as his deputy. Duff Cooper asked Simson to the meeting, and asked him to speak to the War Council about civil defence. Simson said that all he knew about civil defence was some experience of the London blitz but he would talk a little about that, and, when he had done so, he was asked to wait in the ante-room. Called back a few minutes later, he was astonished to hear that Duff Cooper, speaking for the unanimous Council, was offering him the job of Director-General of Civil Defence, subject to Percival's approval.

Simson refused. He said he believed that Singapore would soon come under siege and in such an event the Chief Engineer, which he was, became an official of the utmost importance. He was asked to leave the room again and, when called back, fixed by Duff Cooper's "special stony stare," was ordered to take the post. Simson demurred on the absent Governor's behalf but was given in writing full powers to act, covering both the Island and Johore. Duff Cooper then notified the press so that the news would be in print and beyond recall by the time the Governor returned.

The Governor got back in time for breakfast next morning. Greeted by Jones with all the information about the previous night's meeting, news which apparently lost nothing in the telling, he was furious. He called Duff Cooper's action "a despicable trick," referring to him as usual as "the chancellor," and repeating that as Governor it was for him to make appointments, not for someone sent out in the last few weeks from England, whether he had Cabinet rank or not. He was particularly angry at finding out that Duff Cooper had been saying: "I've put one over on the little man."

Over coffee, Jones calmed the Governor down and advised him to swallow his medicine for the sake of public morale. If the appointment, now announced in the papers, was cancelled, it would bring the War Council quarrels into the open and then anything might happen. Sir Shenton sent for Simson and told him he could be in charge in Singapore but not in Johore, where it might upset the Sultan. Simson said the Sultan was friendly and they might go and talk with him. Sir Shenton refused.

The Governor's amendment was not published in the press, so Simson "spent the rest of the war with the Governor's restricted orders in one pocket and Duff Cooper's plenary powers in the other." Percival sympathised with the Governor's rage at being passed over, but in the end it really was not going to make any difference.[7]

2

The Times reported no action worth mentioning in Malaya for nearly a week, treating these days as a lull or breathing space. Now it printed a dispatch saying that Ipoh had never been meant to provide a stand. All had moved to a prearranged plan "to fall back gradually to more advantageous ground for defensive operations in view of the limited resources of men and material at present at our disposal." [8]

It is worth taking a look at the British newspapers of this period, which tended always to give first place to the American side of the Far East story. Pearl Harbor (understandably), Manila and Luzon generally got most space while Malaya, like a poor relation, was accorded little attention except when there was a real surprise, and these were nasty, like the fall of Penang or, of course, the fall of Hong Kong on Christmas Day. Reading the papers of December 1941 and January 1942, with the knowledge of hindsight, is an eerie experience. Day after day comments appear near the top of the page saying things like "little activity is reported from the north-western sector today," but, if one persists far enough down the column to find a place name and can find the place concerned on one of the minute maps (some papers printed maps showing the whole of Malaya in a space the size of four postage stamps), it becomes ominously clear that, little by little, the names creep southwards.

Reports of Japanese reverses, fully written up, dealt with incidents involving very few men. One such incident happened at a small railway station south of Ipoh, where a captain in the Argylls arrived with his sergeant-major and his orderly to bring rations to the section on duty and find out how they were getting on. They suddenly saw a group of Japanese, about fifteen in number, stealing into the far end of the station under the guidance of a Tamil coolie, while a larger party with bicycles came up the line further off in the distance. The captain told the section to cover the flank, the sergeant-major and the orderly opened up with machine-guns, and a lively scrap took place in and out of the station buildings. In one room the captain, bursting in upon several Japanese, threw away his rifle and attacked with his fists, while the sergeant-major who had run out of ammunition grasped his gun by the barrel (it had blistered his hands, he found out later) and lashed out with its butt. The Japanese kicked and bit and fought furiously; the captain bashed one of them on the head with his steel helmet and knocked him out. Leaving "at least twelve" of the enemy dead behind them, the three got away in the Japanese lorry, taking the knocked-out man along as a prisoner.[9]

This episode, and others like it, were given the full treatment, while reverses involving hundreds of men over miles of country were reported briefly. Bland reassuring statements were quoted. One special correspondent wrote: "All that Singapore stands for in the defensive strategy and in the history and tradition of the British Empire cannot fall in a night." He wrote it on January 3 but it was delayed in transit and was not published until January 6 in London. The following day, readers found: "Many villages have been rendered useless to the enemy. . . . Our artillery has been wreaking havoc among the enemy's positions . . . the scorched earth policy is being applied with greater thoroughness." But a word of caution somehow slipped in here and there. "The battle for Kuala Lumpur cannot be long delayed." [10] Kuala Lumpur! when only eight days before the reports had been comfortably murmuring about "the more advantageous ground" south of Ipoh! when between Ipoh and Kuala Lumpur the distance was over a hundred miles! If the Japanese were advancing at the rate of almost fifteen miles a day . . . then, as Brigadier Simson had foreseen when Percival would not agree about fortifying the north shore, ruin stared the defenders in the face.

3

At dawn on Wednesday December 31 the Japanese made a full-out assault on the dilapidated ferry at Kuantan. Furious scraps raged all day as the fighting flickered backwards and forwards along the river, but by evening Painter's men were all across it, having disengaged at the cost of 500 losses. That night they had an excellent dinner with which to see the old year out. Raffles Hotel in Singapore put on, as a matter of course, the customary New Year's Eve fancy dress ball.[11] In London there were the usual festivities; and *The Times* that day carried among its advertisements "wanted" posts for seventeen companions and governesses, seventeen housekeepers, twelve ladies' maids and maids generally, and forty-two cooks and cooks-general; in a parallel column there were notices that seven companions and governesses, twelve housekeepers, seven maids and two cooks required jobs.[12] The *Guardian* war map showed the whole of Malaya southwards from Ipoh on a scale of

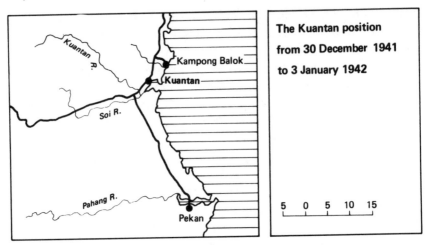

The Kuantan position from 30 December 1941 to 3 January 1942

about fifty miles to the inch, much bigger than most newspaper maps at the time.[13]

The New Year's Day edition of *The Times* led with the Manila situation, and this was being read over London breakfast-tables as the Japanese opened up straight along the Kampar road.[14] Here the British forces were awkwardly placed to receive them, one in a defile on the wrong side of a mountain 4,000 feet high and the other twenty miles away to the south-west near the mouth of the Perak river. The first shock of attack was taken by the British Battalion, who responded "nobly" under shells, mortars, machine-gun fire and air bombings and clung to their unenviable posts on Green Ridge for thirty-six hours.

The Japanese put the pressure on again the following day when Moorhead, seeing the British Battalion threatened by a flank attack that could dislodge them before a few reinforcements got there, ordered Captain Graham and his Sikhs to capture the crest called Thompson's Ridge. Graham had every man served with two drams of rum and started the charge, which went up into "a storm of fire." The first line was taken at bayonet point, and then the second, with severe loss, so that Graham who had "seemed to be everywhere at once" had only thirty men left to lead against the last line. They did it, though, Graham being mortally wounded by a mortar which blew off both legs. His last words were: "Was the attack successful?"

Moorhead reported to Heath by the end of the day that the Kampar position could not be held much longer as his gunners had been in action for three days, the British Battalion was much reduced in numbers, and he had no troops available to relieve either.[15] Down at the mouth of the Perak river Brigadier Paris reported that his men were now too tired to fight effectively and must be disengaged to recover their battle strength. The Japanese in small boats were nosing in along the coast-line, penetrating up the myriad small streams and creeks that wound among the mangrove swamps, difficult to find let alone to attack, and all the while their aircraft came screeching overhead while not a British plane was to be seen.

On the east side the Army had plenty of trouble. Where Painter's men now were the Kuantan river was fordable so that their left flank was under threat. Painter had been told to keep his troops intact (which they no longer were) and to hold the airfield for five days as a protection to the longed-for first convoy of reinforcements now due at Singapore. Unable to obey two utterly contradictory orders, Painter decided that the only solution was to harass the enemy all the time with "aggressive and imaginative" artillery fire, which he now began to do. Reports came in from scouts that the Japanese were moving along the opposite bank of the river to block the escape route, the single road out that led to Jeruntut away to the north-west. With the British begin-ning to move back from Kampar on the west side, a message came up to Painter on Friday January 2 telling him that it would very likely not be as much as five days. Indeed it was not. In the early hours of Saturday he was told to move that night as far as Maran, the fork in the Jeruntut road about sixty miles inland and due west of Kuantan.

Reports, moving unusually quickly, reached London on Friday that Kuantan had been captured by the enemy that day. During daylight on Saturday most of Painter's men managed to get twelve miles along the road to Gambang, reaching it less than an hour and a half before the Japanese, under cover of gathering darkness, opened a "close attack" on the airfield and came along the road sniping from culverts at the rearguard of the British troops. It was "an eye-opener" to find the enemy using a small arms bullet that could, and did, pierce British armoured cars. Two Bren gun carriers collided and started a traffic jam that delayed the retreat still further.[16]

By eight in the evening the airfield rearguard defences, left there to hang on as best they could till nine o'clock and consisting of less than two companies of the Frontier Force Regiment under Lieutenant-Colonel Arthur Cumming, bravely fended off a sharp assault. Cumming and his adjutant, Captain Ian Grimwood, crept up to the perimeter to investigate a burst of firing from the picket line. The Japanese swarmed forward, the two officers fired their pistols and backed separately to safety, which Grimwood reached while drawing the enemy's fire when Cumming's pistol was empty, and Cumming, with two bayonet wounds, reached with the help of the battalion havildar-major who grasped him under the arms and pulled him to shelter. Cumming then led the beating-off of a fresh attack, directed the withdrawal, and took his place in the Bren gun carrier driven by Sepoy Albel Chani and carrying several wounded men in the back. They had a nightmare drive down the road under fire, during which Cumming had his right arm shattered and Chani was shot through the upper part of both legs. Grenades bounced off the wire on the roof and a mine exploded underneath lifting the carrier into the air, but its tracks were not damaged and it pounded on through a road block to safety, whereupon Cumming and Chani both collapsed and were sent to hospital in Singapore. Cumming was subsequently awarded the VC, the first of the war awarded to an Indian Army officer.[17]

It took two days to collect the survivors of this withdrawal, and by great good luck the Japanese did not follow up. The whole move to Jeruntut took three days, the last of them spent in a tapioca plantation, and at dusk on Tuesday a motor transport company arrived to take them out, along a shadowy road with the setting sun glowing red, gold and russet on the trees, up to the Jeruntut ferry, which they reached at ten o'clock to find the river "a rushing torrent" and rain coming down "in buckets." [18]

One other detail remains to be added about that Saturday January 3. The convoy duly docked at Singapore, bringing in the 45th Indian Brigade. "It was not nearly fully trained even for the desert" and certainly it had not had "a day's training for jungle warfare." It was "doomed within less than a fortnight to meet the Japanese Imperial Guards Division and vanish." [19]

4

Matters in Malaya now stood as follows. The British forces in the west of the peninsula were in four sections: one at Bidor, one at Trolak, one at Tanjong Malim, these three like beads on a string in the middle of the road from Ipoh to Kuala Lumpur, and the fourth along the Slim river between the second and third. The forces from the east had got to Jeruntut in the centre of the peninsula, roughly on a level with Bidor.

The Australians from Mersing had also moved over to the middle, to Kluang, where they had been kept busy for days making a road through the rubber. The garrison forces stood to their posts on the Island, and everybody waited for the rest of the reinforcements, who had spent Christmas in Mombasa,[20] to arrive.

A special correspondent sent a report to the *Guardian* after making a tour of the war zones: he said that he found "no signs of alarm in Singapore" and also that the Japanese could expect "increasingly bitter resistance down the peninsula"—optimistic as it sounds, this implies that the Japanese were going to come down the peninsula any way. From the "North Malaya Front" the report stated that the Japanese outnumbered the British five to one and were suffering "enormous casualties." They had what the writer called Whippet tanks. "One came round the corner with a large Rising Sun flag in front. One man, completely unprotected at the back, was spraying either side of the road with a tommy-gun," an officer is quoted as saying.[21]

One reason for the lack of anxiety in Singapore may well have been the fact that reports were so late appearing in the papers. Kelantan, captured on December 8, was not reported until the 22nd, and five weeks after Ipoh was in Japanese hands a press report said it was "suffering bombing." [22]

By Sunday January 4 the Argylls were at the Slim river with orders not to give up the position before the night of January 7-8, an order depressing in itself. It was "the first even semi-prepared position in their experience" and they had reinforcements of a hundred men from Singapore under Captain Drummond Hay who had been implored by every Argyll at the base to let him come too.[23]

The Slim river position looked all right on paper. The river cut across the road and the railway which ran between rubber on one side and the jungle on the other. At the river the road branched off to the east and followed the north bank through Slim Village (Kampong Slim) to the Slim River Bridge, which was to be defended in depth. Paris, back of the line at Tanjong Malim, had anti-tank guns which would have been a lot more use up front. The forward troops at Trolak had two days and nights of repeated air attacks before the Japanese tanks, backed by infantry in lorries, opened the move in bright moonlight at three-thirty in the morning [24] of Wednesday January 7. On that same day *The Times* made two comments of particular interest: "Confidence in ultimate victory pervades the forward battle zones in north Malaya" (it does not say on which side), and "the Japanese have always fought shy of open country." [25] Apart from there not being much open country in that part of the world, there was every reason for the Japanese or anyone else to prefer advancing where there was plenty of cover.

That day, too, the *Guardian* weighed in with a summary of the overall position in the west that was calm and sensible in tone and warned of the wrath to come. It noted the "dogged rearguard actions" that were "delaying the Japanese thrust southwards from Ipoh, chief town of the Malayan tin-mining region," but the left flank was still threatened. The Japanese had made "further landings—not, it is believed in London, in large numbers—on the west coast at the mouth of the Perak and Bernham Rivers" (some accounts spell that Bernam: the *Guardian* version looks a little anglicised), and the "new British line" would be "south of Bidor" given as "about 70 miles north of Kuala Lumpur," at a point where the road from the landing-places met the main route north and south down the peninsula. The report gave the Japanese as "in close pursuit with armoured fighting vehicles, including small tanks" and the defenders as "successfully employing leapfrog tactics to slow them down." A Japanese HQ communiqué was quoted about "mass raids" on the port and airfields of Singapore during the night of January 1 and at dawn on January 3, but gave the British version that these raids had "so far caused little military damage, few civil casualties, and virtually no disruption of essential services." The bombings had been "on a small scale," however, and heavier raids could be expected when Japanese air units were "released from the Philippines." [26]

January 1942 saw many air raids on the Island. Mostly these took place in daylight, according to Mr Barber, and formations of 27, 54 or 81 aircraft flew over, dropping all their bombs simultaneously with devastating results. Brigadier Simson estimated 150 funerals a day though many people in crowded Chinatown disappeared without trace in the ruins, impossible to track down because they had no official documentation such as identity cards and ration books. Hoses and helmets were in short supply, canteens hard to organise, native labour for the burials insufficient. [27]

In the richer residential areas the bombs put the drains out of action and "the stench was nauseating," according to Flight Sergeant McCormac: the government gave free inoculation against typhoid to all who applied. In contrast, the streets in the centre, where the big shops and offices were, continued to be "meticulously" cleaned every day and were "thronged" with Europeans who displayed an "astounding" degree of "serene confidence": "They really seemed to believe the government announcements that Singapore was impregnable."

This confidence persisted in spite of the presence of women from all over Malaya who had come to the Island with nothing but a suitcase crammed with what clothes it would hold and who were living uncomfortably in billets. Even these refugees had little sense of urgency or peril: they refused passages to Australia, preferring to wait for a ship bound for England "where they would be more likely to meet friends." [28] Many of them spent hours in the restaurant at Robinson's drinking coffee and waiting for other friends to turn up, Robinson's being the Malayan equivalent of standing outside Swan and Ed-

The Slim River position 7-8 January 1942

The road down which the British retreated and the Japanese advanced is ▬ ▬ ▬ ▬ ▬ ▬ ▬

The railway is ┼┼┼┼┼┼┼┼┼┼ It was the capture of the bridge (centre right) that was so vital.

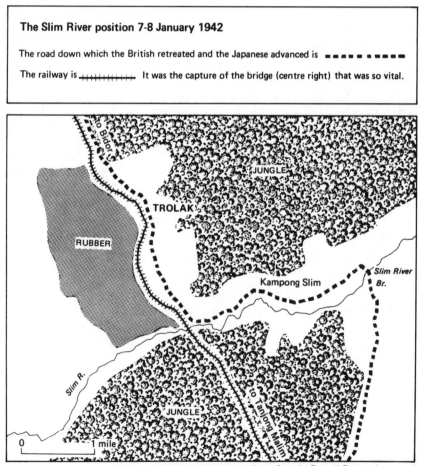

(Details of these maps from Captain Russell-Roberts' account)

gar's in Piccadilly Circus where reputedly one meets everyone one has ever known if one waits long enough. Mrs Buckeridge, wife of the fire chief, worked in Robinson's accounts department, and arranged dozens of loans to those in need, all of which were honoured by the survivors after the war. In the Europeans' houses the servants went on laying out clothes and setting formal meals, but the householders were grateful to be able to use one another's lavatories when their own would not work.[29]

During the night of January 6 Painter's men were shifted out of Jeruntut in streaming rain along a pitch-dark slippery shelf of road with the Malay drivers dropping asleep at every stop. Early on Wednesday January 7 they arrived at Bentong, midway between Jeruntut and Kuala Lumpur. A small town picturesque even in the rain, with its pretty houses surrounded by flowers and clipped yew hedges, it was another world from the one they had left. The sun came out and they rested all day.[30]

There was no rest to be had up at the Slim river. The Japanese had overwhelmed the brave resistance of a Punjabi regiment, bypassed or tanked over and through road blocks, cut all the land communications and forged ahead. By twenty to nine in the morning, after just over five hours of combat, their leading tanks reached the Slim River Bridge.[31] Their advance was deliberate and steady, the light tanks in the lead going at about twelve miles an hour and the heavier ones moving at a walk to match the following infantry. One group was held up by mines on the road for fifteen minutes before they found an unmined side road down which they instantly set off. Many of the anti-tank mortars and Molotov cocktails were damp and would not work. A tank was wrecked on the Trolak road with a line of tanks nose to tail stretching out behind it: "the din that followed defies description," as Lieutenant-Colonel Deakin wrote, hearing tank engines roaring, their guns all firing and crews yelling at the tops of their voices. It was a scene of such chaos that he admitted in his mind "no very clear picture" of what actually happened. The Punjabis at the river had no anti-tank guns and could only fire their rifles.

Major Winkfield of the Gurkhas thought the battle "sounded a bit close" but knew the men were "miles behind the front" and saw no reason for haste when a tank appeared, blazing away with all its guns, going through half the battalion before the Major realised what was happening. More tanks came up, about a dozen altogether, stopped for ten minutes and fired into the surrounding rubber, then went on. The

Major crawled out of his ditch and looked for his battalion: "It had vanished." He made his way alone to base, swimming the river on the way, and next day mustered his survivors: four officers and twenty other ranks left of a full battalion. Within six hours of the start the Japanese had brought their armour nineteen miles behind the supposed front and were unexpectedly halted by a single howitzer set in position by a unit of the Lanarkshire Yeomanry on the Tanjong Malim road and fired by Sergeant Keen, who was killed but whose accurate burst of shot stopped the leading tank.[32]

This whole action can only be fairly described as a major victory for the Japanese and a major defeat for the British. There were heavy casualties among the defending troops: seven battalions mustered after the action and totalled only 1,200 of all ranks, little more than one-fifth of their usual number.[33] For days afterwards, small parties of stragglers came through the jungle to rejoin their units, losing many wounded on the way; some of these tiny groups never got back at all as they fell into enemy hands.[34] Most of these were killed as it was easier for the Japanese to kill them than to be burdened with prisoners in the middle of an advance, and in any case battle fury takes time to die down.

On this same day, by an unlucky stroke of fate, Wavell arrived in Singapore to take up his new appointment. This at least stopped Duff Cooper from constantly talking to Simson about the need for a new Commander-in-Chief, though he kept on about the need for a new Governor and a new Colonial Secretary. Simson had told Duff Cooper about his interview with Percival and his own alarm over the lack of shore defences, and at Duff Cooper's request had drawn up a list of "the ten most important things, military and civilian" that he thought should have been done in the last few months. Duff Cooper sent a copy of the list to Churchill and showed another copy to Wavell as soon as he got there. Wavell sent for Simson and talked to him for an hour, then sent for Percival and asked to be shown the Island defences.[35]

The two generals drove to the north shore, where Wavell saw for himself that indeed there were no defences. He was "very much shaken that nothing had been done," and asked why. Percival replied, as he had replied to Simson, that it would be bad for morale, and Wavell answered, as Simson had answered, that it would be a lot worse for morale if the Japanese started landing, which they seemed likely to do before long. He told Percival to start work on the shore defences at once.

Wavell also went over to the mainland to have a talk with Heath.

He met Gordon Bennett at the same time. Gordon Bennett, an irascible, argumentative man who believed in speaking his mind and was quick to show impatience, told the new Supreme Commander that many of his Australians were quite unready for action, "recruited on a Friday and put on a boat for Malaya the following week." There was still time to give them some jungle training, though, and after all these were Australians: they, under Gordon Bennett, could stop the enemy when no one else could.[36]

Duff Cooper's complaints were now academic. He received a cable from Churchill saying that with the creation of ABDACOM Duff Cooper's mission was now at an end and he should return home by "the safest and most suitable route." [37]

5

On Thursday January 8 Painter's men, with rumours of the Slim river disaster circulating uneasily among them, were prised up out of their welcome rest at Bentong and moved to Rawang, twenty miles north of Kuala Lumpur. The same motor transport company moved them that evening, loading up at five o'clock in the rain and starting away soaked at five-thirty. They got to Rawang at two in the morning and were received by a daybreak bombing raid.[38] This change of base had been planned before Wavell's talk with Heath, in which Wavell gave his opinion that Heath's corps would fall apart if it went on withdrawing across the relatively open country to the south of Kuala Lumpur. As though he had already become certain that Kuala Lumpur could not be held, Wavell proposed preparing a defence line from Segamat along the Muar river. The Australians and the newly arrived Indian brigade would hold the front while Heath's men went back through them and regrouped, all forces gradually coming back to the final line, which was across one of the very few lateral roads in the peninsula, from Mersing through Kluang to Batu Pahat.[39]

A glance at the map reveals the breathtaking extent of the pull back that Wavell was now proposing. From positions, however threatened or unsatisfactory, in the centre of Malaya, the defending armies of the Empire were to retire a hundred and fifty miles in one enormous move, calculated, according to Wavell, to get them clear of the Japanese and give them space and time to regroup, sort themselves out and take breath for the big defensive coming. This proposal was perfectly consistent with the policy expressed by Wavell as far back as lectures he had given at Aldershot in the twenties. Possibly his belief in it had been strengthened by his experiences in the flat wide open desert spaces of North Africa where, whatever else a commander is short of, it is not of room to manoeuvre. Be that as it may, Wavell's remedy was startling and drastic enough to match the situation that had grown up in the one month since hostilities began.

Mr Morrison, in Kuala Lumpur on January 8, met a young staff officer who said there had been "a spot of bother" on the Slim river but the situation was "quite well in hand." When he talked to the men who had actually been there, worn, unshaven, giving him story after story of brave efforts that had come to nothing and narrow escapes, he got a truer picture. He commented that Wavell's plan was a big decision.[40] The press thought so too. Reuter's message out of Singapore that day said: "After nearly five weeks of withdrawals the defending forces in Malaya now appear to be preparing a determined stand." [41]

Painter's men, alerted to another of the interminable small enemy landings on the coast, this time at Kuala Selangor, set off on foot at ten in the morning to the road-river crossing six miles west of Rawang. On the way they were attacked from the air. During one of these attacks Captain Russell-Roberts with a friend and three officers of the divisional staff who had been travelling in a station wagon took shelter for ten minutes; as they dashed into the rubber one of them grabbed a loaf and a pot of jam from the car "so that they could be occupied as pleasantly as possible." They got into position before dusk and "weren't doing badly" when the message came that Wavell had ordered everybody south, so they went across country to Labu, half way between Malacca and Gemas. Passing through Kuala Lumpur on the way they heard the sirens wailing and noticed the shops all boarded up and tank obstacles all over the cricket grounds which was a "very depressing" sight. At Labu, dead tired, they fell asleep at once and then spent "three frustrating days" making ready a position that they "were never called upon to hold." [42]

On Saturday January 10 the great move south began. It jolted into motion in the morning and went on without stopping all that weekend while the endless lines of vehicles rolled by—lorries, cars hastily commandeered, trucks "bearing the names of half the rubber estates in Malaya," motorcycles, eleven steam-rollers and two fire engines, huge tractors whose tracks tore the asphalt surface of the road, trolleys laden with bombs from airfields, camouflaged staff cars, ambulances, repair

trucks, vans full of ordnance and other supplies, every kind of car from
Austin Sevens to Rolls-Royces, all stuffed full of men and material,
driven by British, Australian, Chinese, Malay and Indian drivers some
of whom fell asleep at the wheel or were dazzled by headlights so
that a wreck lay in the ditch every mile of the way. At the railway cross-
ings the long convoy paused to let trains crowded with soldiers go
clanking over. Groups of Chinese and Malays stood in the villages
along the line of march and watched the long parade go by.[43]

The journalists, of course, could not release information about
Wavell's plan, and the papers mentioned the possible loss of Kuala
Lumpur as though it was one more disaster and not part of a considered
strategy. *The Times* headlines on January 10 read: [44]

ALL-DAY BATTLE NORTH OF KUALA LUMPUR
JAPANESE ATTACK WITH TANKS AND INFANTRY
HEAVY CASUALTIES ON BOTH SIDES
SPECIAL DISPATCH FROM THE FRONT
4 ENEMY THRUSTS
FILTERING THROUGH RUBBER ESTATES

The *Guardian* reported a press conference with Heath datelined
"with the Imperial Forces in North Malaya, January 9" in which the
Japanese, "formidable opponents" who combined "the cunning and
resourcefulness of the North-West Frontier tribesmen with the discipline and direction of the modern army," were able to send rested
troops into battle, "while most of our men were very tired by now."
Small tanks could go through "the avenues of trees in the plantations"
which was a danger around Kuala Lumpur, ringed as it was with rubber estates interlaced with good roads. Rubber stocks had been burnt
in the town, and mine and estate machinery destroyed so "the enemy
will not be able to benefit by his conquest for some time to come" (the
positive verb "will" made it look inevitable, though the article went
on to say that the loss "would be very serious").[45]

It was true about the destruction in and around Kuala Lumpur. At
one estate the journalists found the Australian owner distributing rice
to his employees, two months' supply to each, while his old Chinese
overseer looked dazedly at the wreck of the processing plant he had lovingly tended for more than twenty years and had been ordered to smash
up the day before. The manager, who was "heartbroken," pointed to
his perfect trees and the contented labour force that he now had to

abandon: his car, crammed with possessions, stood ready for the journey south.

In the town, which was of course the federal capital, demolition squads were blowing up bridges while columns of black smoke rose into the air from the burning stocks of rubber and the streets were knee deep in paper and cardboard from the stores now being systematically looted. "Every conceivable object" was being "fiercely fought for and taken away"—radios, telephones, sewing machines, rolls of cloth and carpets, tinned foods, golf clubs and tennis balls, sacks of rice—carried off by hand, on bicycles, loaded on ox-carts. The only thing missing was liquor—the Army had collected up all it could find and smashed all the bottles with sledge-hammers.

The reporters went to the Residency, a spacious white house in flowering grounds, and were able to wander in. No flag flew from the roof and the big rooms were empty. A half-finished whisky and soda stood on a table by a sofa, a half-ironed dress lay on a table upstairs, typed letters waiting for signature lay on a desk, the cabinets of display silver, the official files, the royal portraits were undisturbed. In the papers the report has the sentence: "It was as if the owners expected to return the following day and carry on where they had left off"; but what owners, except in direst emergencies, leave drinks half swallowed, dresses half ironed, *overnight?* All the big houses near the Residency were equally deserted.

The reporters took a look at the silent barricaded Government Survey Department. Not a soul was in sight. Mr Morrison ("all of us were in a reckless, truculent mood") smashed a window, climbed in, and found stacks of wonderful maps, many of them tremendously detailed. He wanted to set fire to the whole supply, but a colleague persuaded him not to, saying it would mean burning down all the municipal buildings. "I wish now," wrote Mr Morrison, "that I had done so." [46]

6

It was now the turn of the Australians, whose fiery commander, Gordon Bennett, was preparing for the battle that would decide the fate of Singapore. Already the Australians at Kluang had been sent across to Muar on the west coast, south of Malacca. Here they were "put in the picture" by the intelligence officer, whose picture did not correspond precisely with actual events.

Mr Braddon and his companions heard that half Malaya had been "systematically abandoned," that a scorched earth policy had been "conscientiously employed," that Kuala Lumpur had been declared an

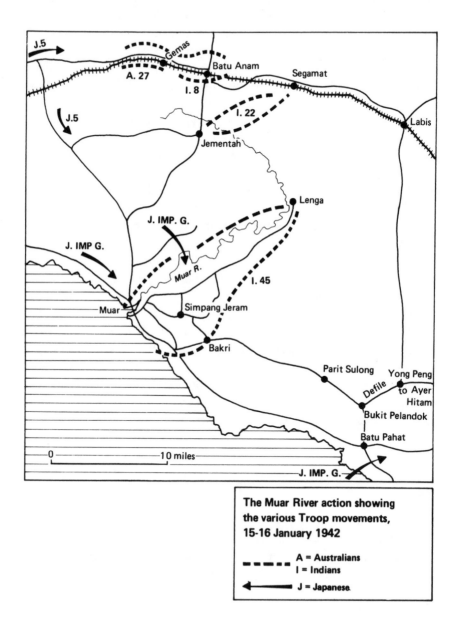

The Muar River action showing the various Troop movements, 15-16 January 1942

- - - - - A = Australians
           I = Indians

◄——————— J = Japanese

open city, and that the Australians were to hold the Japanese on a line
from Muar through Segamat to Mersing. No one mentioned any enemy
landings apart from the one at Kota Bahru, any facts about the constant
withdrawals without full action, any information about the boats abandoned at Penang in which the Japanese were coming along the coasts,
cutting communications on the way and filtering in behind the lines of
troops. The way the Australians heard it, the Japanese were coming
down the mainland and would get the surprise of their lives when they
met men like themselves who could really fight, and there the Japanese
would stop.[47]

As the first step in this happy programme, the Australians began
to move to their assigned positions along the south bank of the Muar
river, alongside detachments of the 45th Indian Infantry Brigade who
had to be hurriedly shown how to fire the rifles they had just been
issued with. They were willing but erratic, firing in any direction "so
long as it was away," and they were shattered by the first air raid on
Muar. They had expected to wait about a week for the onslaught to
begin: they had about three days.[48]

Down in Singapore the legacy Duff Cooper left behind him now
blossomed. The Colonial Secretary, Stanley Jones, got his dismissal.
(At the time he was sharing his house in the Governor's grounds with
the Federal Secretary, Hugh Fraser, and several guests and friends and
they were still sitting down to elegantly served meals though they had
broken with colonial tradition so far as to dress informally.) Jones's
dismissal came in a top secret cable to the Governor, who had to decode
it himself and thought he was decoding his own dismissal until he
came to the name in the last line. The Governor scribbled a note telling
Jones the news and adding that Fraser would take over, and sent it
across to Jones's house where the unfortunate Colonial Secretary read
it just before breakfast. He went to the Governor and begged to be
allowed to stay in any capacity, but the Governor said Whitehall feared
divided loyalties and he must go as soon as he could arrange passage
out. The news was published and the *Tribune* said Jones had been made
the scapegoat for other people's mistakes. The Governor sent a cir-
cular letter to all civil service personnel saying that the day of minute
papers had gone (like the later, terser saying, "the buck stops here"),
and the *Straits Times* replied shortly that this message was about two
and a half years too late.[49]

Matters looked lighthearted enough in the enemy camp, but Yamashita continued to worry and confide his grumbles to his diary. "Five

staff officers have arrived from GHQ Tokyo. I hate them"; "battalion commanders and troops lack fighting spirit—they've no idea how to *crush* the enemy"; "that bloody Terauchi! He's living in luxury in Saigon with a comfortable bed, good food and playing Japanese chess." [50] His men, advancing "talking and laughing just as if they were going to a football match," reflected none of these moody thoughts.[51]

But the opposition had a cheering experience too. Fifteen Hudson aircraft out of the fifty-two promised reached the Island—it would have been safe to send them all in early December, but this was judged impossible; it was dangerous to send them in early January, and this was attempted. Fifty Hurricanes were also sent in crates, arriving in a convoy of American liners, obtained by special permission of the American Government with, apparently, all sorts of heavy reminders about how important it was to protect this valuable convoy against air attacks.[52] In one of these same liners, docking in the rain [53] on Tuesday January 13, came the 53rd Brigade.

CHAPTER VI

Over the Causeway

I

THE 53rd Brigade was a territorial grouping of the 2nd Battalion The Cambridgeshire Regiment and the 5th and 6th Battalions The Royal Norfolk Regiment. As this account concerns itself particularly with The Royal Norfolks, it might be as well to include here a word about their background and circumstances.

The Royal Norfolk Regiment, originally raised in 1685 by James II and named Colonel Henry Cornwall's Regiment of Foot, one of eight new infantry regiments numbered 8-15 and soon to be known as the Ninth Foot, carried on its banners the battle honours of The Boyne, Belle Isle, Saratoga, Vimiero, Corunna, Torres Vedras, Badajoz and The Crimea, among many others, before it was renamed The Norfolk Regiment in 1881. Curiously enough it happened to be serving in Burma at that time. Between then and 1935, when as one of the Jubilee honours it was called The Royal Norfolk Regiment, it served in the South African War and the Gallipoli campaign, and, in peace time, all over the place from Ireland to Shanghai. It had a good reputation. Lieutenant-General Sir Brian Horrocks has said of it that it had always been renowned for its steadfastness and reliability in difficult situations, and was just the sort of regiment that all commanders like to have available in order to plug a difficult gap. This quality of staunchness had been developed over the full period of the regiment's history, and it had needed it, too, for there are several unhappy endings to the actions in which it had been engaged.

> Wherever the fighting was fiercest, climatic conditions most vile and the odds against victory most daunting, the Ninth Foot was sure to be there.

Early in the war the two regular battalions had been supplemented by the creation of four territorial battalions, the 4th, 5th, 6th, and 7th.

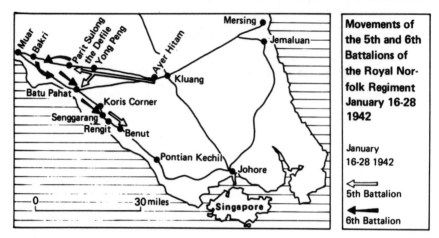

Movements of
the 5th and 6th
Battalions of
the Royal Nor-
folk Regiment
January 16-28
1942

January
16-28 1942

5th Battalion

6th Battalion

It was the 4th, 5th, and 6th that were marked out to come into what Mr Tim Carew in his history of the Regiment calls "a special category of tragedy." [1]

The 5th Battalion's headquarters were originally at East Dereham, with companies at Aylsham, North Walsham and Holt. Like the other two tragic battalions, they spent months doing rather monotonous coastal defence and anti-invasion duties in the period following Dunkirk. In September 1941 when they were issued with tropical kit there were immediate rumours of overseas service, the popular verdict inclining towards the Middle East, and, as training exercises began more and more to have a desert bias it soon became obvious that these rumours were correct. On October 29 they embarked upon the first stage of a colossal journey that took them across the Atlantic to Halifax, Nova Scotia, and then all the way down across the Atlantic again to the Cape of Good Hope. From there they should have gone up the east side of Africa to Egypt, but it was only now that they were diverted,[2] three of the ships going to Bombay and the *Washington,* carrying the 53rd Brigade among the five thousand troops on board, to Mombasa where they spent Christmas, sailing on via the Maldives to join the rest at Singapore.[3]

On the long haul from South Africa the news spread through their ranks that the enemy facing them would be the Japanese, not the Germans. By then it was the end of December and the start of the New Year, and the situation in the Far East was disquieting: the United States fleet had been crippled at Pearl Harbor, the British battleships had been sunk off Malaya, Hong Kong had surrendered on Christmas Day. They did not know the other details: how the Japanese, having estimated it possible to complete the Malaya campaign in a hundred days, had made short work of their initial advance through what the British war maps had for years dismissed quaintly as "unpenetrable (*sic*) jungle," [4] caused Operation Matador to sink without trace, Kota Bahru to fall almost overnight, and in spite of Indian bravery had captured the Jitra position, that nightmare of knee-deep mud, flooded rivers, shaky bamboo bridges, acute food shortages and regiments going without sleep for a week.

By the first week of January, while the four ships were plodding across the Indian Ocean, the Japanese had captured Kuantan, had won the battle of Kampar, and were now finding that it was downhill all the way. Travelling light, advancing on bicycles, living on their carefully measured iron rations unexpectedly supplemented by the masses of stores left behind by the rapidly retreating opposition in front of them, here they were, six weeks from Pearl Harbor, across the line from Batu Pahat through Kluang to Mersing, deep inside Johore. The 53rd Brigade did not know that when the bicycle tyres burst in the heat the Japanese pedalled on on the rims, which in the night made a noise suggestive of armoured vehicles and further demoralised the retreating British troops, nor that the Allied air striking power had been reduced to a barely operable handful, out of action as far as Singapore was concerned from January 26 as it was going to turn out. Johore was now a trap, and it was into this trap that the 53rd Brigade, disembarked in a downpour on January 13 without its guns and without its transport, and given a couple of days to unload, store its winter clothing and issue tropical clothing, was hastily and immediately flung.[5]

They came up to Ayer Hitam, a point on the road midway between Batu Pahat and Kluang, where they were given "a baptism of hellfire." [6] Whereas Sir Compton Mackenzie describes these young soldiers as absolutely mystified by tropical conditions,[7] one of them, John Coast, then a lieutenant, recorded firmly that they were "horribly pitchforked into the mystery and menace of tropical jungle" and that "we always regarded our Division being sent to Singapore as a sacrifice on the altar of public opinion." [8] They were not only virtually raw recruits but had been eleven weeks in transports so crowded that they could have no exercise, and one thing any commander dreads is having to put into action troops that are still soft after a long journey to the battle area. This was precisely what happened. The 18th Division, of which the 53rd Brigade was a part, was not inaccurately referred to as "The Lost Division," and was to have exactly thirty days of combat duty.

2

The alert reader will wonder what had happened, having left the British line following the Muar river to Segamat, to bring it back in three days to the last line in Johore, the Batu Pahat–Kluang–Mersing road. Actually it was not quite as neat as that; for another day or two assorted units muddled about on the roads between Bakri, Batu Pahat and Kluang, but the last withdrawal to a fixed position on the mainland of Malaya was in full operation by January 16.

Gordon Bennett's Australians had made a highly encouraging start, following his cherished plan which relied upon ambush, as he considered Malaya ideal for that type of fighting. His first ambush was set up on the Gemas road, at a bridge that the Australians prepared for demolition. A few men were hidden at the bridge, ready to blow it at the signal, and the rest of a full battalion was concealed in the jungle on either side of the road. They were all issued with rations for four days but did not need them, as the Japanese appeared in two, coming down the road at about four o'clock on Thursday afternoon, many of them wheeling their bicycles. When the officer in charge at the bridge thought that he had let enough come over and there were as many on the bridge as there were likely to be at any moment he gave the order to blow the bridge. Without the slightest warning the explosion went up with spectacular effect and the Australians charged yelling out of the jungle, killing about nine hundred Japanese at the cost of less than a hundred casualties of their own. They then drew back to the south of Segamat, delighted at their success.[9]

The Japanese, deciding that the main road was too expensive a luxury at that price, did what they always did when the road was blocked in front of them: they went round the side. They filtered along the coast to the mouth of the Muar river and began moving inland through the rubber. An Australian officer in one of the observation posts on the north bank reported "calmly" over his field telephone that the enemy was approaching. Sending his assistant off to cross the river and covering his long run with his gun while directing the Australians' fire, he went on for a short time until "his steady voice stopped in midsentence." The battery "had suffered its first loss." [10]

A full scale sequence of engagements promptly developed, with the guns and their crews of the battery fighting their way out of their positions to fresh ones on the outskirts of Muar, the going being made no easier by the constant dive-bombing. The battery commander, a stockily built, dark, bad-tempered man called Major Julius, sent Mr Braddon and another gunner, Mr Hugh Moore, back to rear HQ for reinforcements. At rear HQ just before they left to return in the morning they saw arriving two fresh Australian battalions who came crashing up right away into the savage battle that raged all day around Bakri. That night the Australians formed up in a hollow square (shades of Waterloo) and blazed away at attack after attack, finding in due course that this was a wasteful process as both sides killed a number of their own men. From that time on, the Australians were told, they were to use only the bayonet at night, a dismaying prospect to soldiers who had until then used the bayonet only to open tins.[11]

Among the later arrivals in the Muar area were Painter's men, irritated at being hauled out of their key position astride an important road junction at Segamat and alarmed at seeing the town apparently in flames just as they were leaving. They found out it was neither the Japanese nor the fifth column but the rubber merchants destroying their stocks. The men moved off in the cool night air, seeing the flames reflected in the river and hearing the noise of marching feet and the slow roar of motor transport. As they approached the Muar district, they received the news that the 45th Indian Brigade—just arrived and "as green as could be"—had been "annihilated" by the Japanese, who were now within striking distance of Yong Peng.[12]

The road from Yong Peng to Bakri started in a marsh backed by rubber plantations, after six miles of which the road became a causeway, running straight like a Roman road through a pass called The Defile. Seven miles past The Defile was Parit Sulong, where the road bridged a dark menacing-looking stream.[13] On January 19 the 6th Battalion The Royal Norfolk Regiment was assigned to the Yong Peng area, while for the third day running Percival came up by road from Singapore to see for himself what was going on and to confer with Heath and Gordon Bennett. The War Council in Singapore now had to meet at night.[14]

It is interesting, in a macabre way, to find the following stately comment in *The Times* that week:

> It is learned in London that there is no official authority for the statement telegraphed from Singapore by a news agency that the British should have air superiority in Malaya within three days. It is not in the public interest to disclose air force strengths in this or any other theatre of war.[15]

There were two fundamental weaknesses in the Muar situation. The first was the disposition of troops: it would have been better to put the raw young 45th Brigade at Yong Peng where they would have had a single road to guard than on a wavering front of twenty-four miles along the river.[16] The second was that when the Japanese Imperial Guards came over the river on the evening of Friday January 16 and forced the 45th back upon Bakri with a loss of almost half their numbers, Gordon Bennett did not quite realise how serious the situation was. He sent up a reserve battalion of Australians with orders to counter-attack and then return to Gemas.[17]

The defending troops were now to all intents and purposes split in half, the Australians at Gemas virtually cut off from the men on the Muar, who were still being bombed with hardly a pause. Major Julius spoke to some of them on his way to a brigade conference in a nearby bungalow. A long line of staff cars "so sensibly" led straight to this bungalow and a few minutes later a dive-bomber flew up the line and dropped a bomb on the building, killing most of the senior officers inside. Major Julius was critically wounded and at once many men offered to try to take him back to rear HQ where he could have medical aid. "Protesting in his customary violent language" the Major was put in an armoured car which set out to "run the gauntlet" if it could, knowing that the enemy was all down the road. Within half an hour the armoured car ran into a road block and was shot up by machine guns on both sides. One man struggled back with several bullet holes in him to tell the tale. He was not the Major.[18]

3

Now it was Churchill's turn to realise the truth, and it was a shock. On January 19 he received a melancholy cable from Wavell, who pointed out that all the Singapore defence plans "until quite recently" were based on repulsing seaborne attacks on the Island and at the same time holding any land attack "in Johore or further north." He admitted that "little or nothing" had been done to construct defences on the north side of the Island against a possible crossing of the Johore Strait, though arrangements had been made to blow up the Causeway. The fortress cannon had an all-round traverse, but "their flat trajectory makes them unsuitable for counter-battery work." It reads oddly to see that reference to holding the land attack in Johore or further north when at that moment the defenders were drawing back upon Yong Peng.

For Churchill, on receipt of Wavell's message, the roof fell in.

I ought to have known. My advisers ought to have known and I ought to have been told, and I ought to have asked. . . . The possibility of Singapore having no landward defences no more entered my mind than that of a battleship being launched without a bottom.[19]

Two days before, the Low cartoon in the *Guardian* showed "Singapore's needs," depicting a laid-out petrified Blimp on a slab labelled "Inquest on Malaya Reverses." A crowd stood at the head, at the foot lay a small group of toy weapons labelled "not enough tools," and a hand beckoned the crowd towards these. The caption read: "More attention to the other end, please." [20]

The Europeans in Singapore had been jolted at last. The Chinese shopkeepers heard the news from the Muar, by some mysterious grapevine that outdistanced any official bulletin, and, as they read it, saw the end coming; abruptly they stopped the buying of goods on credit. White Singapore had used the chit-signing system since Raffles's time: it was so established that the worst insult to a Singapore European was to call him "pencil-shy." Horrified settlers now found that "cash only" meant exactly what it said, and more often than not they lacked the cash required.

The Government instantly began paying its employees twice a month and told people to buy in stocks of food, which, of course, made the situation worse. A frantic hunt for all kinds of tinned foods started, people bought quantities of tea and coffee and rice, transferred these to containers that they could seal up (thereby causing a shortage of metal boxes of all sorts), and buried them in their gardens. Fresh food, brought in daily from Johore, now began to get scarce as the Japanese were already fighting in north Johore where the rich market gardens were.

The big stores, however, bulged with newly shipped out refrigerators, books, stoves and fashionable clothes. The Cold Storage * mounted uniformed guards to keep an eye on stocks and Singapore was placed under martial law as a precaution. The Governor broadcast about this and mixed up the rounding-up of fifth column suspects with the martial law proclamation in his speech so that his listeners got nervous. Mr Buckeridge's German-style Swiss steel helmets, issued to ARP and AFS † workers and messengers, caused several

* One of the big stores.
† Auxiliary Fire Service.

panicky arrests by Chinese who said they were enemy helmets, and Mr Buckeridge had to call for them all to be handed in. He had no replacements. The military announced that they wanted twelve hundred bicycles in a hurry and the police rushed round collecting every bicycle they could find; within twenty-four hours this was found to be "a mistake" as the number required was one hundred, which meant that "nine out of ten bicycle owners" could "have their machines back—if they could ever find them." [21]

The 6th Norfolks up on the Bakri road near The Defile had been reinforced by a Punjabi regiment and Moorhead himself, who led a night attack to push the enemy back from the hills bordering The Defile. One company of the Norfolks had worked their way to the top of one hill unknown to Moorhead and shots were exchanged between two friendly groups, killing a number of men, before the mistake was straightened out. When Moorhead's men advanced again they were hit by grenades and hesitated for a moment in case it was not the Japanese, but it was and Moorhead was wounded and died ten minutes later. One of his havildars said: "There will never be a man more brave than he."

After two days of sporadic action, both of which they had spent without rations and one without communication, the 6th Norfolks were drawn back, severely mauled, upon Batu Pahat, where the situation was growing steadily worse. [22] Remnants of the shattered 45th Brigade were making their way as best they could across country, losing men all the way from wounds and exhaustion, some of whom within hours fell into enemy hands where their problems were settled once and for all as the Japanese simply beheaded them.

Some planters whose estates were overrun had difficulty escaping: one was surprised in his house by a Japanese patrol who tied him up and set to work to get drunk on his whisky. One of his Chinese servants crept in and untied him and he managed to move out of the house and run for his life, though he was fired at as he escaped. [23] Others did not have so exact an appreciation of the way matters stood: on one estate the planter angrily accused a British officer in charge of a detachment of ambulances of trespassing on private property and said he would file a formal complaint. The officer said he had better file it with the Japanese as they would be arriving shortly. [24]

Churchill told Ismay on January 19 that emergency defence plans on the Island must instantly be set in motion, employing "the entire male population" so that Singapore would be turned into a citadel and "defended to the death. No surrender can be contemplated." Next day he told Wavell that "every inch of ground" must be defended and "no question of surrender" was to be "entertained until after protracted fighting among the ruins"—the word "surrender" had now been said. This message crossed one from Wavell who warned the Prime Minister that he doubted whether the Island could be held for long "when Johore is lost." A slightly later message told Churchill that "the situation had greatly deteriorated" and that the troops might have to withdraw all the way back not only to Johore Bahru but "eventually" to the Island. He said that "preparatory measures" for the Island defence were "being put in hand" with the "limited resources" available to make them.[25] The fact is that it was not until January 23 that the outline plans were drawn up, details of which were issued five days later: "Not a spade was thrust into the earth until the end of the month." [26]

It was already a week since the *Guardian,* showing the ominous headline "Nearer to Singapore," had printed in its leader:

Japan's offensive range remains remarkable. She gathers the United States island bases in the west Pacific into her hands, takes Hong Kong, advances in the Philippines, drives us southwards in Malaya, and has now launched two new expeditions to Borneo and Celebes. So far there has been no check. But we ought to remember that it was only the British in London and in the Far East who maintained that one piece of territory at least would never fall into Japanese hands. Americans, long before the war began, counted on the loss of the Philippines in any conflict with Japan. They did not expect to hold Guam. The Dutch knew well that they could not be sure of defending any of their many islands without help from strong allies. But the British had no doubts about their power to hold Singapore and not only the Island and base but also the Malayan hinterland, without which the base would lose most of its value. . . . Now it will be as well for people to realise that Singapore is in real danger and without it all the Allied forces in that region.[27]

4

"That the enemy can throw his troops ashore with impunity from waters to which his naval squadrons cannot yet have penetrated, and under air protection alone, is at first sight startling," said *The Times* leader of Tuesday January 20. The Japanese plan, according to that day's dispatch out of Singapore, was now clear. In order to have strong forces ready for the full assault on the Island, they wanted to get through to southern Johore without being involved in "a major action." [28] Avoiding direct confrontation, the Japanese must be hit hard from the air. At that moment there were twenty-eight RAF fighter planes left.

There was a big air raid on the Island that day. Bombs fell near Government House and Fort Canning—in the Colonial Secretary's house Mrs Hay, a guest and alone there at the time, sheltered hastily under the piano. The blast blew the piano top off but left her unhurt. In the Cathedral House garden the Archdeacon's wife and secretary were sitting, the wife doing her knitting and the secretary working on his papers, when a bomb killed him and left her untouched. Twenty-six bombs fell in the Government House grounds, killing a cat and some chickens and setting fire to several cars, and the blast wrecked the telephones and damaged the water system. A bomb exploding close to the Cold Storage broke some of the refrigerator pipes and caused a leakage of ammonia that nearly asphyxiated women doing their shopping.

There were three raids that day and another next morning, the heaviest yet, with more than 100 aircraft killing 383 people and injuring over 700, throwing a car into the billiard room of the Cricket Club and killing a member who had just invited Mr Hammonds to play. Mr Hammonds was thankful that he had said no. Another narrow escape was that of Mrs Buckeridge who had walked down the street from a friend's house to buy a bar of chocolate. The house had a direct hit in her absence. Mr Tim Hudson of Dunlop's, who with his wife had had a narrow escape when a stick of bombs fell across the road along which they were driving, spent the day with his fellow ARP volunteers and made a broadcast that night describing how well the Chinese had worked all those hours. It was something of a contrast to the case of the journalist Mr Leslie Hoffman who had been in the air raid shelter with his old father when "a polite Chinese arrived and announced that he had come to read the gas meter." [29]

Mr Braddon and his companions, negotiating the road back to Yong Peng, found it full of unpleasant surprises. With their CO dead they had to go on their own, and there were plenty of wounded packed into armoured cars to escort along a route that any minute might be shot up by dive-bombers. They had had no food or supplies for two days and found out why when they stumbled on the supply unit, completely wiped out. Just past that they silenced a machine-gun post, and had their first look at the enemy dead: "Not a pair of spectacles amongst the lot. Every one a magnificent specimen of well-developed bone and muscle. The equipment sensible, adequate and light." So much, they thought, for the Intelligence officers' lectures.

During the night they gingerly drove over the Causeway road, guided by the firefly glow of infantry cigarettes on either side, and in the morning thankfully approached Parit Sulong bridge. The leading truck ran into a spatter of gunfire and found the Japanese at the bridge. They refused to let the wounded pass unless the whole force surrendered, so the whole group withdrew into the rubber, grouped the trucks, and made a square round them. They fended off attacks in that place for twenty-four hours and then a few of them wriggled away through the undergrowth and set out for Yong Peng, about fifty miles distant across difficult country. Others joined them in ones and twos all along the way. They hid from dive-bombers in a swamp, got bitten by leeches, had nothing to eat, drank pints of brackish river water and, after going thirty miles in thirty hours and leaving about a hundred infantrymen at one spot for twelve hours' rest, reached Yong Peng. An officer there told them that someone ought to go back for the infantrymen. Mr Braddon and Mr Moore heard themselves saying, to their horror, that they would go. They went. The boatman who had brought them the last miles into Yong Peng agreed (after Mr Braddon showed him a hand grenade) to take them back, and on arrival they were called fools for returning, for the rest of the men refused to move, saying that Yong Peng must have been captured by this time. Eventually nine of them set off after a short night's rest, still without food and feeling utterly exhausted. The idea was to get to Singapore. Within a few hours they walked into a Japanese ambush. Those that survived were taken to Kuala Lumpur and lodged in Pudu jail, where seven hundred men occupied cells and a courtyard designed for thirty convicts. Among them were a lot of Australian prisoners from Gemas. Mr Braddon was captured on his twenty-first birthday.[30]

5

Meanwhile, Painter's men had got back into Kluang where, after an exhausted night arrival, Captain Russell-Roberts went into the streets with their boarded-up shops to see if he could find any food supplies. The Cold Storage building was full of looters. The Captain and his driver got four rabbits and three large fish and so the men had a good dinner. It was Friday January 23.[31]

Two days before, after a flying visit from Wavell, Percival had sent secret instructions to Heath and Gordon Bennett that if they had to withdraw from the mainland altogether each force should fall back along its own lines of communications; Heath would co-ordinate their movements after they had got behind the Kluang–Ayer Hitam line. Mr Morrison interviewed some of the Australians who had managed to get back from Yong Peng. Their five-day stand was heroic and held the Japanese in spite of constant attacks on the ground, from the air, and from snipers in the trees; no sleep, no food, and no drugs for the many wounded. "One day, I hope," wrote Mr Morrison, "an Australian who took part in it will tell the tale." Mr Braddon did so. It was clear to Mr Morrison after this series of interviews that the Johore line had gone and that "there was now nothing on earth that could save Singapore." [32]

The 5th Battalion The Royal Norfolk Regiment was ordered up to Batu Pahat in support of the 6th Battalion, but contact on the way failed because of a muddle over milestones on Friday January 23. They were therefore sent instead to the coast road above Senggarang, starting to move at four in the morning, and when they got there at quarter past seven after a quiet journey they found the Batu Pahat area very far from quiet. In spite of all the bold statements, including Percival's insistence that no one was to withdraw from the Kluang–Batu Pahat line without his permission, further tentative plans for drawing back had been prepared. The code word for the withdrawal was the unexpectedly charming (and, in the circumstances, suitable) one, "Nuts." The discovery of a Japanese battalion concealed in the rubber between Senggarang anw Koris Corner on January 25 caused "Nuts" to be signalled to the CO in the area, Brigadier Challen, at four in the afternoon.[33]

At two in the afternoon of the previous day, Painter's men had gone three miles west towards Ayer Hitam, passing through a rubber estate to the north of the road and covering eleven miles by six in the evening when, about two miles from Niyor, the leading troops found an ambush with a road block awaiting them. They dug in for the night, during which fighting flared up sporadically. In the lulls the very hungry men were fed. The fighting went on all next day and the Sikhs did quite well, but all the men were worried because no news was coming in from anywhere else.

Before they could start a night attack, orders came through telling them to get back to Kluang somehow. The Japanese were working round behind them, uncomfortably close, but the Sikhs fought them off and the withdrawal began. It was a cold night. By two in the morning they were four miles north of Rengam, having covered thirty-three miles in thirty-six hours with eighteen of them in action. When they woke up on Monday morning they found messages of congratulation from Heath and Barstow.[34]

Having received his "Nuts" message, Challen wasted no time, ordering the withdrawal to start at half-past eight on Sunday evening. The plan was that the Cambridgeshires were to move to Senggarang from where they would lead out, followed by the vehicles and guns. The 5th Battalion would pass through the British Battalion and guard the rear from Koris Corner, and as they cleared their sector the British Battalion would move to Senggarang. The 53rd Brigade's orders were to open the road from Senggarang to Rengit, the next place down the coast, by dawn on Monday.[35]

It looks smooth enough on paper, but the troops involved in this leapfrogging manoeuvre found it rough going: by five on Monday morning the Cambridgeshires reached Senggarang in a state of exhaustion. Road blocks appeared all over the place and radio contact broke down again. By ten o'clock the 5th Battalion was reported in depth between Koris Corner and Senggarang and the Japanese aircraft were bombing all the troops they could see, whereupon Challen decided that the two young battalions so recently arrived in Malaya were not fit to meet the sort of conflict that appeared to be facing them. He believed that the only thing to be done was to destroy his guns and vehicles, detach his brigade, and take it across country. He set out, therefore, at a quarter past six in the evening. Divisional HQ signalled all day without stopping, but in vain, for Challen's men vanished from mortal knowledge for nearly twenty-four hours until at six on Tuesday evening a member of the Malay Police, a Mr Wallace, covered with mud and very weary, reached Benut on a bicycle and reported that Lieutenant-Colonel Prattley and twelve hundred men of the missing brigade were resting in a state of complete exhaustion seven miles away. Forty-four lorries were promptly ordered out to meet them.[36]

First thing on Monday morning Colonel J. B. Coates came up to Kluang to confer with Major-General Barstow, Brigadier Painter and Colonel Parkin, and they sat on a large fallen tree-trunk to do it. Briefing arrived a little later that they were all to return to Singapore. One division was to retire down the railway which was going to be awkward as there was one twenty-mile stretch without a road at all so everything would have to be carried. One division was to go down the trunk road from Ayer Hitam, and the remnants of the 11th Indian Division down the coast road. Painter's men left at ten o'clock and by the early afternoon were a mile and a half south of Rengam in "a nightmare position" between the railway and the road which were four miles apart, facing a network of roads all converging on Layang Layang six miles away, where defence measures were impossible. Painter wanted to get into Layang Layang right away but Barstow said they had to protect the flank of Gordon Bennett's Australians, so they "settled down to make the best of a thoroughly bad job," felling trees and digging slit trenches and gun pits, while dive-bombers shot up everything they could see moving.

That night the message came through that "everything on wheels had to be clear of milestone 435 on the railway by five pm next day." The order meant holding on without support for twenty-four hours, digging again after the bomb attacks, and eventually withdrawing between ten and fifteen miles without support.[37] A reconnaissance on Tuesday morning showed the enemy "very strong on the left" and showing every sign of moving round behind them. In the afternoon the vehicles began to pull out, taking guns, ammunition, wounded men and radio sets so that all communication would now have to be by the railway telegraph. Painter, clinging to his orders not to leave the Australian flank exposed, refused permission to go to Layang Layang that night. Fortunately, he did allow a move back of half a mile; the Japanese attacked later and missed the rearguard by less than a hundred yards.[38]

Down in Singapore the same kind of crazy unreality apparent earlier in places like Penang and Kuala Lumpur was beginning to show. The papers still advertised "the usual tiffin dance on Sunday" and offered for sale a European guest house "in select non-military area. Good business proposition." One government department was asked to rush through the printing of new banknotes while another was asked to arrange to burn five million of them if need be. Mr Hudson took a lorry to the ARP stores to collect "desperately needed" picks and shovels and found a note on the door saying: "Back in four hours"—the manager had gone to the cinema. Mr Hammonds came out of the Cricket Club to find two men stealing his car and as he stood "shouting after them" a member whose name he did not know came up and handed him some car keys, saying: "Take mine. I'm leaving in an hour." [39]

From Churchill came a defence plan for the Island containing seven of Simson's ten points in the same order. Churchill sent minutes to the Chiefs of Staff asking them to consider the question of reinforcements, whether to send the last troops already crossing the Indian Ocean on to Singapore or up to Rangoon, as he thought keeping the Burma Road open was more important than the retention of Singapore. Somehow (no one seems to know quite how it happened) the Australian Government representatives in London got hold of a copy of this, and told Canberra, whereupon the Australian Prime Minister, Mr Curtin, cabled Churchill at once that Singapore was understood to be impregnable and its evacuation would be "an inexcusable betrayal." So the rest of the British 18th Division was ordered to make for Singapore.[40] This included the Bedfordshires and the 4th Norfolks, on board the *West Point,* which had sailed from Bombay on January 19.[14]

On Tuesday January 27 Percival, having told Wavell that "we are fighting all the way, but may be driven back into the Island within a week. . . . It looks as if we should not be able to hold Johore for more than another three or four days. Our total fighter strength is now reduced to nine," decided to withdraw completely upon Singapore Island.[42] Brigadier Barclay, acknowledging that only the provision of superior naval and air forces could have saved Singapore in the end, confesses to doubts about how long the Japanese could have been held off. Even when all the difficulties were taken into consideration, he felt sure ("and in this view I am not alone") that a stronger and tougher resistance, however late in the day, would have kept the defence going longer and given those extra precious weeks so greatly needed by Wavell; he comments that Percival's "handling of operations in Malaya is an enigma to me." [43]

Wavell does not escape criticism either. This is made clear in an assessment written by Major-General Sir Francis de Guingand who, like Brigadier Barclay, fully appreciated the tremendous problems of the situation, but stated bluntly that in his opinion Wavell gave unsound advice and failed to see the position as a whole. One does not expect this of a distinguished soldier who was relied upon by Churchill and had been appointed Supreme Commander. General Auchinleck, for example, chimed in from Cairo to say that he hoped the reinforcements would not be diverted to Singapore, and it is this that General de Guingand considered "the final error of reasoning." He says simply: "One would have thought that any experienced soldier would have foreseen the inevitable outcome at that stage." [44]

6

The forty-four lorries picked up the 5th Battalion close to Benut where the indefatigable Mr Wallace had persuaded a Chinese ("a great chap —he had coffee ready for the wounded, and a lot of coconuts and pineapples, and he absolutely refused a cent in payment") to ferry them over the river in ten sampans. The lorries took them on to Skudai, just north of Johore Bahru, starting at three in the morning of Wednesday January 28; by eleven that same morning they had reached the Braddell Road rest camp on the Island. They brought with them seven out of ten of their rifles and one in five of their light automatics. About a hundred and fifty men of the 5th Battalion had moved with the Cambridgeshires. They had a much rougher passage, including a whole day's waiting under aircraft fire within three-quarters of a mile of a road along which Japanese transport was passing all day at Penggor. They were evacuated from their position by night to the Island in small ships.[45] For the next three nights HMS *Dragonfly* and HMS *Scorpion* took off 2,700 men of the 15th Indian Brigade and the 53rd Brigade who had been cut off along the swampy coastline south of Batu Pahat. Percival mentioned the ships in his dispatches. Nearly 3,000 more men of the same brigades were cut off west of Rengit, and Flight-Lieutenant H. Dane in an unarmed plane of the Malaya Volunteer Air Force flew a special reconnaissance to find them, which he did, and told the Royal Navy where they were. The Navy brought them out.[46]

   At half past one in the morning of that Wednesday Painter's men found a railway bridge close to Layang Layang blown up against orders. Their single communication line was cut so that no ammunition or rations could be sent to them. In spite of hearing enemy movements during the rest of the night and knowing that their route was taking them further and further away from the Australians whose flank they were supposed to be guarding, they went on moving south. In the early morning at a railway hut exposed to Japanese fire some of them found some ration stores and there was a scramble to get them out; there proved to be only enough for one meal.[47] The men went on through the trackless rubber with the Japanese very close and coming on a parallel line on the other side of the railway; presently the rubber gave way to tall elephant grass with patches of swamp. At one point the men crossed a stream by a single plank bridge, "twelve feet above a fifteen-foot drop" to the water, a crossing made more difficult by the presence of twenty-five stretcher cases and ten walking wounded.[48] At a rate of a quarter of a mile an hour they went on over a route full of obstacles, the men becoming so tired that they fell asleep wherever the thin column stopped, taking no notice of the leeches and ants that were everywhere. They had a cup of tea on Thursday but on the whole they had no relief, no comfort, no food. Tempers frayed and disputes broke out: some officers wanted to leave the wounded behind, and there was a squabble about whether the officers, who had a mess-basket, should eat when the men couldn't. In the end "they made the right decision," carrying the stretchers along and going without food until all could eat, very much in the position of Henry V's band of brothers.[49]

The country between Layang Layang and Sedenak became more hilly and slippery with rain; midway they stopped for a while on the Hill of Ghosts (Bukit Hantu) whose atmosphere lived up to its name. An enormous vista was visible: great rolling masses of jungle-covered hills with vast belts of rubber, and away in the distance the blue waters of the China Sea. One good point about the Hill of Ghosts was that there were pineapples in plenty so they eventually struggled on refreshed. Descending the slope they came out of cover and camouflaged themselves with greenery like Birnam Wood coming to Dunsinane, so that they were able to hide when the Japanese planes came over. They picked up seven Dogras who said they had been driven out of Sedenek two nights before, a disagreeable piece of information as the party had been aiming for Sedenak all along.[50] It was now Friday morning. Percival had told Heath on Wednesday that the complete withdrawal to the Island was to be an accomplished fact by Saturday morning,[51] so this particular remnant of Painter's force had not got much time.

On Wednesday the *West Point* made her final twelve-hour dash at full speed for the harbour of Singapore, arriving somewhat unnervingly during an air raid.[52] On the previous day Churchill had asked the

Commons for a vote of confidence, including in his speech the sombre forecast that there would be a good deal more bad news to come out of the Far East.[53] To the Europeans in Singapore, this could only mean one thing: Churchill expected the Island to fall. Until that moment the incredible assurance, almost indifference, of these residents had persisted. Perhaps, suggested Flight-Sergeant McCormac, it was helped along by such incongruous announcements as the Government proclamation, with the Japanese barely fifty miles away, that every householder with a garden should start growing vegetables and that fertilizer would be distributed by the Food Production Office.[54]

But now it was serious. Everyone who could leave ought to go as soon as possible. The four big ships that had brought in the 18th Division were still there, so it appeared to be a case of "now or never." A long, hot, anxious muddle followed, with long queues of women and children besieging the P. & O. office through which the Government had ordered all bookings. The office had been moved out of the town centre to the P. & O. manager's private house at Cluny, five miles away. There were raids from time to time during which the queues took shelter in a concrete ditch at the side of the secondary road running uphill to the house. Many women had passport difficulties that took hours to straighten out, for the rules were rigidly adhered to, and the official broadcast that would have told people where to go, what to do, and would have cut through the tangling swirls of red tape was never made.

Down at the docks conditions were chaotic. Many of the warehouses were on fire, piles of rubble blocked approach roads, ambulances stood by with their engines running while people were dug out of smoking wreckage, newly landed troops hurried to unload military equipment and get it away before the next air raid, and the crowd of passengers for the ships flooded into the area, coming as far as they could in cars and then walking. The queues formed up again to pass the narrow gate, moving a yard every half hour, under a sultry sky with the sea like "burnished steel." [55] Mr McCormac, who had managed to get his wife on the *Wakefield,* only just reached it in time. At one-thirty on Friday he brought her along in his car in the middle of an air raid, tearing across "bomb-cratered flats" utterly deserted except for the ship, where they were just starting to pull off the gangway, and in a breathless last-minute finish Mrs McCormac scrambled on board, the last person but one to do so.[56]

The *Wakefield* and the *West Point* sailed on Friday, the *Empress of Japan* on Saturday with the *Duchess of Bedford,* which had come in to Keppel harbour only the morning before full of Indian reinforcements. Afterwards people said bitterly that they had stepped ashore just in time to walk into captivity, and, looking back on it, it certainly seemed like that. The last two big ships out left in the evening, after a blood-red sunset and "the swift pink twilight of tropics" were followed by the rising of the moon. It illumined the bullet-pocked, bomb-shattered buildings, the fires still glowing among them, the pinnacles and palm trees and the uncannily deserted waterfront of the Lion Gate.[57] All four ships reached port safely, the final pair being escorted out by *Dragonfly* to Batavia, where the *Duchess of Bedford* stayed three days for repairs, sailing on Thursday February 5 for Colombo which she reached five days later, and going off for Durban after a further five days.[58] The date then was Sunday Febrary 15.

7

Not all the troops were coming back to the Island in little scattered formations. There were still sizeable units with their COs bringing them out in some kind of order. Broadly speaking the general idea was to come down towards the Causeway at Johore Bahru. On the way groups of troops would be gathered and the less exhausted units would be placed to guard the rear while the rest went forward a mile or two; then the rearguard would be pulled up, changing when necessary, and pressing on. In some places small groups or individuals got separated and captured on the line of march. One of these was Brigadier Challen, who left some Cambridgeshires and 6th Norfolks just after dawn on January 28 just below Rengit while he went to look for the rest of the 53rd Brigade who had not already gone off in the ships. He found a few on the outskirts of Rengit, told them where the others were, and went on with his orderly, who shortly afterwards was badly wounded when the pair nearly blundered into the middle of some Japanese. Challen lay low for the rest of the day, and that night reached the road although he was often shot at, walked some way, and climbed over a road block guarded by two Japanese sentries who paid no attention to him. Challen went on, found a bicycle, rode that for a while until the enemy's presence grew uncomfortably obvious, abandoned the bicycle and struck out across country, spent Wednesday night hiding in a hut and walked out at dawn into an enemy patrol, who sent him up to Pudu jail in Kuala Lumpur.

The rest of Painter's men, separated from the others in the move back to Layang Layang and saddened by the knowledge that Barstow had been killed in a Japanese ambush, struggled southwards in very much the same manner as the first party, shooting up a Japanese picnic on the road and leaving between seventy and eighty enemy dead. They too had to carry their wounded on stretchers across swamps and over steep hills greasy with rain, shelter from air attacks among the undergrowth, were bitten by ants and leeches, went without food, lurching clumsily into the man in front if he stopped without warning. At the halts they sagged instantly into sleep. Some of the wounded died on the way. Just after one particularly harrowing swamp crossing when all the men were asleep a staff captain came by and in an agitated manner asked "what these exhausted men were doing sleeping when it was essential to push along at top speed." [59]

The original party who had passed south of the Hill of Ghosts spent Friday night trying to round up all their worn out number and persuade a few more to be stretcher bearers. One group got lost and remained at large in Johore until the middle of April. At first light on Saturday the remainder started out again and found themselves faced with a large stretch of bog over which it took them hours to feel their way, uncertain footholds tilting the wounded agonisingly in all directions as they went. On reaching drier ground at last, Captain Russell-Roberts reacted by going off a little way on his own and bursting into tears. They had only just avoided stumbling into a Japanese encampment, but that day they found a settlement where they left the wounded men, most of whom recovered and survived their eventual captivity.

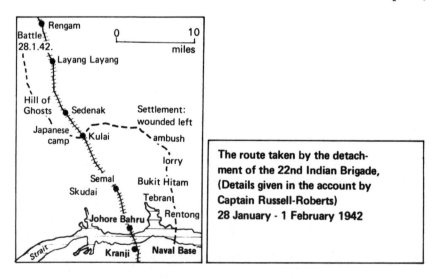

The route taken by the detachment of the 22nd Indian Brigade, (Details given in the account by Captain Russell-Roberts) 28 January - 1 February 1942

Freed from the burden of carrying them the rest of the party went on at a better speed, and found some food too, including a few chickens caught and cooked on the spot in the evening.[60]

By that time the larger groups had converged on the road to the Island. The Argylls, fanning out over the foothills of Johore Bahru, came on in open order with fixed bayonets to cover the retreat, while Royal Engineers squatted on the Causeway drilling holes for the explosives that were to blow it. They stood watching impatiently while the last men came unhurriedly across, apparently supremely indifferent to the enemy hard behind them and the waiting charges on both sides.[61] Their pipers played them over with "A Hundred Pipers" (there were only two remaining by this time), "Jenny's Black E'en" and "Hieland Laddie"; "last of all came Drummer Hardy, almost alone . . . exhorted to hurry, he maintained his own steady pace." [62] The Causeway was blown, tearing a breach in it about thirty yards wide. It was possible for a few latecomers to cross at one point without wetting their feet. The Causeway had taken several years to build and had cost four million pounds.[63]

General Arthur Percival
(*Photo: Mansell Collection*)

General Tomoyuki Yamashita
(*Photo: Kyodo Photo Service*)

THE OPPOSING COMMANDERS

The Eastern and Oriental Hotel, Penang, symbol of prewar gracious living (*By Burton Holmes from Ewing Galloway—Aerofilms*)

Kuala Lumpur Railway Station: a typically flamboyant piece of colonial building (*Photo: Aerofilms*)

Not the easiest country to fight in.
British troops in up-country Malaya
(*Photo: Keystone*)

Ayar Hitam is where the 5th Battalion first went into action
(*Photo: Aerofilms*)

A refugee train comes south over the causeway to Singapore Island
(*Photo: Keystone*)

The Japanese invasion of the Island, first week of February 1942
(*Photo: Keystone*)

The centre of Singapore. St. Andrew's Cathedral and the cricket club (*Photo: Aerofilms*)

The bombing in Singapore (*Photo: Mansell Collection*)

Pier built by prisoners for
General Saito, 1944

Changi, Singapore, 1942

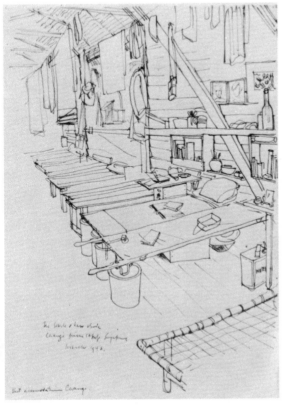

Two drawings by Ronald Searle
(*Ronald Searle and Cambridge
University Press*)

Two drawings by a prisoner, G. S. Gimson: (*above*) Tarsao, landing place, November 7, 1942; (*below*) Chungkai, railway cutting, 1943 (*Imperial War Museum*)

A very rare photograph: a concert party entertainment at Chungkai Camp. All present, despite appearances, are soldiers (*Photo: by courtesy of David Arkush*)

The dentist's room used by David Arkush (*Photo: by courtesy of David Arkush*)

Part of the railway from the air (*Photo: Aerofilms*)

After the surrender. Australian ex-prisoners watching the Japanese filling in trenches (*Photo: Keystone*)

CHAPTER VII

"A Corner of Hell"

I

THE defending armies of the British Empire had now retreated 450 miles in fifty-three days,[1] and had lost Malaya. Plenty of questions were asked, some openly, others more discreetly, trying to find out exactly how this had happened. One important factor was certainly the bold and skilful outflanking tactics of the Japanese. Almost from the moment when their troops stood on the west coast at Penang they had sent by night small launches towing strings of barges filled with soldiers who were landed wherever a launch could put in south of the British lines. In tens, in scores, in hundreds, the Japanese would come ashore and lie concealed in the jungle for anything up to a couple of days, then strike. Roads were blocked, lorries ambushed, cars stolen or hijacked, stores looted or fired, enemy groups would be found in areas where none were known to be, uncannily appearing wherever they could do quick decisive damage.[2] It was this more than anything that made the British believe they were outnumbered, this more than anything that contributed to the overall lowering of morale.

For a day or two after the blowing of the Causeway little parties of British and Indian soldiers came back to the Island. Captain Russell-Roberts's group numbered about a hundred when they woke chilled and stiff at dawn on Sunday, but during the morning they had a bad time at a Japanese ambush and only thirty-two men were pushing on together after midday. There were enemy planes about but none attacked; eventually the group commandeered a contractor's lorry full of Chinese and an Austin car, drove three miles south through pineapple plantations and caught up with a party of Garhwalis from their brigade. The lorry was sent back to tell the Brigadier where they were but it did not return; by great good luck they found another and set off at top speed in a cloud of red dust, joining the splendid main highway from Mersing to the coast.

All Johore seemed dead. At the coast they stood opposite the Naval Base which made no signal; the water was covered with oil and the rain was falling. The men found a weatherbeaten sampan and pulled across the Strait, landing at the Naval Base Yacht Club steps. There was no sign of defence anywhere and very few people about. The over-riding thought in the Captain's mind was to find his wife. At his HQ, a solid white house on the Naval Base road, he had a bath in three inches of water and asked for a pair of shoes or boots—his own had been lost in one of the swamps. The shoes were provided by Brigadier Billy Key, a short, thick-set, hearty man with a round face, strong chin, and "a bulldog look of defiance in his eyes." The Captain got a lift after some trouble and reached his wife's flat in Lloyd Road in the middle of the night. By dawn on Tuesday the brigade survivors were mustered: sixteen officers, a British signalman, and forty-six men.

The Captain told Key the whole story of the journey out of Johore and now spent a few days between HQ, Fort Canning, and the flat. He picked up a fresh outfit at Robinson's which was still stocked with masses of clothes and furniture, lunched at the Cricket Club, swam at the Tanglin Club, and visited the Raffles Hotel where there was danc-ing as usual every night.[3] The great dance halls such as the "Happy World" were packed to capacity each evening. Right up to the last moment the British civilians in Singapore included those who dressed for dinner, ordered their servants, drank their sundowners, met for cock-tails, and excused themselves from ARP practices on the grounds that they were engaged in the tennis tournament and couldn't get away. This reminds the present-day reader of the behaviour of some of the passen-gers on the *Titanic*. But the *Titanic* sank too.

Now, according to Captain James, Britain was really up against it. A mixed civil population of a million "squatting" on the Island from coast to coast "in undisturbed occupation of nearly all the so-called strategic points"; no related system of fortifications; a mass of mixed troops, about 85,000 of them, mostly raw, and the whole thing admin-istered by "numerous defensive committees, civil and military governors, high and low commissioners, commanders-in-chief, GOCs of all three Services," as well as Whitehall—all this with planning "on a higher level leaving the low level of the beaches to look after itself." There was, James said, no team spirit.

All the wires of communication ran across crowded native villages and that meant they were a security risk. Indeed at some moment in the first week of February the troops arrested two Chinese who had been flashing signals across the Strait to Johore Bahru and took them to the police station at Bukit Timah. A Malay Police officer released them before the troops returned next morning, but promised that the Security Police in Singapore would report the whole thing to the Governor. Nothing more was heard.[4]

2

Technically the siege of Singapore started on Saturday January 31 at a quarter past eight in the morning. The sound of the explosion on the Causeway was the first most people knew about the complete withdrawal from the peninsula. The weather was perfect and remained so throughout the first days of February: [5] blue sky, little white clouds, blue sea, green palm trees rustling in a light breeze, the sun shining warmly on white buildings, green parks and brilliant tropical flowers and birds, a dream travel poster come to life.

There was a lull in war activity for a few days, too: both sides were getting ready as best they could for the climax.[6] Reporters went up to the north shore and sat among coconut palms looking across the Strait, where from time to time they could see the enemy. He did not look particularly menacing from that distance: a few soldiers went along the waterfront, a staff car stopped for an officer to gaze across at the Island. It all seemed quiet and normal.

The Island was well supplied, two dairy herds had come over the Causeway during the past few days, there were 9,000 cattle and 125,000 pigs, and so much flour that the Food Controller asked Mr Morrison if he could arrange for several thousand tons of it to be shipped to Ceylon. Every person was allowed two tins a day of fruit and vegetables, milk and sugar were not rationed and the butter ration was four times the size of the English amount. There was plenty to drink. The water pipes over the Causeway had of course been broken, but the Island reservoirs were full and could supply seventeen million gallons a day.[7] It did not seem like the sort of siege described in the history books.

Mr Morrison and the other correspondents ran into trouble with the censorship over this. They were forbidden to use the word "siege" in their reports. They were, however, told that they could substitute the curious word "besiegement," or, if they preferred, "investment." The man who laid this down also expressed the opinion that the Japanese were not going to strike at the Island but would bypass it. One journalist was stuck for a story and wrote a pleasant little account of how he was doing his own washing and how he had bought and cooked a leg of pork for lunch. This housewives' choice dispatch bothered the censors who thought it must be some obscure kind of code, and the reporter was actually "ordered up to Fort Canning and interrogated," prohibited from sending any more reports, and forced to appeal to the Chief of Information, Mr Rob Scott, who got him off the hook.[8]

On the opening Saturday, Percival issued an Order of the Day which said:

> Our task is to hold this fortress until help can come, as assuredly it will come; this we are determined to do. Any of the enemy who sets foot in our fortress must be dealt with immediately. The enemy within our gates must be ruthlessly weeded out. There must be no more loose talk and rumour-mongering. Our duty is clear. With firm resolve and fixed determination we shall win through. For nearly two months our troops have fought an enemy on the mainland who has had the advantage of great air superiority and considerable freedom of movement by sea. Our task has been to impose losses on the enemy and gain time to enable the forces of the Allies to be concentrated for this struggle in the Far East. Today we stand beleaguered in our island fortress.

Already comparisons had been drawn between Singapore and Malta. They were not realistic comparisons. Malta, the heroic bone in the throat of the Mediterranean, was a thick chunk of rock standing well out of the water and honeycombed with caves and shelters. Singapore, divided from the enemy by the Strait which was less than a thousand yards wide in some places and never more than five thousand, was a low-lying swampy diamond, seamed with creeks, supremely approachable and virtually shelterless. Its highest point was a hill at Bukit Timah, less than six hundred feet high. Whatever it was, at no time in the 123 years of its history since the day Raffles landed had it been a fortress.

Conflicting theories exist regarding the defence plans for the Island. Brigadier Barclay explains one of them clearly, saying that the Japanese preparations included "a most elaborate deception plan" to make the British think that the main attack would come on the north-east coast. He says this was completely successful because the freshest troops were put there (the 18th Division, of which the 4th, 5th, and 6th Battalions

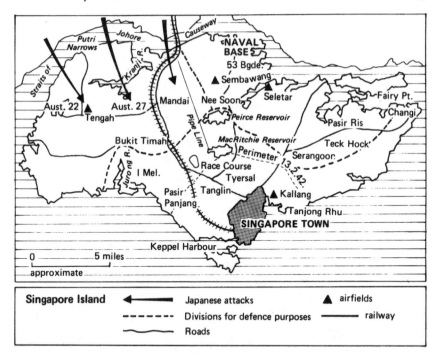

Singapore Island

- ◄━━━ Japanese attacks
- ▲ airfields
- ------ Divisions for defence purposes
- ━━━ railway
- ───── Roads

The Royal Norfolk Regiment were a part), and when the attack came it was on the thinly held north-west corner.[9].

Mr Bateson's viewpoint presents a contradictory series of ideas. He says that Wavell believed the Japanese would land on the north-west part of the Island and that the strongest defence troops should be there to meet them. Percival did not agree, thinking that the attack would come in the north-east, and disposed his men accordingly.[10] Mr Barber indicates that Percival stubbornly refused to give way to Wavell in the matter.[11] Other writers, however, Churchill included, drew different conclusions and stated that the original idea had been to use the freshest troops in the north-west, as it was there that they expected the assault; the Strait was narrower, the coastline shorter and more deeply indented, narrower fronts could be set up.

The freshest troops were, on the whole, those most recently landed, but Percival decided finally to allocate the north-west coast to the Australians, possibly because their bellicose CO was longing for a fight and had vociferously said so. There may also have been a faint feeling of compunction at the prospect of using the newly arrived and raw 18th Division to meet, head-on, a full scale invasion.

Which of these theories is correct it is now hard to decide, probably impossible. They may all be wrong: it is natural to duck behind the one that offers the best self-justification and it may as well be left at that for the purpose of this account.

The Island was divided into three sectors to meet the coming attack. Wavell believed after the loss of Johore that Percival ought to be able to hold out for several months. A couple would make all the difference, as America had promised "large numbers" of aircraft and other weapons within "a short time," so eight weeks of stubborn resistance, or even six, would probably turn the tide.[12] The Island did not lend itself to a battle of manoeuvre but the troops were allocated as though it did. The northern sector ran from Changi to the Causeway and was the most strongly held in terms of numbers and artillery, being assigned to III Corps, which consisted of the 11th Indian and the 18th British Divisions. The western sector, stretching from the Causeway to the Jurong river, was assigned to Gordon Bennett, with the 44th Indian Division who had landed on January 22 from the Jurong to the Berih river, the Australian 22nd Brigade with a nine-mile front between the Berih and the Kranji rivers, and the Australian 27th Brigade from the Kranji to the Causeway. The southern sector, the whole south coast curving from the Jurong up to Changi, was defended by the 1st and 2nd Malaya and Straits Settlements Volunteer Brigades, which "had not yet seen action but which were to fight staunchly." [13]

The Bedfordshires and the 4th Norfolks, who had landed on January 29 and been given "a dollop of local transport," were rushed off to the north-east corner of the Island where their units were split up and allotted "rather haphazardly" to local COs.[14] This was close to Changi, which had a large barracks and a jail, and they were going to come to know both very well later under other circumstances.

Now for all the troops on the Island began the process of working all day to set up the sorely needed shore defences—gun positions, underwater obstacles, barbed wire, searchlights, trenches and support lines—in other words "to try to make up in eight days for fourteen years eaten by the locusts." [15]

The pace of communications between London and Singapore now speeded up. Churchill wanted to know what plans were being made for the relief of Singapore, suggesting running convoys in of reinforcements, troops, aircraft, and food; yet whatever plans existed for this relief or any other could not be carried out without command in the air, and this was no longer even a possibility. Wavell withdrew what fighter planes were left to Palembang in Sumatra, saying that three of the four airfields on the Island were within range of the Japanese artillery on the mainland. (The fourth airfield, Kallang, reclaimed from a swamp, was in any case almost unusable. It was pitted with craters which were brimming with water much of the time.) Churchill wanted to know why Wavell had done this, as at first sight it looked like an act of despair.[16] It appears so at second sight, too. The situation reminds one of the state of affairs in Georgia in 1864 when the Federal armies came down the railroad towards Atlanta, fighting an action, outflanking the Confederates, fighting another action, forcing the enemy all the time to "fight and fall back! fight and fall back!" * To General de Guingand it seemed that Wavell gave up the Island as hopeless as soon as Johore was lost: he gave "such bad advice" and should have approached his problems "more realistically and with greater skill." [17]

The soldiers were now kept busy for hours at a stretch in the mangrove swamps, trying to dig trenches in the oozy ground and setting up barbed wire.[18] But the civilian population now had something else to think about. On the north coast two huge black clouds of smoke were darkening the blue sky: they came from the oil dumps at the Naval Base, and had been burning for three days when the journalists were called to a press conference and, listening in horrified silence, were told that the Naval Base had been evacuated. Not only that: it had been evacuated before the last troops crossed the Causeway.

3

One reporter asked: "But I thought they'd been withdrawn to the Island to defend the Base?" There was, as Mr Barber found out from Mr Hammonds who was present, no answer.[19]

Mr Morrison, with Mr Rob Scott and a correspondent called Henry Stokes, went to see for himself. It was, he said, his most tragic memory of the whole campaign. The Indian sentries at the gate let them pass without a word. Inside was a scene of confused desolation: deserted barrack blocks, piles of clothes and equipment lying about, a few lorries loading some stores at the waterside warehouses, four oil tanks on fire, row after row of enormous workshops full of priceless untouched machinery and stocks including aircraft parts, radio parts of every kind, hundreds of boxes of electric bulbs, rope, wire, all silent and abandoned.

* Margaret Mitchell, *Gone with the Wind.*

The three men put fifty of the gas masks in their car, knowing the hospitals had none; they took a crested china beer mug each from the police mess as a souvenir. They saw an unfinished meal on a table, three dartboards just inside a door, a football by the goal posts on one of the seventeen pitches. All the rooms and offices used by the Naval Commander-in-Chief Rear-Admiral Spooner, and his many staff, stood empty and lifeless. A wall map and a few books were left, some desks and chairs. Rubbish lay outside the kitchens, attracting flies, rats, and a few scavenger dogs. Three enemy planes circled overhead, and the journalists were sniped at from over the water as they had a look at the shore.[20] The Army took 120 lorries up to the Base every night for a week, each lorry making three trips, to move out portable stuff, especially clothes, food and cigarettes. One soldier told Mr Hammonds that it was like "pinching the rings off a warm body." [21]

Mr Morrison, Mr Scott and Mr Stokes left the Base and went over to the neighbouring airfield at Seletar, the one that had been so comfortable according to Flight-Sergeant McCormac. It was not comfortable now: black skeleton buildings, wrecked aircraft, large craters, a few soldiers with machine-guns down at the water's edge where boats were tied up at the Yacht Club, no other sign of life. The three men quietly climbed into their car and drove away, oppressed by the knowledge that the Naval Base which had cost sixty million pounds and taken seventeen years to build had been used in war just once, sheltering the two British battleships for a few days, and had been abandoned like the *Mary Celeste*.[22]

The Admiralty had told Spooner on January 21 to remove his skilled personnel from the Base and he had done so, transferring all the Europeans to Singapore town. Many of them were then sent straight off to Ceylon. Any scorched earth work would be done by the Army, he decided, but he did not tell Percival this, nor, in fact, any of Malaya Command. He had, in addition, dismissed his civilian labour force.[23] It is interesting to discover that none of this is in the account, otherwise fairly detailed, that Churchill later wrote.

4

During the few days of grace that opened February, Yamashita systematically grouped his delighted warriors for the assault on Singapore. He made his advance HQ at the top of the tower in the Sultan of Johore's palace, from where he could look out through wide windows at the Strait and that part of the north coast that was soon to come under bombardment. After the surrender, one of the British prisoners was asked by the Japanese why the palace had never been shelled, and was told that no one imagined any commander being so foolish as to make his headquarters in "such an obvious target." [24]

Yamashita had three divisions on hand, all closed up now after the conquest of Malaya, and another division standing by in Japan. He was short of ammunition, especially shells, and irritated by a recent visit from Terauchi's Chief of Staff, Lieutenant-General Osamu Tsukada, who brought him "voluminous notes" on how to capture the Island and left without thanks for the lunch Yamashita had given him. Tearing up the notes, Yamashita reflected crossly in his diary that whenever there were two alternatives, "Southern Army always insist on the wrong one." The Air Division ignored some of his specific strike requests. But at least he had 300 landing craft, and each day his troops practised the drill. The 4,000 men of the first assault wave had all fought in China and were "masters of seaborne landings." [25]

All the Japanese worked under a clearly established system with a fixed hierarchy and a single line of discipline running from the Commander-in-Chief to the private and understood by every man along the line. In addition they were all elated by success: with mounting incredulity Yamashita had become aware of the lowered morale of Percival and his staff, of the speed and ease of the infiltration tactics and the pace of the opposition's retreat. He had no defeats, no crippling losses, he could count on plenty of air support. He had only to keep his nerve, and the biggest single prize of the war in the Far East would be his.

"Singapore," wrote Mr Morrison sombrely, "was crying out for leadership." He was conscious of a sense of defeatism, not alleviated by the editorials appearing daily in the *Straits Times,* which was, as it had always been, "splenetically hostile" towards the local government and the civil service. The Europeans' defeatism affected the Asiatic population, and native labour dwindled to a trickle, forcing the authorities to divert troops to urgent unloading, delivery and defence-building jobs. Native crews deserted from ships in the harbour; shop-owners took refuge in Island villages, leaving their shops boarded up; office and hotel staff drifted away. The Governor talked to Mr Morrison and said he thought the officials had done well, that Singapore could hold out through a long siege, and might well "write an epic in imperial history"; he was, thought Mr Morrison, "Sanguine to the verge of complacency."

Later the same day, Percival gave a press conference and explained the general outlines of the situation: much of his talk was "sensible" but Mr Morrison had never "heard a message put across with less conviction." In his opinion Percival had "considerable personal charm" if one met him unofficially, but with all his ability to present clear schemes on paper he always "saw the difficulties" before he "saw the possibilities." Mr Morrison thought the best military leader on the Island at the time was the "rasping, bitter, sarcastic" but "tough, ruthless, aggressive" Gordon Bennett, unconventional, proud of his Australians and spoiling for a fight.[26]

It was surprising how many activities went on just as they would have done in peace time. The Governor was presented every morning after breakfast with the day's menu. He no longer insisted on dinner jackets for evening, but his staff still had to wear collars and ties. The Swimming Club went on presenting its monthly bills. Robinson's was full at coffee time. Hundreds of people queued for the cinema: it seemed to help. Mr Bennitt had a new gas heater installed in his bathroom. Shops that were still open were doing well, sales increasing in food, drink, clothes, and books, garages had a run on repairs because cars kept running into the cattle in the blackout, firms continued to produce Tiger beer and soda water. Women had their hair done, had facials and bought cosmetics, and the soldiers crowded Change Alley to buy souvenirs. In the evenings there was always dancing, and many residents played bridge. Many more did a lot of drinking.[27]

Against this background the work of defence struggled on. Machine-guns were moved from the south to the north coast, boats were looked at and noted, slit trenches dug, barbed wire and searchlights set up, fire lanes cleared. There was little local labour to call upon, and the troops' work was not made easier by frequent difficulties and protests raised by the residents. A major in the Argylls, wanting to cut down trees to improve his field of fire, was told to get permission first from "the competent authority"; when an officer took his men to the golf links he was told that he was on private property; when that same golf club was to be made a strong point, the secretary said nothing could be done without first having a meeting of the committee.[28] The barbed wire kept running short wherever it was most urgently wanted so that one exasperated colonel set out to fetch some himself from the Base Ordnance Depot; on arrival he found the Depot closed for its customary half-holiday.[29]

Bombing raids added to the confusion and the usual unscrupulous characters thrown up by such crises took advantage of these to do a considerable amount of looting. All sorts of rumours and reports went round, some of them reaching print, as did one dispatch out of Chungking quoting "a Chinese Army spokesman" saying that "the Japanese 16th Division" had been "virtually annihilated" in the Johore fighting and "the ashes of over ten thousand Japanese dead" had already arrived in Saigon.[30] Wherever the Japanese 16th Division was, it was not anywhere near Malaya. Yamashita's three divisions were the 18th (the Chrysanthemum), the 5th, and the Imperial Guards. By Wednesday February 4 he had completed his reconnaissance and settled his plan.

Like all Yamashita's war plans, it was clear, simple and practical. The Imperial Guards would move on Saturday to take Palau Ubin island, close to the north-east Changi area, which was nothing but a piece of rock surrounded by muddy beaches, no use to anybody. Certainly it was no springboard for invasion of the Island, but Percival might think it was and waver between the north-east/north-west alternatives again. On Sunday night the other two divisions would attack the north-west coast, and the Imperial Guards would switch back to come in behind them. Fake camps had been set up on the coast opposite the Naval Base and lorries went along there by day and returned by night. This worked. For some time Simson had been stacking piles of materials in the north-west sector, petrol, wire, mines, lights, vital defence supplies of all kinds in great quantity. In organising all this he was stimulated by the confidence that the Japanese must invade, or attempt invasion, in that quarter. The approach roads, state of the ground and the water, width and shelving of the Strait—all were favourable west of the Causeway and bristling with difficulties east of it. Percival, alarmed by signs of activity opposite the north-east sector, ordered Simson to move all his precious stocks across there at top speed.

Aghast at the thought of his carefully laid stockpiles uprooted for what he was sure was a chimaera, Simson none the less obeyed, and his Royal Engineers managed to shift the stuff by Thursday morning. During that Thursday Gordon Bennett's reconnaissance reported heavy troop concentrations beginning to build up close to the coast facing the north-west sector, and this of course was reported to HQ, whereupon he told Simson to move all the stockpiles back again. By now Yamashita's guns had opened the preliminary artillery bombardment, which went on for two days.[31]

On Thursday night, Mr Hudson gave a broadcast. Speaking openly and angrily, he said that it was no use comparing the Island with Malta: Malta had shelters, Singapore had drains and trenches.[32] "The official shelter policy," he stated, "has been bungled." There were scores of tin miners on the Island now, from up-country, who were expert in tunnelling and ought to be given something to do. If the Government was unable to find the labour, Mr Hudson guaranteed to go out and get it himself. The effect of this talk was "electric": listeners jammed the telephones with praise and offers of help, all the reporters were delighted as all mention of shelters had been censored since the raids began, and Mr Hammonds, determined that there should be no slip-up this time, rushed to the Cathay Building, got a copy of the script, and sent it out to London "within half an hour." Next morning the *Straits Times* commented on "the very forthright nature" of the broadcast: "so entirely out of tune with what we are accustomed to hear from official spokesmen." Mr Hudson was reprimanded by the "official spokesmen" who told him that he had damaged public morale and that "several senior members of the government" were very angry with him, but Simson sent for him and praised the broadcast, telling him to go ahead.[33] The official policy on shelters screeched to a halt, backed up and reversed itself, but by then, of course, it was much too late.

5

On Sunday February 8 Mr Morrison and Mr Stokes, with another journalist, Mr Yates McDaniel, went out with Colonel Dalley, "a cracker-jack of a fellow," to have a look at the Chinese volunteers known as Dalley's Desperadoes, then stationed in a mangrove swamp among the Australians on the north-west part of the Island. The position was being shelled and the three reporters had to keep flinging themselves flat and trying, as Mr Stokes said, "to squeeze our bodies under our tin helmets." Mr Morrison admitted: "I was windier that day than I had ever been before during the Malayan campaign."

It was pouring with rain, everybody got soaked, but there was a difference in the atmosphere among the Chinese who, unlike the rest of the men engaged in the defence of Singapore, had "a personal venom" against the Japanese because of the "China Incident." They were inspired by a genuine, intense commitment to battle, and when the time came they fought savagely. The corresponding reprisals just over a week later were proportionately severe.[34]

There was a Free French ship in the harbour, the *Felix Roussel,* due to sail that night, and for those Europeans in Singapore the day was one of wrestling with agonising private decisions followed by a rush to get tickets and pack for the few wives remaining who would go. Mrs Hudson, Mrs Glover, Mrs Buckeridge reluctantly agreed to leave, but the American Freddy Retz, who had married Dr Philip Bloom two days before in a hasty ceremony interrupted by an air raid and sandwiched between bouts of duty at the hospital, refused. Mr Buckeridge drove his wife to the harbour, went on board with her, and then found that her travel pass had been made out in both their names. It would have been so easy to stay there. Mr Hudson, also on board seeing his wife settled, heard a sergeant marshalling passengers up the gangway say that if he had any sense he would stay on board. Both men, sorely tempted, said goodbye to their wives over a last drink and then left together, returning to the Buckeridges' flat above the fire station for "a scratch meal of sardines and bully beef and beer." Mr Glover went with Mr Hammonds to the reserve *Tribune* office at Dulverton to work on next morning's issue of the paper.[35]

All that day the Australian positions in the north-west sector had been steadily bombed and shelled, the intensity of attack increasing through the afternoon, and there had been no reply from the Island artillery. This has never been satisfactorily explained though there is a theory that Percival and Gordon Bennett both thought it was the first of several days of this softening-up process, but as it was in fact the fourth day of bombardment this explanation does not quite fit. The rain had stopped and the night was clear and starry by soon after nine o'clock when the troops of Yamashita's first wave moved quietly down to the boats.[36] The guns had fallen silent and for a little while there was a kind of pause. Clouds of smoke hung in the air from the earlier gunfire and the burning oil still sending out acrid black plumes high into the sky. The assault craft chugged out into the Strait and the Australians strung along an eight-mile stretch of coast saw the black shapes and heard the outboard motors. The guns opened up again with terrific force on both sides: Mr Morrison in Singapore, going to bed very tired at about half past ten, heard them sounding continuously "like the rumble of wheels on a road." [37]

Apart from the gun flashes and the occasional fiery glow from a boat that received a hit, the assault sector stayed obstinately dark. The plan had been that as soon as the enemy was sighted all the searchlights along the north coast would blaze out and light up "the killing area" to daylight brilliance. But no lights came on. The troops had been told on no account to pull a switch without orders, and the orders could not get through because the afternoon bombardment had cut every line of communication to the coast. Suddenly observers in the city saw blue and red rockets bursting in the northern sky.[38] It seemed a peculiar time for fireworks. What it meant was that the first assault wave of the Chrysanthemum Division and the 5th Division had got their foothold on the Island.

Percival rang up the Governor and told him that the attack had started,[39] and a few other wakeful and alert Europeans heard that something more dramatic than usual was going on scarcely twenty miles away. There, matters were chaotic. After ten o'clock Captain James, sent out to reconnoitre and finding conditions slightly misty, groped through closely planted rubber and creeping mangrove (where exploration was bad in daylight so it was well nigh impossible in the dark), over ground held between the Australians and the Indians of the 44th Brigade, and was appalled to hear Japanese voices out of the thickets in front of him calling "Yose-atsumeru, tsume-yoseru"—"Gather together." The Captain backed away as stealthily as possible and sent a runner to the Divisional HQ to report the enemy positions; six hours later a reply came back asking him to confirm his report.[40]

By then of course the whole situation had changed beyond recognition. The Japanese were making a double-pronged attack on either side of the Kranji river. Against the first landing craft the Australian gunners did well, but their shooting enabled the Japanese to see quite soon where their guns were concentrated and to steer in between them, in many cases landing at the second or third attempts. On reaching the shore the Japanese made their way inland as fast as they could and then worked their way round behind the defence posts where hand to hand fighting developed.

As each outpost was silenced the next landing craft came in without opposition so that the weight of the assault built up steadily. The commanders of each unit had compasses strapped to their wrists like watches and were therefore able to lead their men consistently south and southeast.[41] The first big defence position inland from the coast was between the headwaters of the Kranji and Jurong rivers, cutting across the whole west side of the Island, an excellent stop line for an army with prepared defences against an army that had no boats. Neither of these conditions applied to the early hours of Monday February 9.

Mr Morrison, sitting in the press room of the Cathay Building and typing up a report on the previous evening's bombardment, was interrupted by a colleague, Mr Ian Fitchett, who burst in with "the breathless news" of the landing; almost immediately the radio bulletin was heard making the announcement. Mr Morrison pulled the sheet of paper out of his typewriter, crumpled it up, dropped it in the waste paper basket, and rolled in a fresh page. There were, he believed, "some three or four thousand Japanese shock troops" at present on the Island; [42] only much later was it discovered that 13,000 had landed that night and another 10,000 soon after dawn.[43]

The High Command issued a communiqué during the morning. It said that "offensive action is being taken to mop up the enemy." [44] Percival sent a message to Wavell in Java: "Enemy landed in force on west coast last night and has penetrated about five miles." Having sent this off, he settled down to draw up his plan for the perimeter defence of the city.

Crowds stood around the Cathay Building, waiting for news. Other crowds filled the Cathedral.[45] Like the military, they had left it very much too late for heavenly intervention.

6

The Japanese advance opened a gap between the Australians and the Indians at the precise time when they were moving back on orders to their stop line, on which there were no prepared defences. In the end the withdrawing brigades "overshot the mark, and before they could be redirected the enemy had passed it." [46] Gordon Bennett had a visit from Percival that afternoon and had to report that "all battalions were out of touch with brigade. The enemy bombardment had destroyed all beach lights and beach guns and machine guns and caused heavy casualties." Percival, he said, seemed very worried, as indeed he might be. The 22nd Australian Brigade was split up into groups trying to find their way back, some managing to reach Bukit Timah in the centre of the Island, some even getting as far as the city, but many died and many lost their way, and within twelve hours of the start of the landings the Brigade "was no longer a conclusive fighting force." By sunset on Monday the Japanese were in possession of the Tengah airfield.

That evening Percival met Heath and Major-General Keith Simmons, CO of the southern sector, and explained to them his perimeter line, which ran around Bukit Timah and the reservoirs and included the swampy Kallang airfield, and after the meeting the plan was issued in writing "as a secret and personal instruction" to all the senior commanders.[47] That evening also Simson visited the Governor to ask permission for the fullest possible scorched earth policy to be started without delay. The Governor, who knew that the Asiatic businessmen would be expected to carry on whether Singapore was ruled by British or Japanese, felt that Simson was being too pessimistic in drawing comparisons between what had happened in Malaya and what was likely to happen on the Island. He demurred, saying that there were at least forty Chinese-owned engineering works that must not be touched (all well equipped, containing new machinery and vehicles) because it would be bad for morale. This left forty-seven British-owned plants for Simson's men to smash up. It must be remembered, as Mr Barber very fairly pointed out, that it was difficult to scorch the earth of a fortress it had been ordered to defend to the last man.[48]

Percival was talking to Heath and Simmons in his office at Fort Canning and Sir Shenton was talking to Simson on the Government House veranda over a whisky and soda, but over on the other side of the Island Yamashita had come to have a look for himself. Crossing the Strait in a small barge so crowded that they all had to stand up holding on to one another's shoulders, they got ashore and stumbled over something soft that moved under their feet; Colonel Tsuji, switching on his flashlight, found rows of captured British and Australian soldiers lying roped together: "The symbolism," wrote Mr Swinson, "was too startling to be missed." [49]

Captain James, back at Tanglin Barracks after a heavy day, remembered seeing "hundreds of bedraggled Australians" streaming back that morning along the Bukit Timah road. One had said to him: "Chum, to hell with Malaya and Singapore." Another young soldier had described his platoon "spread all to hell and gone in the rubber" among the close timber full of drifting smoke. They could see little of the enemy although "there must have been thousands of them." He asked bitterly: "What could we do? Ever try to scoop water with a piece of torn fishnet?" and wondered why there had been no artillery support.

Malaya Command had reported austerely that the Very light signals were not seen, the cable communications had been severed, nothing came through on the field radio and the beach lights failed to function.[50] Reuters printed a report describing a brigadier and his staff sitting on upturned petrol tins under a large bush, reading maps. The brigadier had his dog with him.[51] As the end drew inexorably nearer, the Singapore Europeans took their dogs to the vet to be destroyed rather than leave them to the mercy of the surrender.[52] This was perhaps the most heartbreaking thing they had to do, worse even than smashing up the machinery that had been their livelihood for years.

And it was being smashed up, though by no means all of it. At one place Simson's squads were half way through demolishing a large garage when they were stopped by the owners waving a written permit of exemption in front of their eyes. Something else being got rid of was liquor—a total ban was coming into force on Friday, but in the meantime the Governor had asked for stocks to be destroyed. Mr Buckeridge wrote that he never realised how long it took to pull twelve bottles out of a case and throw them against a wall. Over in the Treasury Building they were burning money, which took a day to do as the numbers of the notes burned had to be recorded before the bundles could be pushed into the furnace.[53] All this activity went on amid almost continuous air raids. It was easier for the Japanese to manage now that the target area had dwindled to the compact measure of two-thirds of the Island.

All this time the 18th Division had been standing by in the northeast sector, making trenches and stringing wire, with no enemy in front of them. Percival moved them only when the Tengah airfield went and the Japanese started a fresh coastal bombardment near the Causeway, signalling unmistakably their intention to come across east of the Kranji in fresh force. At that point Percival called the Norfolks and Cambridgeshires to defend the reservoirs and part of the Bukit Timah area, the front of which was held stubbornly by the Argylls.

On Tuesday February 10 at various times the north end of the Jurong line, the outposts at the south end, and the positions below the Causeway were all abandoned, though "none had been subject to attacks that could not be met." Wavell paid what was to be his last visit to Singapore. It was a most uncomfortable one, interrupted by air raids: at one point a bomb fell at HQ forcing Wavell, Percival and Gordon Bennett to "scuttle for cover beneath a table," which Percival called "an unedifying spectacle"; fortunately the bomb did not go off. Wavell said that the British must recapture the Jurong line, though as Captain James shrewdly pointed out, it is easier to plan counter-attacks than do them.[54] Captain Russell-Roberts, sent to Tanglin Road where he had lived in such comfort so short a time before, stopped near the Golf Clubhouse where there was no telephone, no transport and no automatic weapon to be seen. A forward post there overlooked the eighteenth green; it seemed "sacrilege" to dig a trench on that grass "within a delicate chip shot of the pin." There was at least "plenty of food and wine." [55]

Mr Morrison, now reduced to getting about on a bicycle, went to Kallang airfield. There, half a dozen Hurricanes were doing what they could to stem the tide of attacking enemy aircraft. As the runways were holed with craters, they had to take off from the road running alongside the airfield. Two Hurricanes that had crash-landed lay by the side of this road, "other burnt-out hulks" littered the field and the hangars were "charred ruins." In the western part of the city troops were moving, some to action stations, in battle order with a purposeful air, others drifting aimlessly about. Military cars and lorries sped along, the native population sat huddled in groups in doorways and parks. The sun shining in the blue sky was hidden by smoke clouds, and the crash of shells and bombs and the chatter of machine-guns never stopped for a second. Wild rumours of the Japanese pushed back or reaching the botanical gardens three miles away, of parachutists landing or the Americans coming ashore at Penang, circulated around the city. At midday the Governor broadcast: "We are all in the hands of God." Gordon Bennett advised an Australian journalist "to get out while he could." Mr Morrison wrote: "I gave Singapore thirty-six hours." [56]

It was not going to be quite as quick as that. Lieutenant Coast called the battle of Bukit Timah without doubt the main battle for Singapore. It lasted several days between the Race Course and Forest Reserve Area and the Golf Course and the Adam Road, a mile or two nearer Singapore. He wrote a most vivid account of what being there was actually like: in that strange place, full of rustling shadows, trailing creepers, noisy insects and frogs, every tree could and sometimes did conceal an enemy, though "heaven alone knows how many rounds were pumped into surprised nuts." All this, and shots being fired, red Very lights soaring up into the night sky, attempts to take up positions in isolated houses upon which the Japanese rapidly got the range, periods of crouching down into slit trenches under mortar barrage, heart-in-the-mouth investigations of the nearby road in the half light of dawn with a battle clattering away to the right, and one battery firing inaccurately because they were doing it from a map.

At one point an enemy position was found in a clump of flowers from which the Japanese could have rolled grenades into the British trenches; at another, Lieutenant Coast managed to have a hasty cold bath with soap in a house where the roof gaped and bullets flew. Throughout the battle the men did not feel hungry, but longed for drinks. There was a night, too, spent in wet grass, after three days without a moment of sleep; the final positions were near, and in, a quarry, in slit trenches surrounded by jungly scrub, where the average visibility was about ten yards.[57] Tuesday's Low cartoon in the *Guardian* echoes this: called "forgetfulness of self at Singapore" it shows British gunners in a bombardment saying: "They must be pretty tough, those Yanks in the Philippines." [58]

Wavell and Percival, leaving Gordon Bennett's HQ, saw "an undisciplined-looking mob of Indians" carrying rifles and wearing blackened uniforms; Percival felt "more than a bit ashamed of them and it was quite obvious what the Supreme Commander thought." He found out later that the Indians were retrieving rifles by order of their "good quartermaster" and that the blackness came from oil smoke: "Many of our troops looked more like miners emerging from a shift in the pits than fighting soldiers." "It is difficult," wrote Sir Compton Mackenzie, "to write with restraint about the folly of that scorched earth policy in Malaya." [59]

Churchill, however, was still writing about it. On the Tuesday he cabled Wavell that the British greatly outnumbered the Japanese and should be able to wipe them out; there must be "no thought of saving the troops or sparing the population." At all costs they must fight to the end; the 18th Division had the chance "to make its name in history," and commanders "should die with their troops." Referring to the honour of the Empire and the Army, he relied upon Wavell to "show no mercy to weakness in any form."

As Wavell left Singapore on Wednesday, receiving Churchill's message just before setting out, he slipped on the quay in the dark and fell off it, breaking two small bones in his back. This may or may not have affected the way in which he replied to the Prime Minister that night in a hopeless comment that, even so long afterwards, creates in the reader an unpleasant sensation of rage and despair. Saying that "everything possible" was being done to "produce a more offensive spirit and optimistic outlook" but that this had so far been unsuccessful, he stated:

> Morale of some troops is not good, and none is as high as I should like to see. . . . He [Percival] should however have quite enough to deal with enemy who have landed if the troops can be made to act with sufficient vigour and determination.[60]

Yamashita had ordered the Imperial Guards to cross the Strait after his Monday visit. Their commander, Lieutenant-General Nishimura, stalled over this, partly because the Guards felt they had lost face at the Muar, partly because Yamashita had gone over his head in appointing a new CO to his own old regiment. For some time off-putting messages passed between the two generals. "It looked to me," wrote Yamashita, "as if he was still upset about not being able to lead the attack. I ordered him to do his duty." Nishimura sent a staff officer along to see Yamashita, who snapped at him: "Go back to your divisional commander and tell him the Imperial Guards Division can do as it likes in this battle." Nishimura was sufficiently stung by this to order the advance, and on Wednesday the Imperial Guards, cream of the army, crossed the Causeway.[61]

7

Mr Morrison, after a last look at the city from the balcony of the Cathay Building, cycled down to the docks, which were in "appalling confusion," passing on the way the wreck of a Japanese Zero put on display near the Cathedral. He hired a sampan, and was rowed out to a Dutch cargo ship anchored in the roads. The skipper agreed to take him, and within an hour or so the ship picked its way cautiously through the minefields en route for Batavia. Mr Morrison stood on deck looking back at the Island. The sea was deep blue, the sky, seen clearly at last, blue and cloudless, except over the Island, where black smoke still hung, and one tall column of white looking like a volcanic eruption. All the landmarks he knew so well stood out sharply, fires burned in several places, the rumble of guns came across the water.[62] Civilian casualties in air raids had reached two thousand a day. A million gallons of spirits were being destroyed so that by Friday the streets would be streaming with alcohol and rain.[63] Lorries were lined up bumper to bumper along roads and in public parks, roads were blocked with craters, broken telegraph poles and tangles of wire. Clouds of smoke blotted out the sky. Looters and rioters were everywhere. The last defensive perimeter was beginning to tighten inside the gathering enemy noose. Singapore was "a corner of hell," its smoke visible to Mr Morrison 120 miles away twenty-four hours later, at anchor by the palm-fringed white sand of a storybook tropical island. On the deck of the ship, camouflaged with foliage, were six huge crates holding Glenn Martin bombers. The ship had brought them to Singapore two weeks before and they had never been unloaded. Now it was taking them back.[64]

CHAPTER VIII

The Ford Works Building

—————

I

AMONG the films on in London that week was the zany classic *Hellza-poppin.* This matched Singapore's situation better than another release, *Blood and Sand*: [1] on the Island the sand might give place to mud and swamp, but the blood was there in plenty.

By Wednesday February 11 the two fighting areas had come closer and closer together, moving in upon the village of Bukit Timah. One pair of defending brigades, the 22nd Australian and the 44th Indian, had fallen back between the Kranji and Jurong rivers, leaving the western part of the Island to the enemy; the 27th Australian Brigade with part of the 11th Indian Division and several regiments from the 18th British, had been pushed back in sections from the Causeway-Kranji area and the west side of the Naval Base towards the precious reservoirs.

One particular hill in the Mandai district seemed bewitched: two sets of troops had left it in a hurry without being attacked and a third had shied at attacking it when it was empty.[2] Within forty-eight hours of the invasion some of the Argylls were cut off two miles in advance of the British lines and, just as they and other detachments had been forced to do on the mainland, they began to struggle back piecemeal to their base. One group ordered to hold the pipeline now consisted of a corporal and two privates, ragged, exhausted and burnt by the sun. Advised to get some sleep inside the British lines the corporal replied that if these three were the last of their battalion he was the senior NCO and they had been told to hold the pipeline, whereupon "all three turned back toward the enemy." [3] Gordon Bennett inexplicably moved the 27th Australians during Wednesday morning without telling either Malaya Command or III Corps, which left a single Australian company and a Baluch regimental battalion to hold the Mandai road and four reduced battalions to try to recapture Bukit Timah village, into which the Japanese had now penetrated.[4]

Singapore town was in absolute chaos: long trailing lines of native civilians were clogging the roads, already blocked by traffic, towards the eastern part of the Island. They carried their belongings on their backs, in handcarts or abandoned rickshaws, in one case in an empty coffin. Those who were trying to drive somewhere on official business found that it took over an hour to go two or three miles. All the hospitals had received direct hits, and one of them, a group of huts at Tyersal Park, was burnt to the ground; most of the people there were killed, either in the fire or by machine-gunning from the air. The Cathedral was filled with stretcher cases.

On Tuesday a rumour started that the nurses were to be evacuated, and the chief of the civilian medical services, Dr R. B. MacGregor, got in touch with the Governor to see if this could possibly be true. Sir Shenton checked with Percival and reported back to MacGregor that no such idea had been considered. A heavy air raid now opened up on the docks and the officer in charge there telephoned Simson to ask for advice: he said that the senior European officials of the Harbour Board had left the Island on orders from the Governor. Simson at once checked with Sir Shenton and the Governor admitted that it was true, he had been told by Whitehall to send the Harbour Board officials out as they were experts and needed in India, and by an oversight he had forgotten to tell Simson.

The responsibility for destroying the docks machinery now lay with the ARP under Mr Hudson, who was asked to start the demolitions that afternoon, but the Japanese beat him to it. They came over in precision formation, dropped their bombs as usual all together, hit a fuel dump, a rubber warehouse, a sugar warehouse, set fire to shops in the Keppel Road and a Chinese junk out in the water, and threatened a sawmill and a timber works. A shell fired at the same time exploded on a paint shop and set it alight. Mr Hudson drove some casualties to the General Hospital where he found a mass burial going on, the many dead being placed in two huge pits and sprinkled with lime. Inside the hospital they were running short of water. Mrs Bloom had a bath in hot water prepared for washing bloodstained uniforms, and the operating theatre staff had to wash their hands and sterilize their instruments in soda water.[5]

It is difficult to sort out the events of those last days into any kind of orderly narrative, partly because plans were changed or not made clear and partly because few people kept any precise record of their actions. Even if they had, it would give a false impression: the movements were never co-ordinated and never orderly. Told to hold in one place, a commander would do so for a while and then inexplicably pull back. One group of Australians close to the Causeway held on splendidly, their CO having been refused permission to withdraw; in the morning the Japanese gave up trying to push further in at that place. Yamashita waited an hour or two, asked for a fresh reconnaissance report, and found to his amazement that the Australians had gone. The CO had withdrawn them, saying he had permission, Gordon Bennett indignantly denied giving it, and whoever was to blame the result was that a gap lay open where yesterday there had been stubborn and successful resistance.[6] It was a carbon copy of the withdrawal on the previous night from the Jurong Line. In the light of events like these it is not surprising that Wavell wrote later: "I left Singapore on the morning of 11 February without much confidence in any prolonged resistance."

2

The official Orders of the Day, including Wavell's own, still called for all-out fighting and he referred to the Americans at Bataan, to the Russians and the Chinese. As it turned out Bataan was overrun in the end, and as for Russia and China, neither of them was really comparable to an island not much bigger than the Isle of Wight. Incidentally, a rumour that spread during the campaign claimed that the War Office had actually sent out maps of the Isle of Wight, though it wasn't made clear whether this was supposed to have happened by accident or whether by design on the principle that anything was better than nothing and supplies of the correct maps were short. The frightening thing about this apparently silly story is that considering all the mistakes that had been made, it might just conceivably (people felt) have been true.

On the Wednesday Yamashita had a letter for Percival dropped from a plane. It was a courteously worded request that he should recognise the situation as hopeless and give in without further delay. As a matter of fact speed was essential to Yamashita as well. His chief of supply had warned him that stocks of ammunition and petrol were running dangerously low and it would be as well to bring matters to a close as soon as he could. He thought carefully and decided to bluff it out. The aircraft went on raiding, the guns went on firing, as though both were inexhaustible and supplies would last for ever. Percival telegraphed the gist of Yamashita's message to Wavell, adding that he did not propose to reply as he had no means of dropping a message; the answer "would of course in any case be negative." [7]

There was still a dribble of people leaving the Island. Mr Glover and Mr Hammonds were persuaded to get away and left on Wednesday night on board an elderly coastal steamer. The Governor took over the *Straits Times* as a government publication and 7,000 single quarto sheets appeared in print on Thursday morning, the lead story consisting simply of the official communiqué, stating that "enemy pressure slackened during the night," that "no change in the situation" was reported from various places. They were piously hoping "to stabilise our position." [8] In a way it was no more unreal than the report that day in *The Times* which quoted a man from Nova Scotia saying in Singapore that the Japanese were "scared to death of cold steel." [9] The *Guardian,* under the headline "Singapore's Fate," said that the Japanese claimed to have entered the city area; "this may relate to penetration of the north-western suburbs." [10]

Captain Russell-Roberts, hearing that all troops were to come back inside the defensive perimeter as they were holding their own nowhere except for the 1st Malay Regiment stubbornly clinging on near Pasir Panjang, went into the town to say goodbye to his wife who was leaving at three that afternoon on a small ship called the *Mata Hari,* and then "drove like mad" to the Golf Course where the rest of his regiment was to be found. They were about to be sent forward of the Kay Seang road to "fight it out to the end." It took longer to move than they had expected and they did not reach the new position until after first light on Friday.[11] During Thursday, Government House had its worst shelling so far, killing twelve of the domestic staff.[12]

Heavy fighting went on that day around the village of Nee Soon, the Imperial Guards hammering away at a regiment from Baluchistan that gave a good account of itself in spite of being faced by tanks, which were now coming over the Causeway which the Japanese had not taken long to repair.[13] The perimeter line was large when it came to numbers of troops defending it, but small to contain the administrative units which now had no work to do but were not given other jobs and were still cluttered up by enormous quantities of useless equipment. In all the muddle there was no way of keeping security, and

Japanese agents went on sending their reports out by radio with complete confidence.[14] Friday the thirteenth dawned fine and clear. In his ARP post at Tiong Bahru school, where he had slept in the headmaster's study, Mr Hudson was just contemplating breakfast of corned beef, bread, and stewed tea, and reading the second edition of the Governor's paper with the words printed across the top: "Singapore must stand; it *shall* stand," when bomber planes droned overhead and a stick of bombs fell across the school. When Mr Hudson picked himself up from the floor and staggered dazedly outside he found the building half demolished, three cars wrecked, and seven people dead, among them his own houseboy. The ARP post was shifted into the College of Medicine where the wardens were told to bury the dead "anywhere, anyhow"—"it was like the Black Death all over again." Since the telephone kept cutting out, Chinese dispatch riders carried the messages, most incoming ones reading: "Japanese approaching, please give instructions." [15]

On that Friday, accompanied by a mass of hasty consultations, list-compiling and altering, argument, persuasion, recrimination and refusal, about three thousand supposedly key people were shipped out in a flotilla of small craft to destinations in Java and Sumatra where their skills might be useful. Among them went several who had been ordered to stay at their posts till the last, including Group Captain Nunn, head of the Public Works Department.[16] Others who went included Spooner and Pulford.

Much comment, verbal and written, since then has attempted to work out the rights and wrongs of these individual departures, but the whole question is academic: the ships never reached freedom. Some were sunk as they left the Island, some were captured at sea, some surrendered, some lost their way in the dark and made landfall on small islands where the people on board managed to get ashore but eventually died of illness or starvation or were picked up by the Japanese and brought back.

Pulford and Spooner died,[17] so did Nunn, though he got a lot further than most—he and his wife, arrived in Sumatra, went aboard an old Dutch steamship, sailed for Colombo and were lost when the ship went down in four minutes after a torpedo hit from a Japanese submarine. Mrs Nunn was put in the single lifeboat with eighty others but only four survived long enough to be captured and only one of those, Lieutenant Gibson, lived to tell the tale after the war.[18] Captain Russell-Roberts' wife was captured (his baby daughter had been safely taken to England by friends), and died in captivity.

3

On Friday evening the Governor left Government House for the more secure shelter of the Singapore Club. Lady Thomas, who had been very ill for some days with amoebic dysentery, was taken out first by ambulance. The stately white house, now under shelling so constant that no one dared to go upstairs, was almost empty, a ghost of the splendid past already.[19] Sir Shenton made a quick trip upstairs to grab a few clothes which he stuffed into a suitcase while his ADC in the kitchen "shovelled any tinned food he could find into a hold-all." The two men eventually drove off down the long drive, where the sentry at the gates presented arms as the Governor passed through for the last time.

The Singapore Club was crowded, four or five sleeping in single rooms, queueing for meals (dinner that Friday was corned beef with potato salad out of a tin, and tea made with tinned milk), while the whole of the ground floor was full of wounded for whom the impossibly overworked nurses fetched water from a standpipe out in the street.[20] Over at the Dunlop warehouse Mr Hudson (his dinner that night was sardines and baked beans, with "a stiff brandy") had just arrived to make his nightly check for the European manager when he was visited by four Chinese who offered him half a million dollars in cash for the thousand tons of rubber the warehouse contained. The Chinese told him they had a cargo boat ready to take the rubber to Java, if they didn't take it away the Japanese would get it and they knew how much there was. The rubber belonged to all sorts of people who could not be traced as it had been built up for weeks from shipments sent out of Malaya but, of course, it was not Mr Hudson's property and he simply couldn't do it. The four Chinese, in their tidy white suits, shrugged regretfully, picked up all the bundles of notes and put them back into their briefcases, and Mr Hudson saw them out.[21]

Captain James had had a fairly eventful day. He was in Orchard Road when a stick of bombs exploded across it, setting fire to a petrol station which blazed up in seconds and punting two cars into the air like footballs. They bounced several times and burst into flames. One house collapsed under a direct hit and "looked like a caved-in slaughterhouse." No local ARP people seemed to be around so Captain James rushed off to find an ambulance. He found dozens of them parked by the Cathedral and sent some off to Orchard Road.[22] Moving about in the streets was harder than ever: the town was clogged with people.

In the Municipal Building there were "solid blocks of Australians sitting on the stairs." [23]

On paper, Captain James supposed, Singapore could have held out for many days; [24] but not like this, in the actual conditions of muddle and damage, looting and despair, with the bombs and shells crashing down all the time and the thick black smoke pouring up. Great holes had been smashed in the roads and buildings and telegraph poles stuck grotesquely out of the wreckage, cars and lorries choked every street and sporadic bursts of firing were heard inside the city itself, some of these coming from troops firing at suspected infiltrators. At the Woodleigh pumping station the engineer and his wife were still working hard to keep the water supply going, but more and more it was running to waste out of holes in the pipes.[25]

The hard-pressed fighting troops were being split into smaller and smaller pockets of resistance, the Bedfordshires losing six officers and twenty-six men of one regiment in the first five days. Grimly counting their shrinking numbers, they felt that they "never had a chance to fight." [26] Captain (now Lieutenant-Colonel) Reginald Burton of the 4th Norfolks knew that his men felt they had "done as well as could be expected" in their fighting, especially against an opponent who had the "advantage of position" and good air cover. Knowing that instead of pushing the Japanese off the Island they had been made to withdraw puzzled and depressed them. They had been in quite a good defensive place, and were pulled back only a short distance, where they had to "dig in and wire all over again"; this was "rather the last straw." If they could have stayed where they were and allowed the enemy to walk into their fire it would have been better, he thought.

At this stage Captain Burton found himself envying the men who had been wounded and sent to hospital—they were honourably out of the situation, though "that they were in reality far from being out of it didn't enter my head." [27] If any of them were in the Alexandra Military Hospital they were in a far worse case than Captain Burton. The Malay Brigade had held on valiantly for two days at Pasir Panjang, the ridge protecting the Alexandra area, and were now almost wiped out. The Japanese overwhelmed the remnants of them, making straight for the hospital, where a young lieutenant named Weston met them on the steps, carrying a white flag. He was killed at once and the Japanese went through the hospital and killed most of the patients and staff inside, including one man on the operating table. About two hundred of the patients were herded into the old servants' quarters and left there for the night. All but three were killed when a shell scored a direct hit on the building.[28]

During the day, Captain James picked up two very precise Japanese maps and passed them on to HQ. On the flagged veranda of the guardhouse at Fort Canning he handed them in, but the reaction was one of "no interest." [29]

4

Fort Canning had been having a bad day too. Percival called a meeting at two in the afternoon for all the divisional commanders and staff officers to discuss counter-attack possibilities, which all the commanders opposed. They had to consider their exhausted, hard-pressed troops as well as the civilian population, faced now with the prospect of street fighting. Percival was certain that the end was near, but thought they could manage to hang on for a little longer. He telegraphed Wavell that the Japanese were now "within five thousand yards of the sea-front"—the whole town area was now within range of their field artillery. There was danger of running out of water and losing food stocks if the enemy overran them. He quoted the commanders' opinion about the state of the troops.

> We would all earnestly welcome the chance of initiating an offensive, even though this would only amount to a gesture, but even this is not possible, as there are no troops who could carry out this attack. In these conditions it is unlikely that resistance can last more than a day or two. My subordinate commanders are unanimously of the opinion that the gain of time will not compensate for extensive damage and heavy casualties which will occur in Singapore town. As Empire overseas is interested I feel bound to represent their views. There must come a stage when in the interests of the troops and civil population further bloodshed will serve no useful purpose.[30]

This telegram bristles with unanswered, and unanswerable, questions. Was it really true that *all* the troops were too exhausted? Why say "earnestly" when one looks for the word "eagerly"? Why was it so clear that "this would only amount to a gesture"? "*No* troops who could carry out this attack"? Just how unanimous were all the subordinate commanders? What views of the Empire overseas are represented in this message? And (the sixty-four-dollar question) how many lives were saved, and whose, by caving in then, now that it is known what happened afterwards? What made Percival think that bloodshed would cease when the fighting stopped?

Wavell's reply was uncompromising.

> You must all fight it out to the end as you are doing. But when everything humanly possible has been done some bold and determined personnel may be able to escape by small craft . . .[31]

One bold and determined person at least was preparing to do this. Gordon Bennett (who had privately cabled the Australian Prime Minister that if the Japanese got into the town he was going to surrender "to avoid further needless loss of life" without saying a word about this to anyone in Malaya Command), had for some time been working out plans for his own escape. He had discussed the subject with the Sultan of Johore, with whom he had become friendly: the Sultan had entertained Gordon Bennett to meals in his palace and had given the General many presents (on January 28 an entry in Gordon Bennett's diary read: "He entertained me at lunch and appreciated the visit. As usual he displayed his generosity by presenting me with gifts"). Gordon Bennett had asked the Sultan to let him have a boat to escape by if the need arose. In his opinion it had arisen now.[32]

5

Wavell cabled a summary of Percival's situation to Churchill. It went against every grain of Churchill's nature to say so, but he had no choice any more, and had reluctantly to signal back that in agreement with General Brooke, Chief of the Imperial General Staff, he realised:

> You are of course sole judge of the moment when no further result can be gained at Singapore, and should instruct Percival accordingly.

Wavell meanwhile had signalled Percival that the fight must go on.

> You must continue to inflict maximum damage on enemy for as long as possible by house-to-house fighting if necessary. Your action in tying down enemy and inflicting casualties may have vital influence in other theatres. Fully appreciate your situation, but continued action essential.

Sir Shenton Thomas weighed in at the same time with a message to the Colonial Office.

> General Officer Commanding informs me that Singapore City now closely invested. There are now one million people within radius of three miles. Water-supplies very badly damaged and unlikely to last more than twenty-four hours. Many dead lying in the streets and burial impossible. We are faced with total deprivation of water, which must result in pestilence. I have felt that it is my duty to bring this to notice of General Officer Commanding.[33]

The lowered morale was not apparent among the men of Captain Russell-Roberts's party who had spent Friday less than a mile to the rear of the Alexandra Hospital, digging in in high spirits, surrounded by plenty of supplies in a private house they had taken over as HQ, which was well fitted with a complete set of modern furniture and had a small car in the garage. The men set up guns on the verandas and anti-aircraft spotters in the bathrooms and sent out foraging patrols.

Buller Camp near by was on fire and so were the oil installations not far off.[34] Over by the reservoirs the 11th Indian Division, or what was left of it, was "still standing firm"; on its left the 5th Norfolks and the 2nd Cambridgeshires, "heavily engaged" throughout the weekend "until the moment of capitulation," "did not flinch." [35] To all the defending troops who were not in the upper echelons of command, that is to say to every soldier from the colonel to the private, the idea of surrender had never occurred. They were all caught absolutely unawares and to the many who wept when the news eventually reached them it was a heartbreaking experience.

Yamashita had his thoughts, too, which he wrote in his diary.

> My attack on Singapore was a bluff—a bluff that worked. I had 30,000 men and was outnumbered more than three to one. I knew that if I had to fight long for Singapore, I would be beaten. That is why the surrender had to be at once. I was very frightened all the time that the British would discover our numerical weakness and lack of supplies and force me into disastrous street fighting.[36]

Percival, no bluffer, never imagined that Yamashita could have been worried, and estimated the Japanese forces at about 100,000, indignantly refusing to believe that he could have been forced back to the wall by a smaller army than his own. He seems to have thought at one time that the Japanese were fewer in number, for his Order of the Day of February 10 said: "It will be a lasting disgrace if we are defeated by an army of clever gangsters, many times inferior in numbers to our own"; [37] but by the end of that last week he had come round to the belief that all this brilliant and confident advance, carried out so quickly, could only have been accomplished by an enormous body of troops. He could not know how Yamashita's men were short of water, down to a hundred rounds of shells for each field gun and less for the heavy guns, and were approaching, just as Percival's soldiers were, the limit of endurance at which Wavell thought surrender could no longer be put off. [38]

Short or not, Yamashita was still keeping up the pressure. It seemed by now that the air raids went on all day so that Buckeridge and his squads from the Fire Department never had a break. Some fires blazed while others smouldered sullenly on. There were constant outbreaks too among the warehouses where rubber, sugar and paint were stored. Perhaps the most dramatic incident occurred when a warehouse full of Chinese New Year firecrackers caught alight and the fireworks banged off in all directions. The car park on Collyer Quay caught a cloud of incendiary bombs that burned out hundreds of vehicles. The oddest fire was the one on the Pulo Saigon bridge over the Singapore river, described by Mr Buckeridge as "a bloody great fire where no fire could possibly be": a burning oil slick floated up the river on the tide, setting fire to the packed sampans and then to the oil dripping down the bridge from broken oil-pipes that ran along it. "Constructed entirely of steel girders," wrote Mr Barber, "this ancient Meccano-like structure . . . was ablaze from end to end." Crowds inured by now to fires stood staring in astonishment as the lace-like ironwork and the asphalt roadway through it slowly burned itself out by ten o'clock that night. [39]

The looters were having a field day. Even the Bishop of Singapore repaired a punctured wheel on his car by pinching a tyre off an abandoned vehicle. Mr Bennitt bought razor blades in every shop that sold them. Groups of men stripped deserted market stalls bare. Through all this, rickshaw men hopefully offered "sightseeing tours." [40] There was a rush on Kelly and Walsh's bookshop, and another rush to get (of all places) to the dentist. Scuffles broke out in tobacco shops where Europeans who had stopped bothering about stocks of food were trying to pile up stocks of cigarettes. The manager of Robinson's issued two free sets of clothes to every European child.

On Saturday night, before going to bed, the Governor wrote in his diary: "Much quieter night in the Club." [41]

6

Captain James kept on wondering why the 18th British Division had been sent to Singapore. It had only completed its disembarkation on January 29, just over a fortnight ago, and in any case it had never been used as a division. Arriving in pieces it was thrown into the battle in pieces "until it lost its value as a fighting force under its commander, Major-General Beckwith-Smith." The Captain wrote later—much later —that "one-third of this gallant Division died, not in the fighting but as prisoners of war." [42]

In the different patches of action the dawn conferences of Sunday February 15 all took the same line of dogged persistence. Colonel Jimmy Larkin told his men: "Gentlemen, we fight, and if necessary die, in our present position." [43] Brigadier Stewart of the Argylls spoke to his small group, two officers and fifty men "black and greasy from fire-fighting," and reminded them of his two promises, never to order them into battle without enough guns and never to say Go On, only Come On. He had to break the first promise now, there were only too clearly not enough guns, but the second promise still held. Would they, he asked, come into this last battle with him? Nobody spoke. Slowly the men all rose to their feet and stood waiting. The Brigadier led them off towards the guns in the distance. [44]

Colonel Larkin's men were under fire by this time. Shells burst in the garden of their HQ, sending shovelfuls of black earth flying in at the windows. The riflemen, heartened by having some real work to do at last, fired away enthusiastically. [45] The last detachment left of Moorhead's Punjabis threw the enemy back from a small hill with all the dash and valour they had shown whenever opportunity had afforded all the way down from the Patani road.

But it was all useless. Wavell's last cable had come in at Fort Canning.

So long as you are in position to inflict losses and damage to enemy and your troops are physically capable of doing so you must fight on. Time gained and damage to enemy are of vital importance at this crisis. When you are fully satisfied that this

is no longer possible I give you discretion to cease resistance. . . .
Whatever happens I thank you and all troops for your gallant
efforts of last few days.[46]

It was the twelfth birthday of Percival's daughter Dorinda, and he
started the day by going to Holy Communion, celebrated in the Fort.
He was not the only one. Places of worship were crammed that morning, and dozens of services were held in hospitals. At nine-thirty Percival held a short meeting, lasting only twenty minutes, in one of the
Fort's bomb-proof rooms, with the senior commanding officers, and he
listened quietly as each one gave his appreciation of how matters stood.
They were very well turned out in their fresh uniforms—it is curious
how centuries-old habits persist—and their verdicts were unanimously
negative. Gordon Bennett recorded in his diary: "Silently and sadly we
decided to surrender." [47]

The melancholy formalities of capitulation were straightforward
enough. Yamashita had made them known in the letter dropped for
Percival on Wednesday, Japanese Empire Day. It requested the "parliamentaire" to be sent to the Bukit Timah road carrying a large white flag
and the Union Jack. The two men selected to carry out this distasteful
task were the Colonial Secretary Hugh Fraser and the Chief Administrative Officer Brigadier Newbiggin.

Knowing what Yamashita's own position was like at the time it is
interesting to see how he expressed himself in the letter to Percival.

Your Excellency:

I, the High Command of the Nippon Army based on the spirit
of Japanese chivalry, have the honour of presenting this note to Your
Excellency advising you to surrender the whole force in Malaya.

My sincere respect is due to your army which, true to the traditional
spirit of Great Britain, is bravely defending Singapore which now
stands isolated and unaided. Many fierce and gallant fights have been
fought by your gallant men and officers, to the honour of British war-
riorship. But the developments of the general war situation has already sealed the fate of Singapore, and the continuation of futile
resistance would only serve to inflict direct harm and injuries to thousands of noncombatants living in the city, throwing them into further
miseries and horrors of war, but also would not add anything to the
honour of your army.

I expect that Your Excellency accepting my advice will give up
this meaningless and desperate resistance and promptly order the

entire front to cease hostilities and will despatch at the same time
your parliamentaire according to the procedure shown at the end of
this note. If on the contrary, Your Excellency should neglect my advice and the present resistance be continued, I shall be obliged, though
reluctant from humanitarian considerations, to order my army to
make annihilating attacks on Singapore.

On closing this note of advice, I pay again my sincere respects to
Your Excellency.

TOMOYUKI YAMASHITA [48]

This may have been a bluff (as it was) but it has the authentic courtly
ring ("What is thy name? I know thy quality"). Very different from
Major Toyama, who told Captain James after the surrender: "You de-
fied Dai Nippon, you surrendered and must accept the consequences,
you should have died fighting like Japanese soldiers; stop complaining
and reconcile yourselves to lifelong imprisonment." [49] Of course the
Major did not know just how short a line his own army was working
on. Yamashita, who had also started that day in prayer (it was Chinese
New Years Day, incidentally, and there should have been fireworks),
went up to Bukit Timah during the morning to the Chrysanthemum
Division HQ. Here Lieutenant-General Renya Mutaguchi reported that
the enemy were firing less than before. Yamashita told him to stand by
and went back to his own HQ, and some little time later one of Mutaguchi's patrols reported a white flag "among the trees ahead." [50]

If this was Fraser and Newbiggin, it must have been more than a
little while later. Carrying Percival's letter to Yamashita and the two
flags requested, they set off from Fort Canning at half past eleven. Their
car had to turn back twice because of craters in the road, and they were
held at gunpoint by a British patrol at the Duncan Road. Because of
minefields on the Adam Road they had to go forward on foot. It was
nearly half past one before they met any Japanese. An armed patrol
came out of the rubber by the canal, where orchids flowered on the
bank. After a cautious approach and some explanation by the interpreter, the Japanese took quite a time before escorting the British anywhere; they wanted to take photographs. They posed Fraser and Newbiggin and the interpreter to face the light—it was steaming hot and
everybody was sweating—and took pictures. When at last they were
satisfied and sent for their senior officers who of course came hurrying
along from HQ at top speed, it was past two o'clock.

Yamashita would have none of it. He would deal with Percival in person and the firing would not stop until the General came to meet him. He sent a note back with the two British envoys, who were escorted to Adam Road by Japanese troops. Although they were returning over the same ground they had covered coming up, Fraser and Newbiggin were blindfolded, a puzzling precaution and a frightening one, too, as they walked back during a British shell barrage. At the Adam Road barrier the Japanese left them and they got back into the car. At the Stevens Road a British sergeant fired his pistol at them, missing them by a miracle. They re-entered the Fort at just on four in the afternoon.[51]

7

The place chosen by Yamashita for the surrender ceremony was the Ford Works Building near Bukit Timah. It was the biggest covered building left sufficiently intact, though it had been damaged by shells and was pocked with bullet-marks, part of the roof had fallen in and many of the windows gaped open, the glass shattered by shot. In that sultry late afternoon the acrid smells of burned rubber and petrol and charred wood seeped out across the principal section, now cleared for this meeting. A long table with a white cloth on it stood in the middle, and chalk marks all over the concrete floor showed where all the officers and reporters summoned to witness the ceremony were to stand.[52]

Right up to the last minute Yamashita was nagged by doubts. Was this a trick? Acutely aware of his own position, his men living on two bowls of rice a day, five gallons out of six of everybody's water supply pouring away through holes in the pipes, rifle ammunition down to one hundred rounds a day for every soldier, he worried until the moment of truth, shortly after five-fifteen, when he came into the building and was face to face with his adversary at last. One glance at Percival's tragic expression was enough to reassure Yamashita, but he had to make certain: the colossal gamble had paid off, the enemy had let him get away with it, but it had been done by a perilously narrow margin. Time was as precious to him as ever it could have been to Percival, and he simply had to come to terms that day. His men could not have stood up to a really determined counter-attack at that point, and he knew it. Accordingly he came prepared to put the boldest front on it, to drive the hardest of bargains, assumed a fierce, uncompromising attitude, and clipped out his words to the interpreter, Mr Hishikari: "The Japanese Army will consider nothing but unconditional surrender at ten pm Nippon time."

This meant half past eight, barely two hours away. Percival said: "I can't guarantee it—we can't submit our final reply before midnight."

Yamashita banged the table with his fist. "Are our terms acceptable or not? We are ready to resume firing."

According to one account, one of Yamashita's aides now put a paper with questions written on it in English in front of Percival. The first question read: "Does the British Army surrender unconditionally?" Another account reported Yamashita as saying: "Answer me briefly— do you wish to surrender unconditionally?" Both accounts record Percival's request to wait until next morning. Yamashita said: "In that case we shall go on fighting until then," and, pointing at Percival, he told Mr Hishikari: "Tell him to answer yes or no."

Percival, weary, anxious and beaten, hesitated; at some point Yamashita asked: "Have you any Japanese prisoners of war?"

"None at all."

"Have you any Japanese civilians?"

"No, they have all been sent to India." (This exchange comes in the Japanese account and seems a little peculiar: if this was so, what about all the informers, infiltrators, fifth columnists? But perhaps it was thought best for the Japanese not to hear about those.)

The big question came again. "Do you consent immediately to unconditional surrender or do you not?"

Percival, with his head bowed and speaking "in a faint voice," said: "Yes."

The instrument of surrender was laid before him. Before signing, Percival asked that the Japanese troops should not enter the city before morning, and agreed that his own troops should be disarmed at once "except for a thousand who would maintain order during the night." Yamashita warned him that any breach of this agreement would start the fighting up again. Then there was a further question. One account gives it as: "Will the Imperial Army protect the women and children and the British civilians?" The other quotes it as: "What about the lives of the civilians, and the British, Indian and Australian troops? Will you guarantee them?" There is a significant difference in the two questions. There is not much variation in the reply.

"Yes. You may be easy about that. I can guarantee them absolutely"; or: "Please rest assured, I shall positively guarantee it."

Percival signed. One account says it was seven o'clock, the other that it was ten past six. The two commanders shook hands while the flashbulbs popped and the reporters scribbled in their notebooks. Yamashita wanted to say something kind to his enemy who looked so tired and thin and defeated. He could not speak English, he knew how hard it is to convey any feelings correctly through an interpreter, so he tried to make his meaning clear with a look and a sympathetic handshake.

It is doubtful whether Percival noticed. He stood up very straight as he turned on his heel and left the room. Yamashita picked up his papers.[53]

8

"It was for Egypt and for Russia," said the *Guardian,* "that we sacrificed Malaya."

Jubilant broadcasts in Berlin and Tokyo reported that Sir Shenton Thomas and his officials had left by air, that most of the British and Australian troops left the Island on Friday for Sumatra, that those remaining, numbers varying between 65,000, 45,000, and 30,000, had quickly been assembled "in the Changi fort." [54] On the Allied side the reaction was stunned disbelief. Franklin Roosevelt sent Churchill what comfort he could. "It gives the well-known back-seat driver a field day, but . . . I hope you will be of good heart in these trying weeks." [55]

Simson, seeing that his part would be over by about six, had got all his arrangements lined up to leave the Island, but Percival had forbidden him to go. Gordon Bennett, who consulted nobody, issued an order to his Australians to remain at their posts until eight-thirty the next morning and that foolish actions should not imperil the cease-fire, arranged for new clothing and two days' rations for everybody, and went down to the docks with two officers who were coming with him. He apparently hoped to get to Malacca, but he met a party led by Mr M. C. Hay, Inspector of Mines, and they all got on board a junk which, after a brisk hectoring of the Chinese skipper by Mr Hay, sailed south a few minutes later, leaving behind the dying Lion Gate and the equally dying military career of the Australian commander.

Promptly at eight-thirty the guns fell silent. News of the surrender began to spread, received for the most part with horrified incredulity. Some sought the comfort of food, opening hoarded tins for a "surrender dinner"—one such meal consisted of steak and kidney pie, Christmas pudding and strawberries and cream. Others crowded the space left in the Cathedral among the ranks of wounded and joined in a service led by the Bishop, including, oddly, the hymn "Praise, my soul, the King of Heaven." Mr Hudson packed a bag, picked up a couple of bottles of whisky from the Dunlop warehouse where he had hidden them, and went with Mr Buckeridge to Robinson's, where there was quite a party.[56] People ate tinned meat and pineapple from the shop kitchens, drank out of restaurant glasses, had baths using the ladies' hairdressing soap and the household department baths, and went to sleep on the luxurious beds and sofas of the furniture department. Among the sleepers there that night was Captain Russell-Roberts.[57]

When last heard of, the Captain was out near Tanglin, where in a last gallant barrage of rifle fire, his men were giving all they had got "for the first and last time" even though the range was too impossibly great. They heard that the white flag had gone forward; darkness fell, quiet and full of rumours. Eventually the surrender message was read out and was received with emotion. The men went in to Singapore by way of River Valley Road, and were quartered in a large building close by Change Alley while the officers went into Robinson's to have their last good sleep for nearly thirteen hundred nights "on those heavenly sofas." [58]

Captain Burton, who had been slightly hurt in the last bursts of fighting, was lying on a mattress on the floor when the news of the surrender reached him. When he heard that a car with a white flag had been seen heading towards the enemy lines he thought it was "just another story." But finally one of his men came up to him and told him that it was all over. Feeling sick, Captain Burton turned his head away and "lay for a long time, trying to think clearly." The strongest feeling he had was what a waste it had all been—the long voyage, the short battle, and now the prospect of captivity: for how long? involving what? where? Filled with despair and fear, trying not to think but unable to prevent the whirl of thoughts, "this was one of the blackest moments of my life." [59]

This is not the reaction of a beaten man. Neither was that of Mr Buckeridge, who wrote in his diary:

We'd given up. Or someone had. The gang of men round the table was as weary as I was, but I'm sure that every single one was willing and eager to carry on the struggle. But there was no struggle. It was over. We talked as though we shared a dreadful secret. Dreadful it was, but secret, no. We didn't know what the hell had gone wrong. We were damn sure it wasn't us.[60]

9

Yamashita gave a cocktail party at HQ, with chestnuts and dried cuttle-fish and wine.[61] Later he would accept General Wainwright's surrender of the Philippines. But even in the chaos of war a pattern emerged, for in Tokyo Bay on September 2, 1945, when the Japanese formally sur-rendered General MacArthur would have both Wainwright and Perci-val beside him. He would sign his name in fragments, using six pens: one for his wife, one for his aide, one for West Point and one for the Archives, but "the first pen went to Wainwright. Percival got the next one." [62] It made a sort of rounding-off, after the "1,297 days" that lay between now and then.[63]

But that Sunday, Yamashita, emerging from the Ford Works Build-ing, was the man who had found the pot of gold at the end of the rain-bow. It had been a staggering feat of arms on his part. Against all the odds, all the expectations, operating on a shoestring, at the price of 3,000 of his soldiers' lives, he had caused the great showpiece, reputed bastion of imperial British power in Asia, to fall within seventy days of the start of hostilities. Expensive British roads and cheap Japanese bicycles had done it. He had not depended on lorries and trucks that could break down, catch fire, get jammed in bottlenecks or halted by road blocks.[64] His total casualty list was less than ten thousand. The British had just experienced the greatest military disaster in their his-tory. The whole glittering prize was Japan's within ten weeks. "Thank you very much, you have done a good job," he told his staff. "Now you can all drink as much saki as you like." [65]

PART TWO

THE LONG WAY
ROUND

———

CHAPTER IX

The Fortress in the Sun

I

On Monday, February 16, 1942, it was possible for a person living in London to have a lively evening out. Which theatre should it be? Priestley's *Goodnight Children,* Coward's *Blithe Spirit,* Esther Mc-Cracken's *Quiet Weekend?* Or stick to a classic and go to *The Merry Wives of Windsor?* What about Edith Evans in *Old Acquaintance* or Robert Morley in *The Man Who Came to Dinner?,* or Hermione Baddeley and Hermione Gingold in *Rise Above It?* While hesitating over so tempting a choice in *The Times,* a man with a healthy bank account might consider buying a 1936 Daimler with 24,000 miles on the clock and in excellent running order for £225, or, if he went in for that sort of thing, a hundred raspberry canes for twenty-five shillings, while a woman might decide to spend six and a half, eight and a half, or ten and a half guineas among what was described as a wonderful selection of dresses for Queen Charlotte's Ball.[1]

Waking up to a flawless morning in Singapore, with the palm trees rustling gently in a light breeze from the sea and the grass looking soft and green under a clear blue sky, victors and vanquished alike knew that whatever faced them there was precious little choice about it.[2] The far from quiet weekend was over, the only blithe spirits were Japanese and most of them were weary, dinner was certain in neither time nor quality, one's oldest acquaintances were very far away, and who knew what it was that one must rise above? At least there was a little comfort left for those who had slept on the beds and sofas in Robinson's: they went into the ladies' hairdressing salon and freshened up, some of them washing in Eau de Cologne, and then, smelling loudly of scent, made a hearty breakfast of bacon, eggs, sausages, and grapefruit. Raffles Place was crowded with British, Australian and Indian troops sitting on the pavement, talking, smoking looted cigarettes, in some cases gambling with a pile of money on the ground between them. One Australian soldier was wearing a top hat. Many men, particularly the officers, went into Kelly and Walsh's bookshop and came away with the thickest books they could find—Captain Russell-Roberts chose a twelve-hundred-page collection of Somerset Maugham's stories and a complete Kipling.[3] Next door in the British Dispensary they stocked up with toothbrushes, sponges and, with a notion of things to come, aspirin.[4]

It was the military who were abroad in the streets that morning, not the civilians, except for a few British. The Chinese and Malays for the most part stayed behind the boarded-up shop fronts. It was as well they did for during the morning eight Chinese coolies were beheaded for looting. There was no doubt that in the early stages it was the Chinese who came in for the severest reprisals.[5] According to one Chinese commentator, it took the Japanese three and a half years to make all Singapore anti-Japanese, by which time, of course, it was more pro-British than ever before. The Japanese re-opened the schools after two or three months, made the learning of the Japanese language compulsory, and preached Co-Prosperity, provoking the reaction that the Chinese would have the Co and the Japanese would have the Prosperity. Certainly the Chinese had a struggle to survive. For some, a major item of diet for a while was a kind of porridge made from looted supplies of British Army dog-biscuits.

There was no doubt about something else, too: one world had come to an end and another, an unknown one, was beginning.

2

The Tiger of Malaya, as Yamashita was now known (nicknames of this kind have often been bestowed with less justification) realised at once that he had a fresh set of problems to face. Singapore might look quiet at first sight on this Monday morning, but in fact it was full of unburied dead, smouldering fires, looters, weapons and general wreckage. In particular it was full of crowds of people—enemy soldiers, far too many of them to manage neatly. It all needed organising, there was a great deal to be done. The first thing Yamashita did—he had no choice —was to order the British civilians to carry on as usual if they held important administrative posts. The only difference now was that Singapore, sealed in on itself, was at last the fortress it had always vainly claimed to be.

The attitude of the Japanese to their prisoners of war was relatively

clear cut. Brought up in the tradition of Bushido, the Way of the War-
rior, and the Samurai Imperial Guards encouraged to accept the theory
that on the Emperor's death it was the duty of his senior military officers
to commit suicide in order to accompany him in a fitting manner into
the next world, and to think that capture was a disgrace second only
to desertion in the face of the enemy, they were hardly prepared to treat
with forbearance those soldiers who had descended to that depth and
who were so lost to all sense of shame as to survive defeated. Japan
had signed the 1907 Hague Convention regarding prisoners of war,
and the later, more humane Geneva Convention of 1929, but this latter
signature had not been ratified by the Japanese Government. In practice
the Japanese despised the prisoners, were quite indifferent to their suffering and death, thinking that they had only themselves to blame, considered them a great nuisance in clogging the wheels of Japan's war
effort, and saw no reason why they should not be made to work like the
slaves they appeared to be.

Something of the individual Japanese quality in war is shown in
a vivid appraisal by Mr John Masters who calls them the bravest people he ever met. In any Allied army most of them would have won the
highest decorations. Mr Masters dismisses the popular view that such
bravery is mere fanaticism: if one believes in something to the point
where one is willing to die for the slightest thing that would help to
achieve it, "What else is bravery?" The Japanese would go on attacking when no other soldiers in the world would have done so, far past
the stage where all hope seemed lost: they simply kept on going, and
the only thing that stopped them was death. In defence "they held their
ground with a furious tenacity that never faltered," so that finally it
would become necessary to kill them, one by one.[6]

How would such fighters regard prisoners of war? Yet there is another side to the coin: Colonel Laurens van der Post puts it in a conversation between a former prisoner and his former Japanese guard,
when the Englishman explains that he used to tell his men who were in
despair that "there is a way of winning by losing, a way of victory in
defeat"; the Japanese reaction is "truly moved": he calls that "a very
Japanese thought."[7]

Naturally, some Japanese were more humane than others, so it was
largely a matter of the luck of the draw. In addition, the Japanese concerned with the sorting-out in Singapore in the early weeks were fighting
troops and their attitude was slightly closer to that of one professional
to another. They thought the British reacted as if they had lost a sport-

ing contest. Later, these troops were needed in battle elsewhere, and were replaced by others who had neither the same status nor experience, and who proved far more callous and uncomprehending. Later still, too late for many of the prisoners, those attitudes gave place to a mixture of contrition (when the war tide turned against Japan) and belated panic at the awkward questions that were certainly going to be asked when peace came.

When peace came! Ahead of them all on that fine morning stretched a long road: it would take three and a half years to pass along it. For the defeated, it led to Changi and the Burma-Siam railway, through starvation and disease, pain and suffering and a death rate of one in three, past places they had never heard of, Kanchanaburi, Chungkai, Hintok, Konkhuta and the Three Pagodas Pass. For the victorious, it led to Midway and Leyte Gulf, Kohima and Rangoon, to the desperate heroism of the kamikaze and the smouldering horror of the Urakami Valley, and at last to four words spoken on the deck of the USS *Missouri* in Tokyo Bay on September 2, 1945: "These proceedings are closed."

But just now that time was a long way off, and somehow Singapore must be restored to order. The British and Australian troops were given until five in the evening of February 17—forty-four and a half hours from the official cease-fire—to assemble in the Changi area. They spent the interval in gathering together what kit they could, foraging for food and tobacco, eating messy scratch meals, sleeping in utter exhaustion on concrete floors or out in the open, trying to rustle up lorries that would still go and to keep track of friends, finding a book or two to tuck in a bulging kitbag, looking at the evidence that the take-over was beginning, and attempting to adjust to the new situation.

The General Hospital was under orders to evacuate completely by Tuesday afternoon, and somehow this was done, although all the Chinese boys and amahs had disappeared and the business of moving ambulances through the streets was a nightmare in itself. Those patients who could walk at all were sent home or to their units. The other civilian patients were sent to the Asylum, from which the inmates had been taken to an island in the harbour. The military patients were crammed into the Cricket Club, the Singapore Club and the Victoria Memorial Hall. In the midst of this chaos the Archdeacon performed a marriage ceremony in the matron's office between Lieutenant Alastair MacKenzie and Nurse Sybil Osborn. The bride wore white but it was a nurse's dress and it was stained with blood, and the Archdeacon wrote out the certificate from memory on a piece of hospital paper. The main room of the Singapore Club was packed with wounded like a tide washing around the marble pillars and the long bar, which still dispensed lime juice. At the Asylum a British woman doctor with a lot of orphaned Chinese and Malay babies to look after gave some of them away to Chinese and Malay parents whose children had been killed in the air raids.[8]

The rising sun on Tuesday February 17 revealed hundreds of little Rising Suns on flags that had appeared overnight throughout Singapore. The Cathedral was still crammed with stretcher cases, Japanese soldiers with small tanks were beginning to restore order among the dockside warehouses and stores, Japanese staff cars sounded their klaxons in the streets, where the native population was very much playing the situation by ear, and very soon it was obvious that it was going to be an extremely hot day. The sun blazed in a deep blue sky, the sea glittered, the flame trees glowed brightly, and by ten in the morning over two thousand civilians were assembled on the Cricket Club lawn, ready to be sent to their first internment camp, nine miles away near the Sea View Hotel. Some drove out there, when they were eventually allowed to get moving at nearly one o'clock, but many walked, including the Governor, who had turned up in fresh white ducks.[9]

It was fourteen miles to Changi, where the jail and the big groups of Army barracks stood, and that was where the military prisoners had to go. The long, long column set off, headed by at least four files of brigadiers and full colonels, with here and there a lorry on which some soldiers hitched a ride for part of the way.[10] The housing shortage was acute enough but the food shortage was worse, so of course the prisoners went hungry, and had to manage as best they could to buy something to eat from Chinese traders as they made their way out of Singapore town towards the north-east corner of the Island.

Having reached the subject of the surrender in his *Regimental History,* Mr Carew says of the 4th, 5th, and 6th—"these three fine battalions"—that there is "unhappily little else to tell." [11] Looked at from another viewpoint, there is quite an amount to tell, though it takes some finding, for those involved are often, understandably, reluctant to speak or write too fully about their experiences. However those who managed to overcome this reluctance have almost always found that they gained considerable ease of mind from doing so.

One point of cardinal importance must be made here, firmly and at once. Courage, as everyone knows, is a relative thing, inconsistent and variable as all human qualities are—many a VC has been terrified of mice, or the dentist, or women. Courage in battle (which may be the courage of the fool who does not see the risk or the higher kind that shrinks from the terror and still goes ahead) is, rightly, recognised and awarded with decorations. But there is a higher kind still—that of solid endurance, when there is no way of knowing how long one must go on, when there is no sign of light at the end of the tunnel, and always the inner fear that one is forgotten. Sometimes ex-prisoners have felt almost ashamed to admit that they were in captivity, not realising that as prisoners who managed to survive they can justly be regarded as being in a special category of bravery. News, action, hope, company and the cheers of the multitude reinforce the soldier in battle; no such comfort is available to the soldier in enemy hands, whose daily companions are silence and despair.

3

The interned civilians had to sleep on floors and some of the children fell ill, but in a haphazard, dream-like way they managed. Some who had cars were allowed out on foraging trips, from one of which the former Defence Secretary brought back a pile of books (and had one confiscated by the Japanese officer because it was called *The Code of the Woosters*).[12] The volunteer nurses at the Singapore Club stocked up with clothes left behind by members' wives who had left on the ships.[13] The big ships got away safely, but the little ones were nearly all sunk or captured; those which reached some island or other fared no better, for the few who escaped death through starvation or disease were later captured.

While the civilian population, British and native, was on the scrounge and the military prisoners were straggling into Changi, the Japanese Army made its official victory march into Singapore. No one can deny that they had earned the right to it. But the high-ranking officers of that army were preoccupied, on the one hand, with the problem of over eighty thousand enemy soldiers to deal with and, on the other, with the difficulty of tidying up. The rubble of the bomb, shell and fire damage must be cleared, main services repaired, transport organised, stores unloaded, dead buried, supplies distributed, stocks found and sorted, people accommodated. Wrecked aircraft were lying about, a Blue Funnel liner was burning in the docks, railway carriages were burning in the station, piles of coal were on fire, the warehouses were in chaos, one station platform was littered with abandoned Army equipment, dead people and cows lay decaying in the streets.[14] The two problems matched like a pair of gloves: the prisoners could do the work.

At Changi the men were crowded to the extent of two hundred to a space used by twenty in ordinary conditions. The whole thing was regarded as temporary. A few weeks, a few months at most, was the expected term; all kinds of rumours circulated and were readily believed; depression and irritability were as common as dirt, and before the first week was over one highly significant thing happened which did not appear important at the time: the first Japanese-issued rations arrived, and they consisted of sacks of rice.

To the soldiers, this was something new. The only rice they had met so far was in the homely rice pudding. Rice as a staple of diet was peculiar: some said that it would swell up inside so that nobody would be able to manage more than two or three ounces of it a day, others thought this unlikely but didn't know exactly how much they would be able to take in or how it would affect them. At first a sticky half plateful was all that the men could force down, with plenty of drinking water. An hour or two later they were surprised and indignant to find themselves ravenous again. The amount was raised, ounce by ounce, to half a pound or more. They were still hungry and now they found it an effort to walk half a mile, their legs felt weak, they had to keep sitting down. But they now had two strong preoccupations which helped to keep them going: to get more of it, and to learn how to cook it properly.[15] It was stated that the worst hardship was the perpetual hunger, a state of near-starvation which made it harder than ever to rise above their wretchedness.[16]

Major Basil Peacock, who was unlucky enough to be a prisoner of war twice (captured by the Germans in World War I and now, a quarter of a century later, in the hands of the Japanese), wrote simply that for three and a half years they were always hungry. Real starvation, he said, is rare in Europe, and it must not be confused with having to wait a long time for a meal, or living on slim rations: it is a torment made worse by dreams of delicious food. The old saying that "he who sleeps dines" is shown to be nonsense; the worst part of being consistently hungry is the degradation at finding oneself so preoccupied with food that one becomes indifferent to the needs of others. The Major, considerably older than most of his fellow-prisoners, and more widely experienced, had a philosophy and detachment that kept him balanced; in writing of this experience of persistent hunger, he just comments that if one remained free from disease it was not too difficult to survive.[17]

Mr Morrison, back in England, was asked quite often how the Japanese were treating their Singapore prisoners. He said that he did not have enough information to be certain but, having lived in Japan for several years and having developed a high regard for their good qualities, he would be "sadly disappointed" if their treatment of the prisoners did not "conform with accepted international usage and convention." [18]

4

The prisoners were now organised into working-parties, some of which, for the sake of greater convenience, were moved into quarters nearer their place of work—schools, empty buildings of all kinds, tented camps on cricket fields, do-it-yourself huts in patches of lalang grass near coconut plantations, the best of which, according to Lieutenant Coast, aimed at being like Oriental hen-houses, but mostly approximated nearer to those for pigs.[19] From all the varied bases the men went out on the daily jobs in charge of their own officers and NCOs. On the whole they did not mind this too much: they were kept busy, they were able to move about the town, sometimes picking up a little extra food or some cigarettes or a scrap of news, for the Japanese were in their opinion extraordinarily casual in guarding them. There were tempting opportunities for a little gentle sabotage such as puncturing oil drums, and they could see for themselves how many hundreds of other soldiers were in the same boat.

Captain Burton was put in charge of a mixed group of about a hundred Royal Norfolks and Suffolks and sent to Havelock Road, in the centre of Chinatown, across a small river from another camp, River Valley Road.[20] The name sounds nice and River Valley Road had been described as a good camp: so it was, according to Sergeant Kenneth Harrison, for the bugs and lice, but for nobody else.[21] Later, Captain Burton's group went to Tanjong Rhu. It was on a peninsula ("tanjong" means "promontory") beyond Kallang, the swamped airfield, had been a Chinese slum district, been bombed and now looked like a ghost town, or an abandoned film set. The prisoners cleared away rubble and dumped it into the sea, ostensibly to make a wharf and, in their leisure moments after work and roll call, would sit on the sea-wall, watching the tranquil water that they could never forget divided the bound from the free.

Still later, this same party was sent to work in a quarry at Pasir Panjang, west of the harbour. The work was much harder and more unpleasant: in the gruelling heat the full effect of the near-starvation diet made itself felt. It was a test of endurance that the men, clinging to their regimental tradition and discipline, met with some reserve of strength.[22]

The most popular place for working-parties was the docks, where among the big go-downs and their wreckage there was always a chance of looting something edible. Sometimes a Japanese guard could be persuaded to take a couple of jars of Marmite for himself while the men pocketed everything else in the crate at top speed. Sometimes diversions had to be caused: one useful idea was the introduction of a small dead snake so that a good snatch could be made during the subsequent confusion; on one occasion bottles of A1 sauce were found and the men drank it down neat as if it was lemonade.[23] They found spare radio parts and hid them in their hats. Some Australians discovered a petrol supply dump and with superb coolness actually set up a small stall just off the Bukit Timah Road, and sold an incredible quantity of petrol to the people of Singapore at five dollars a gallon.[24]

The resilience of most prisoners showed itself in their amusement over incongruous incidents. Sergeant Harrison refers to a Two Star Private named Ito, a pleasant, rather shy man, who told his squad of prisoners that they had to make shirts. They looked at one another bewildered, but then Ito, with the Japanese talent for improvisation, took off his own shirt, unpicked every stitch of it, and, laying the pieces flat on the table, said that there was the pattern; the prisoners, catching on enthusiastically, traced out these shapes on the khaki drill, cut them out, and stitched the pieces together with results that threw all of them, including Ito, into fits of laughter. By the end of the day, to their surprise, they had a pile of shirts in one size, without collars, and looking almost presentable.

A week later six of them were called out after the morning parade and bundled into a truck where they were told by the Three Star Private in charge that their duty for the day was to tune pianos in the houses of ill fame patronised by the Japanese officers. Charmed by this, and untroubled by the fact that not one of them, the Japanese guard included, had the faintest idea how to tune a piano, they set off, provided with piano wire, pliers, screwdrivers, and the information that the sergeant would be highly displeased if the job wasn't done properly. They went to four houses, where they tightened and loosened the piano adjustments to the point where one of the party said it "sounded all right to the naked ear." [25]

One day in the go-downs Mr Braddon's party found a mixture of goods, many of them edible, and they made the most of it. Chocolates, cough sweets and cough mixture, cod-liver oil, bay rum, essence of vanilla, handfuls of sugar mixed with handfuls of herrings in tomato sauce—it all went down, while they smeared oils and lotions all over themselves in equally wild blends and sold dozens of lipsticks to the Chinese outside the back door. They came out smelling to high heaven of face cream, hair cream and antiseptic, and with the money from the illicit sales fastened under their arms with adhesive tape. Though they were severely thrashed, they were pleased at having got away with it at the time, with the party atmosphere of the looting, and above all with having stuffed themselves full.[26]

Mr Braddon was at River Valley Road, where he shared Sergeant Harrison's view about the bugs and lice, and said that there were masses of mud everywhere and a dirty little stream alive with frogs. The men gambled on frog races, a sport officially prohibited, and kept lengths of slow-burning rope in the huts to satisfy the eternal requests for a light.[27] They smuggled radio parts and other useful objects in their water-bottles—one man made a point of offering the guard a drink each day and reaped the reward of his enterprise when his was the only water-bottle not ordered to be emptied when a guard, taking a swig from the first bottle to hand, took a mouthful of machine oil and bicycle chains.[28]

For most of 1942 the 5th Battalion The Royal Norfolk Regiment was quartered at Serangoon Road camp, where Colonel Prattley was the senior British officer. Almost all the survivors of the Battalion were there; this "gave them the edge over everybody else" because they felt they were still a complete unit. So many units had been split up and people had been separated from their friends. Having their own officers and NCOs they maintained, better than most, their spit-and-polish, and an air of smartness and neatness, with parades and bugle calls, that caused other groups to refer to "bloody Aldershot Serangoon." It paid off, however. The camp had a good health record compared with others, and seemed "a paradise" after (for example) Havelock Road, River Valley Road, or Pasir Panjang.[29]

In all the camps the officers realised that idleness was the great reducer of morale so all kinds of activities were organised: lectures and classes, construction and cookery, coconut parties which were officially forbidden because the incompletely ripe nuts gave the men stomach upsets, and the creation of all kinds of supervisory jobs rather on the principle of class monitors in schools, but with a distinct flavour of Parkinson's Law about them. It helped, however, even if a job turned out to be watching other people doing work that they were quite capable of doing on their own.[30]

Not only idleness was countered by these activities but hunger too. Throughout the years of captivity, the men created gardens whenever they stayed anywhere for any length of time. In these early days they explored old overgrown gardens near by and cut roots and experimented in growing, or trying to grow, all the edible plants they could find. This eventually became a regular and valuable source of food, though they cultivated the local Black Markets as well. Close to the camps the prices were high, but out and about on the Island the working parties did better. The basic idea was that trucks going to fetch cement or gravel or granite chips could always pack in a few pineapples or a tin or two. Plenty of cheerful bootlegging went on.

Changi was always the main prisoners' base, and there the men evolved one of the best activities of all: the concert parties. Some Japanese proved unexpectedly helpful with these, finding in the town such objects as costumes for a play, or make-up, or musical instruments for the camp orchestra. It took a while for this to develop, however: Captain Ernest Gordon arrived in Changi when it had been functioning as a camp for about three months and did not mention plays or concerts. He said that the administration was all done by the prisoners, the officers commanded their own units, although they were not permitted to show any insignia of rank [31] (but Mr Braddon wrote that the officers looked gorgeous wearing their pips so that no one would mistake them for anything else).[32]

The resourceful men in captivity, said Captain Gordon, had already done a good deal to make their situation endurable—shacks had been built from discarded lumber and fitted with bunks, bedding made from old sacks, soup tins converted into eating and drinking pots, oil drums into cooking pots.[33] By the autumn of 1942 the full lecture and concert programme was under way: lectures on such subjects as winter sports, contract law, Communism, or tiger-hunting, classical concerts and recitals, musical shows with songs composed by such men as Slim de Gray and Ray Tullipan, and scenes that provided warming laughter and the great Changi catch-phrase, the melancholy-faced Mr Harry Smith's mournful "You'll never get off the Island." [34]

Bits of news filtered in from outside, but never enough. The Japanese finished their victorious sweep—on March 11 President Quezon and his staff left Manila, and so did General MacArthur, on orders from Washington (that was when he coined *his* famous catch-phrase, "I shall return"); on April 8 General Wainwright withdrew to Corregidor and less than a month later surrendered the Philippines to Yamashita, who thus completed the double achievement. In May came the indecisive Battle of the Coral Sea which made history by being the first naval engagement ever to be fought entirely by aircraft-carriers. The Japanese were intoxicated with victory, the "victory disease" that made them careless. In the first week of June they lost the Battle of Midway, *Red Castle, Increased Joy* and *Green Dragon* receiving their death blows within six minutes and *Flying Dragon* joining them later in the day. Although this proved a mortal wound it was more than three years till the Japanese surrender.

The prisoners heard little of all this, just the regular comments from the guards—"Nippon number one" and "War finish one hundred years" —but heard plenty of rumours. The daily crop were known as "borehole" rumours as they were passed on at the latrines. Captain Gordon found morale low at first, the pain of defeat still fresh. All kinds of gossip went round about Singapore's having been handed over too easily and quickly, perhaps corruptly, and the men had heard a lot of atrocity stories which frightened them. [35] They had not come to terms with their situation and, indeed, it was a situation to tax all their spiritual and physical resources. They were spared only one dilemma.

The one problem that, from first to last, bothered the Japanese a good deal less than it ever bothered the Germans, was the prospect of their prisoners trying to escape. Apart from their being on an island, there were only two ways out from Singapore: by land and by sea. By sea was out of the question, as small boats could not pass beyond the neighbouring islands, which were also Japanese-held, and no large vessels belonging to Allied or friendly nations came in and out of the harbour. By land meant going up through Malaya. Recognisable at a glance, escaping prisoners would have had all the odds against them: no weapons, so they could not live off the country; infinite miles of jungle to traverse, with all their climatic difficulty, animal and insect life, and few natives, who in any case would hardly feel inclined to help since large rewards were offered for the recapture of escaped prisoners; the certain knowledge that attempts to escape were capital crimes to the Japanese; and little or no language skill to assist them. It is notable how very few people even tried and of those less than a dozen succeeded. Invariably the ones who did get away achieved this in the early stages and with an unusual degree of luck—Sergeant McCormac was one of them. He and a tough Australian called Donaldson took more than five months to escape, by way of Sumatra and Java, helped by fishermen, road gangs, guerillas, lifts in a lorry and a goods train, and finally the exodus to Darwin in a Catalina.[36] Lieutenant Hew Crawford escaped for a while and had many adventures with Malay villagers before illness and starvation drove him to seek the dubious asylum of a prison camp where he was able to infiltrate himself safely.[37]

But the vast majority made no attempt to escape, and there was seldom even a discussion of the chances. It seems that everyone realised from the start that there was too much going against the idea to make even the working out of a plan worth while. In the early working-party days there was plenty of dodging out, of course, short periods of overstaying one's time in clandestine visits to friends in other camps and being neatly covered by one's camp fellows. But this is not escaping. It is likely that it was the nuisance potential of over eighty thousand men, even unarmed and half starved, which influenced the Japanese in their decision to send many of them up to Siam, rather than any particular worry about mass escapes of the kind that made the Germans turn their prisoner of war camps into the fortress strongholds with which the war films have made us all agreeably familiar. The Japanese-held prisoners were fastened in securely by the landscape itself, by every endless yard of it.

5

A number of reasons operated to attract the Japanese towards the projected railway.

They needed one. Japanese troops in Burma had to be kept supplied, and a rail link between Siam and Burma would shorten the supply routes by hundreds of miles and relieve pressure on sea transport, which had run into difficulties of its own—the speed of the Japanese expansion had stretched shipping resources to the limit. Rice was not plentiful in Malaya, but Siam was full of it. The prisoners would find it even more daunting to think of escape up there, for in Siam they would be separated from the nearest Allied forces by over a thousand miles of thick jungle, and a Japanese army, and they would, moreover, be scattered in camps across a far larger area than they were now occupying on the Island.

There was also the challenge of creating the rail link, which would prove that the Japanese could succeed where no other nation had even attempted to try. In the mid-nineteenth century the vogue for canals had inspired two Indian Army captains, Captain Fraser and Captain Furlong, to suggest cutting a canal across the Isthmus of Kra and, when that idea was not followed up by either the British or the French governments, to propose a railway there instead; a few years later there were tentative arguments about a railway link from Rangoon to Bangkok but these also came to nothing.[38] The government of Siam made surveys during the twenties and thirties and consulted many engineering experts, including German technicians, but all had taken one horrified look and said it was impossible. The jungle—the densest in the world except for the Amazon basin—the climate, and the roller-coaster nature of the ground, convinced them that it was not only impossible but that it would cost more than anyone could pay.

The question of cost did not trouble the Japanese now. They had an enormous potential labour force, free for the asking, and expendable. If civilian workers in peace time died on the job somebody would want to know why; no such consideration protected the prisoners. There were few tools except picks and shovels, although they had plenty of blasting powder, but this was outweighed by their being able to call upon a far greater number of men than any other circumstances would have permitted. What they were really doing, though it probably did not strike them at the time, was carrying out a project of the same order as the building of the pyramids. For in 1942-1943 a huge engineering work of the greatest technical complexity was hacked out of the earth by the power of human muscle and very little else, something which makes the railway unique in this period of history. The cost in money was negligible. The cost in suffering and blood was astronomical. Some worked it out at one life for every seventeen and a half feet of track, others that it cost one life per sleeper, or railroad tie.[39]

One factor that raised the cost in lives was that the Japanese, understandably but unfortunately, were in a tearing hurry to get the railway finished. If they needed that line, and they did, they needed it soon. As it turned out, the final irony was not lacking either: no sooner was the line completed than the Allied forces started bombing it. Very few

Japanese supply trains in fact used the railway, and those trains that did run seldom ran the length.

The route chosen started in the south from Bampong and Kanchanaburi, crossed the Meklong River, and then followed the course of the Kwai River (full name Menam Kwa Noi which means Mother of the Waters) to the Burmese border at the Three Pagodas Pass, from which point it would join the line coming to meet it from Moulmein over the watershed. Modern maps do not mark all the places, and often enough the names have been changed over the last quarter of a century. But the River Kwai still follows its course, the charmingly named Three Pagodas Pass is still there, and it is possible to trace the route adequately on even a small-scale map with few marks of identification.

The line began in the north at Thanbyuzayat in Burma and the two ends met just below the pass at Nikki, sometimes spelt Nieke, in the late autumn of 1943, having completed altogether a stretch of two hundred and seventy-three miles through an impossible terrain of mountains, streams and swamps.

The basic working plan, like the tools with which to carry it out, was

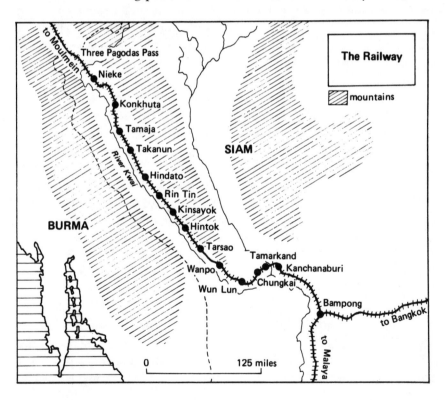

simple. Starting from Bampong at one end and Thanbyuzayat at the other, staging camps were set up along the projected line of construction, following the water as far as possible, as supplies could always be brought along the river and the few roads were poor at all times and impassable in bad weather. The procedure laid down for all these camps was that the guards' house had to be built first, cookhouses next, then huts for the working parties, and finally provision, if one can call it that, for the sick.

The camps were all of a pattern, hastily constructed for the most part. Few of the men had done any building before, particularly with the sort of equipment they had to use now. The huts were shaped like ridge pole tents with low sides, and because of the way they were built they could be any length. The framework was made of bamboo poles: a row of these, twenty feet high, ran down the middle, with other long poles on top to make the ridge. From that the framework sloped away to meet and overhang the side poles. Before the roofing was put on, it looked like a criss-cross pattern of varying lengths and thicknesses. The roofing was made of attap, a thin cane or split bamboo, with leaves from a certain kind of palm folded round it and fastened by thin pieces of rotan. This makes a kind of tile three feet long and a foot wide, and, if well laid, will keep out tropical rain. The proper ratio is six, or at least four, to the foot. The prisoners had two to the foot, and consequently did not stay dry.

These leaf roof tiles were fastened in place by ties made from the soft stringy underbark. The only tools needed to build a hut like this were a saw or axe that would trim the poles and a spade to dig the holes in which the uprights were set: no nails at all were used. The furniture of the living-huts was as simple as their shape: two long sleeping platforms, two feet high, also made of bamboo, split and hammered flat, with slats across the top to lie or sit on. Each man had a space of about two feet by about six, like a grave space. One macabre feature of this kind of building was that the huts never stayed rigid, in time warping and twisting out of true into strange writhing shapes. But, as Major Peacock pointed out comfortingly, this elasticity was sometimes an advantage during storms, as a collapsing hut would fall slowly.[40]

Lieutenant Coast, arriving at the start of the line, Bampong, said it was a typical camp, and that it was deep in black mud so that crossing it was like walking through treacle. There were flies everywhere. All the cooking was done in giant iron frying pans. The huts were full of bed bugs, and the latrines were alive with large grey-white maggots. The hospital hut was permanently flooded and swarming with mosquitoes. The drinking water all came from a single well half a mile away down a rough path.[41] In the camps actually on the river, the river itself, according to Sergeant Harrison, would soothe and bathe wounds, provide priceless drinking and cooking water, and also bring to many disease and death.[42]

All agree that the Kwai was a beautiful river. The country around it was thinly populated, and the whole area was almost unknown to Europeans until the prisoners came into it. The surrounding mountains are echoed in the graceful curves and sharp points of Siamese roofs. Along the water, here and there, stood houses on stilts, and all around the jungle came crowding up close. In the higher parts the river flows fast and there are rapids, but most of the time these can be navigated. During the rainy season the water level rises sixty feet. Into this picture-book background now came the setting up of the camps, where the prisoners, referring to themselves with wry accuracy as coolies, lived in the utmost squalor.[43]

One lieutenant who had heard something about the railway in advance told his Australians that the proposed line had been surveyed by "umpteen other nations" who had promptly turned the idea down. When asked why this was, he had told them to "take your pick, chaps" of diseases, mountains, impassable rivers and monsoon floods—"I wouldn't want to frighten you gallant people"—and he ended off-handedly: "Apart from that, it's said to be quite a pretty country . . ."[44]

6

First of all, the prisoners had to get there.

Some went up into Siam comparatively early and others much later, the first groups moving off in May 1942 and the whole operation covering the span of more than a year. The various accounts of the way in which the prisoners were briefed and of the journey north from Singapore agree in almost every detail. Before leaving, each group had a pep-talk from a Japanese officer, dressed for the occasion in full uniform with pale lavender gloves, and usually speaking through an interpreter. The talk began with a lengthy preamble in which the new era of the South-East Co-Prosperity Sphere was extolled as exemplifying the wisdom and greatness of the Emperor, and went on to say how everyone concerned would benefit from the new system. The men were

then told about their future quarters. All were given the impression that
they would find good, pleasant accommodation and fine food, plenty
of medical care and "splendid facilities for recreation." As Captain
Gordon said, it sounded like "advertising copy for a health resort." [45]

Sergeant Harrison heard that they were to go to freshly constructed
rest camps in a land overflowing with rice where the natives had the
highest standard of living in Asia; [46] Lieutenant Coast understood that
their destination had splendidly healthy mountain air, running water,
wooden huts and a complete orchestra for every thousand men; [47] Major
Peacock, who went among the earliest, said of those who followed that
they had been bluffed into thinking they were coming to hospital camps
or sanatoriums in the fresh hill air.[48] Mr Braddon heard that the sick
men would be included in the party lists so that they might recover in
comfortable camps with plenty of food.[49] Captain Burton wrote that
they were assured of a good camp: "Rumour had it that there were Red
Cross camps in the Malayan hills . . . Some of the promises made by
the Japs gave strength to this rumour, but I had secret doubts." [50]

All of them were optimistic: in happy ignorance of what actually
lay in store for them, they hoped for the best, welcomed any kind of
change, looked forward to going into the country where there ought to
be plenty of fruit and vegetables and imagined that the wet heat would
be left behind. "It is perhaps as well," wrote Lieutenant Coast, "that
there was no soothsayer in our midst." [51]

Some took with them as much as they could carry—according to
Major Peacock and Mr Braddon they were encouraged to do so [52]—
while others found, like Captain Gordon, that packing was "a simple
business; I had only to wrap up my blanket, a pair of shorts, two tin
cans and a toothbrush." [53] There was however one Australian party
with a piano which actually got as far as Bampong, and some Indian
Army officers made a wheeled hencoop which they trundled along full
of cackling birds. Others, who had kept ducks and chickens in their
camps on the Island, reluctantly decided to kill them before leaving,
and at least enjoyed a few days of gorging on poultry. Captain Burton's
men were told to cut their baggage down to bare essentials, which was
all some men had any way, and he found this the best advice: "Many
failed to heed this, only to learn wisdom the hard way." [54]

Most groups assembled quite cheerfully in the rubber-tiled hall of
Singapore station when their turn came, laughing at odd items of others'
equipment, excited at the prospect of a change of scene. Their first
sight of the trains put an end to the gaiety. These trains were long

strings of iron or steel box-cars, eighteen feet long and eight wide, with sliding doors in the middle of each side, with a chain across. Thirty-one, thirty-two or thirty-three men were crammed into each truck, with all their kit, so that they could stand up (after a fashion: the roofs were low) or sit bolt upright with their knees drawn up, or squat, but could not stretch out or lie down. This made sleep impossible except in short, restless snatches. Some trains set off with a Japanese guard in each truck; others, carrying as many as eight hundred prisoners, had a single Japanese sergeant and half a dozen guards for the lot. As the trains bumped over the Causeway, the length of each train, the roar went up. "You'll never get off the Island."

Most writers on the subject agree that the journey took four or five days, though it seemed much longer. The box-cars baked in the heat so that they were like ovens, froze at night like ice-boxes, and when it rained the water streamed in. Halts were few and rations grudging: some had one meal a day and occasionally two.[55] Drinking water was scarce and thirst a torment. The trains stopped for hours in steaming sidings to let the regular trains go through—trains in which passengers on upholstered seats, and being served off china and glass in dining cars with white tablecloths, gazed curiously out at the prisoners. At times there were glimpses of lovely scenery: the twinkling lights of beautiful Penang, and, crossing the Isthmus of Kra, the moonlit blue waters of the Gulf of Siam "creaming on lonely golden sands";[56] then the weird limestone peaks sticking up abruptly out of the plains like the jebels of the Sahara.

All the writers record the thankful relief of their arrival at Bampong station, where they could move about and stretch their cramped limbs; and all of them were unpleasantly surprised by the sight of Bampong camp, the quagmire in the clearing, crowded with prisoners and surrounded by clamouring Siamese (including saffron-robed Buddhist priests) wanting to buy anything the men would sell them, particularly Parker pens. The later they were to reach Bampong the greater their horror, for as time went on disease had spread and become more virulent so that former companions had often become unrecognisable if they were not already dead.

Some groups were taken from Bampong to Kanchanaburi by truck, but others had to walk the twenty-five miles, a "very stiff ordeal" that took place over two nights; the Bedfordshires "did the last ninety miles on foot, forty of them through jungle."[57] On the first night, Captain Burton found himself hypnotised by the white bowl strapped on the back of the man in front of him. It moved with the man's movements and Captain Burton followed it mechanically. Mr Braddon kept on counting steps, thousand after thousand to the verge of madness.

His own march lasted seven nights and was remarkable for two things: no singing, and the magnificent help and example of Major Kevin Fagan, the Medical Officer, who kept them going when nothing else could.[58]

On all the marches they tried to keep to the routine of march customary in the British Army, fifty minutes of walking and ten minutes of rest. Each time they struggled to their feet after a rest period they found it more difficult. At the first dawn they halted and dropped to the ground where they stood, or bathed in the river; they all got into the river sooner or later, a great luxury which was almost miraculously refreshing. Provisioned by the native traders who swarmed around, some managed a good meal before setting off again, often the last good meal they would have for many long months to come. Often the last good wash, too, as it turned out.

The second night of march was worse than the first. "Each of us suffered his own personal agony," said Captain Burton, "though it was generally hidden by cheerfulness of a macabre nature." The road here was a surfaced one that seemed about the same in quality as a secondary English road, and a bus service ran along it: the Japanese guards used the buses to bring in the stragglers during the later part of the night. As the hours went by, starting again after the rests became "absolute torture" so that the men "pressed on in grim silence in a sort of mental stupor." Captain Burton found that he could no longer think about the others because his own personal struggle was so great; the journey took on the quality of "a death march" and on arriving at Kanchanaburi (where in the distance they could see the old walled city) they reached "the last flicker of endurance," falling asleep as they crumpled up on the ground, unable even to crawl to what shade there was. When they came to and looked around, they felt they were at the end of the world, "certainly on the threshold of Purgatory."

All the rumours that had filtered back, and it must be remembered that Captain Burton was among the later groups to be sent up into Siam, were full of foreboding. The "inhuman drive" to finish the railway, the slave-like state of the men building it, the "cruelly enforced marches" and death camps: all these had by then been heard of, talked about, and were dreaded. The prospect before them could well have created a suicidal frame of mind; it was only the knowledge that survival "hinged on making the best of things" that forced them to hang on. Captain Burton admitted that to him the future had so nightmare an aspect that his brain refused to accept it.[59]

Lieutenant Coast, referring to the marches from camp to camp, said that they were all alike: for the first hour one talked to one's neighbour, but during the second and third hours backs and necks stiffened, kit weighed pounds heavier, conversation dwindled and died out; after that one simply trudged grimly along in silence, and, with feet blistered, fevers rising and backs ready to break, wondered: "How many more days, how many more days?"[60]

CHAPTER X

Something Worse

I

So far we have taken a look at the accommodation the prisoners had and how they reached it. It is necessary now to consider the work they had to do. There was no delay in their starting it: within minutes of arrival, sometimes, they were set to work on what Sergeant Harrison summed up neatly as the building of a reasonably level strip fifty feet wide from one end of Siam to the other.[1] This was precisely what they achieved. It meant clearing trees and rocks away, making embankments and bridges, cuttings and viaducts. Bearing in mind the fact that all this had to be done virtually by hand and within a time-limit, one must also remember that a fixed percentage of men at each camp had to form the working-parties. In order to make up the numbers, this percentage always included men who were unfit to work at any given time and had to be carried or driven to the working sites. Mr Audric had this explained to him when he visited the railway. He learned that if a sick man could do no more than break a few stones in the course of a whole day even this was considered useful: "It was of no account if the effort proved too much, and he dropped dead beside his pitiful labours."[2]

As each camp was established, the men in it had to build their stretch of line that would in due course join up with those of the camps on either side. The jungle growths were cleared first, which was back-breaking work. One of the hardest parts was uprooting large clusters of bamboo, for each stalk had to be pulled out separately, which took at least ten men on a rope. Twenty men might move a large clump in one day. The cut or uprooted trees had to be carried to the side of the clearing, where they formed great tangled piles that in their turn were hard to shift. The earth and rocks were loosened by picks and shovels and the rubble carried away in small baskets or on stretchers.

On the whole length of line, of which Major Peacock saw more

205

than a hundred miles, there was only one petrol-driven rock drill, and this soon went out of action.[3] The larger rocks were blasted out with explosive, placed in boreholes; these holes, a yard deep, were made by the laborious process of chipping patiently away with a long drill shaped like a chisel, and an eight-pound hammer. The hammer and tap men, as they were called, worked in pairs. One sat on the ground, holding the drill between his legs and turning it a little after each blow from the other man's hammer. The risk of a smashed finger or splinter in the eye made this, as Sergeant Harrison put it, not a job on which to let one's thoughts wander. The making of one of these holes often took a whole day.[4]

The work was divided into three parts: earth-moving, hammer and tap, and rock-rolling. The earth movers shovelled away the topsoil to expose the rocks, the hammer and tap men followed and smashed the rocks up, and then, when the explosive charges had been rammed into the holes and fired, the third group moved in to clear away the rocks and boulders. They prised out the pieces with crowbars, sometimes taking a couple of hours on the bigger ones, and, in spite of the strenuous nature of the work, its danger, and their pitiable condition, they found it exhilarating to send the boulders crashing down the steep hillside. Some of the rocks were much larger than the men who shifted them. Sergeant Harrison described the feeling: after a final look to see that all was clear, and a nod from the soldier in charge, the great rock, delicately balanced on the brink, would be pushed quite gently, and roll over the edge in slow motion, going faster as it fell, finally bounding in joyful leaps to the trees below, where it crashed like thunder; then a hush followed in which they could hear screams of anger and defiance from the baboons they had disturbed.[5] Sometimes the guards would throw stones themselves, small ones, usually at the prisoners.[6]

At some of the larger rock cuttings the Japanese had tubs to move the rubble in: these ran on little narrow-gauge iron spur rails and were pulled by the prisoners. This was particularly dangerous if they were on a gradient.[7]

There were culverts and bridges to be made too. These were built of timber cut in the jungle and dragged to the sites. The timber was mostly teak, one of the hardest woods in the world; but included whatever was available, from teak to kapok, all of it green and uncured, possessing varied properties when it dried. If particularly large pieces were needed, they were floated down the river and then cut to size and shape on the job. Two-handed saws were used for the cutting, a laborious task. Major Peacock reported that the strongest officer-prisoners were used for the bridging work, operating in parties of twenty.[8] Later, higher up the river, elephants were brought in to shift the timber, and these were welcomed by most of the prisoners whose task they now took over, even if some of them did feel it was rather degrading to be told by the Japanese that one elephant was worth twenty officers.

The bridge-building methods were altogether primitive. There was no steel, no nuts and bolts, no heavy construction equipment. Issued with iron spikes, baulks and ropes, the prisoners walked up to the sites. They floated heavy square beams out into the river and rigged up pile-drivers on scaffolds. Men sat on the ground and cut the ends of the piles into points with sharp knives called changkols. The piles were to be driven into the ground by teams pulling on the dozens of ropes that worked the piledriver. The driving force itself was usually a log with an iron cap, suspended above the foundation log by a rope going up over a pulley. The men, pulling and sweating in "that accursed team like slaves of the Pharaohs," hauled up the weight, released it to thump down on the foundation log, and drove it further in with each blow.[9] The blows were directed by a Japanese standing on top of the scaffold, and it took two or three pulls to raise the weight. Hour after hour, with the team leader shouting, "One-two-three! One-two-three!," this went on: "pick up the rope, strain five or six paces back, let go, pick up the rope—as close to being galley slaves as one could wish." [10] When the beams had all been driven in, and were level, the rest of the structure was erected on top.

Lieutenant Coast worked on two bridges, each about forty yards long; Captain Gordon's party took under two months to build one several hundred yards long and about "five storeys high out of the water"; [11] Sergeant Harrison's group made a bridge eighty feet high and four hundred yards long, using wooden wedges, bamboo ties, attap lashing, wooden dowels, some iron spikes, and a good deal of faith.[12] While the piledriving teams pulled and hauled, and the pilepointers sharpened their giant pencils, others on another rope and pulley brought new timbers up from the river. The rest of the men either carried them to stack or broke stones and piled them. They had been told beforehand that they would be privileged to do skilled work daily, parading after breakfast, having their midday rice brought out to them, and working until six every evening. No account was ever taken of Saturdays or Sundays. Every tenth day was considered a rest day unless a great "speedo" was ordered, something which in most places occurred quite soon. Piece by piece, with cross-beams whose joints were mostly dovetail or butt joints held by iron staples, these monstrous erections rose slowly to the level of the track. There were occasional mishaps, like the famous "pack of cards" bridge at Hintok, which fell down three times before it was completed, and it seems surprising that it remained standing then, considering the variety of woods used in it.[13]

The Japanese in charge told the men that they would be treated well if they behaved well, but that if they did not carry out orders they would be killed. They were also warned that they must cherish their tools as there would be trouble if any were lost or damaged. It was also clear to them that they would have to work unless they were hospital cases. Lighter sickness or diseases that did not obviously show were passed as fit.[14] Rising in the dark, eating a mug full of ground rice without salt or sugar, known as "pap," paraded at the first pale light of dawn and marched up to the sites, they worked until the midday break, when the lunch rice was sour after six hours in its cans in the sun, and at six in the evening they went down to bathe in the river, their skins sunburnt, their hands blistered and bleeding. So it went on for days, weeks, months. The men lost all count of time: to them it was only 1943 and the railway.[15]

2

Rumour had not misled them when it spoke of the frantic hurry to get the railway finished. The Japanese had originally estimated eighteen months for the complete building of the line. When construction started later than they had planned, they compressed this into twelve months, not altering their original deadline date, which was met. As the pressure increased, applied downwards from Tokyo, they started on an unprecedented reign of terror.[16] It is all very well to point out now that better food and medical care would have produced better work, more efficiently and quickly done, but the Japanese in 1943 were not in the mood to reason. Captain Burton thought it highly probable that someone at the Imperial Japanese Army HQ in Tokyo had "lost his temper and kicked someone. The kicking had continued downwards and had now reached us the labourers, the lowest form of life." [17] Lieutenant Coast said the same thing: they were to be Very coolie of Very coolie.[18]

Sergeant Harrison and his men felt it too—working on "Hellfire Pass," the notorious six hundred yard cutting that became the most infamous section of the line. When they were first taken out to the site they looked in awe at the ribbon of river far below, the miles of hills stretching away to the west, and the mountain crest through which the cutting had to be made.[19] A Siamese engineer whom Mr Audric met after the war considered the Wun Lun viaduct one of the most difficult and dangerous constructions, and "marvelled at the skill of the men who built it." [20] Partly it was laid on a ledge cut out of a steep cliff; some of the upright wooden supports were over sixty feet high and embedded in the rocks lower down.

During the periods when the work was speeded up, the prisoners were kept at it throughout the hours of daylight, eating their morning and evening meals in darkness. At some stages the building went on through the night hours as well, creating a scene that no one who was there is ever likely to forget. Flares cast a lurid light across the wreckage of stones and trees and the men who moved them, against the dense black of the night sky.

The main bridge on which Captain Gordon was working was the one that gave the title to the celebrated novel *The Bridge on the River Kwai*. He makes an interesting observation about the book, calling it "an entertaining fiction" but pointing out that to let such a fiction go unchallenged would be unjust to the officers and men, living and dead, who worked on that bridge. "They did not do so willingly, but at bayonet point and under the bamboo rod, and they risked their lives continually seeking for an opportunity to sabotage the bridge." [21]

In the novel, a key situation arises from the wrangle over the thorny issue of whether the officers should be made to do the same work as the men, and alongside them without distinction of rank, or whether they should command their own men as officers are expected to do in ordinary conditions. The colonel in the story, it will be remembered, was for ever referring to the Geneva Convention in support of the latter principle. This is true of dozens of occasions in the actual captivity of soldiers under the Japanese: the rights and wrongs of officers working was a vexed question that was only partially solved on the Kwai by the formation of an Officers' Battalion, which worked exactly like the rest of the coolies, and suffered a proportionately high percentage of casualties.

3

Moving north up the course of the railway, starting from Bampong, the following camps are mentioned (with variable spelling) in all the available accounts: Kanchanaburi, Tamarkand, Chungkai, Wun Lun, Wan Po, Tarsao, Hintok, Kinsayok, Rin Tin, Hindato, Takanun, Tamaja, Konkhuta, and Nikki. Just above the last, the Three Pagodas Pass crosses into Burma. There the two ends of the railway met, the upper part being pushed southwards by a second army of slaves, mostly Dutch, Eurasian, Malay and Tamil prisoners. Several of these camps had distinguishing features, although the basic layout of each was much the same. Bampong was the starting point of the long two-night march up to Kanchanaburi: the troops usually called it Kanburi and it was built on flat mud and had little to recommend it. Tamarkand was approached past fields of peanuts, clusters of elephant grass, and patches of scrubby jungle. Chungkai, by the broad river, shaded by huge trees, groups of mangoes and enormous prickly bamboos, had narrow, overgrown paths leading to remote villages and vanishing into the hills.

About four miles up the line, separated from Chungkai by wide and unexpectedly attractive stretches of what looked like common land with areas of bamboo growths, was Wun Lun, where the station had two sidings, each about a hundred yards long. The solitary platform was a raised bank of earth with a small attap hut on it with a telephone that rang all the time. The huts in the camp were low and as no Japanese-designed hut ever had doors more than five feet four inches in height the men were for ever banging their heads; and it was a hazardous business getting in and out in the dark.

Wun Lun had a market by the river, approached across a mud square and past a plantation of kapok trees which were quite beautiful with their stiff, regular, silvery trunks in symmetrical rows, little tufts of green leaves at the ends of the branches, and uniform thirty feet of height. The kapok appeared in pods like small brown corncobs stuffed with seeds like cotton wool. This was attractive, but the camp arrangements were not. The cookhouses were situated over a quarter of a mile from the huts, and reached by crossing a wavering plank bridge with a single hand-rail above a steep cleft. In the frequent wet weather it was glassy with mud. But Wun Lun did not prove too bad for Lieutenant Coast and his fellow-prisoners, compared with other places. Their work was relatively unhurried, there was less supervision, and they could relax in the river. Every day they heard frightening stories of some dreadful sort of "speedo" going on higher up at Wan Po where two thousand men were hard at it day and night making a huge cutting: it sounded like an inferno.[22] This was, of course, Sergeant Harrison's "Hellfire Pass."

Near Wun Lun the river curved in a great loop, and the camp there was known as Monkey Bend, from the vast number of apes living in the trees. From Wun Lun Lieutenant Coast's party went up to Takanun, and, before making that fatal stage of the journey, he paused to take stock. They had now been in captivity for fifteen months (this brings it up to May 1943), labouring each day for a wage of four pence, on a semi-starvation diet and with little or no medical care. Resistance, sapped by the climate, by disease and lack of vitamins, was low; most people were now anything from fourteen to thirty pounds under weight; the officers, especially the younger officers, were in little better case than the men. They, too, had been on the working parties, some of them in the officers' working party, which was three hundred strong, some out with groups of Other Ranks. In addition to the construction work, these officers were all the time responsible for the constant and tricky mediation between the Japanese and the troops. The officers had had their share of illness and hospital treatment and although their diet was better supplemented than that of the men it was still poor—no Siamese would have dreamt of eating it. The reader who makes the trip up the line with Lieutenant Coast will realise that all concerned were in a wretched state to face the worst ordeal they had yet to encounter.[23]

They set off by night on top of a fully loaded goods train, pulled by one of the usual Siamese wood-burning engines, clanking along at about ten miles an hour, while they lay on the tarpaulins gazing up at the stars and the fifty-foot feathery bamboos, and listening to the loud noise of the cicadas sounding all around them. They passed through Bankao, where Mr Audric was later told that the discipline had been far more severe than in the camps lower down,[24] and then came a long upward gradient. It seemed immensely long, and it felt cold and damp in the open. The train stopped and they all listened for some order to be shouted. When it came they slid down into the muddy puddles beside the track, and hurried to put their own kit in some spot that might be dry to the touch. The guards shouted orders while the rest of the camp baggage was unloaded, the engine whistled and the train moved slowly away, stopping (they heard it) further up the line. No one seemed to know what to do next. They sat about on the rails as the driest place to sit as the dawn came up and they saw a big flat-topped hill, tree-covered, identifiable as Arrow Hill near Wan Po, about sixty-five miles north of Bampong. They also saw, close by, several sidings and a few attap stores glistening in the rain under the spiky bamboos surrounding them.[25]

After an apparently endless wait they were told to draw their breakfast rations, which consisted of a pint of boiled rice and half a teaspoonful of sugar for each man, and were ordered to march in an hour for Tarsao, over twelve miles away, a journey made after a sleepless night and with no further rations. The long straggling lines of men, one on each side of the track, made their way slowly over loose ballast and mud, passing on the way the groups of camps at Wan Po, now empty, and then seeing the river curving in a great wide bend round steep limestone crags. Clinging to the cliff face, thirty feet above the water, ran the huge bridge which the two thousand slaves had built in seventeen days: gazing in stupefaction they could hardly believe it.[26]

They walked across the bridge, which like all Japanese-sponsored bridges was a nightmare to cross, shaking at every step, and then began to approach wilder country full of thick green vegetation that steamed with oppressive heat. The march grew more and more tiring; the last three miles were like wading through sand. At least they did not take the wrong fork as Mr Braddon's party did and have to walk four extra miles—"twelve thousand exhausted paces." [27]

Finally they came to Tarsao, where, said Mr Audric, most prisoners came at some time or other. He calls it the mid point of the line,[28] but Lieutenant Coast makes it about seventy-eight miles one way and a hundred and ten the other.[29] Mr Braddon simply comments that it was very likely the foulest of all the staging camps.[30] At Tarsao they found that people had been coming through for days on their way to Takanun or Nikki. The first thing that happened was a furious tropical storm, in which the rain stung agonisingly and soaked them as wet as if they had been standing in the river. The officers finally fell asleep on the floor of the sacrosanct Camp Office where they slept instantly in spite of exhaustion, the pouring rain, and the "hellish chorus" of bullfrogs.[31] When Mr Braddon arrived at Tarsao it was not raining, but the sight of all those squalid huts behind the bamboo compound fences of the camp was not inspiring. They had been carrying a man for twelve miles who turned out to be dead when they got there. They went down to the brown river and swam, relaxing in the water and spitting it at each other in a friendly way. The river bank was full of

Siamese offering to buy the men's clothes. On the way up to the camp a lieutenant who looked rather harassed stopped them and warned them that every drop of water had to be boiled as it was infected with cholera. They went the rest of the half mile in uneasy silence.[32]

Lieutenant Coast's party went off the following morning on a roller-coaster of a road, all mud and ruts, through the trees. Before leaving they had news of H Force and F Force, prisoners who had left Changi only two weeks before (among them Captain Burton), including many sick and weak men, entirely unused to jungle surroundings and completely do-it-yourself camps, whose treatment was far harsher than that given to the comparatively hardened veterans who had been in Siam some months already. They were, in fact, hearing about Captain Burton's "death march." Mr Braddon's party also stayed at Tarsao for one night, but they made their march through the darkness, passing warnings of low branches and protruding stumps back down the line and feeling bitterly that "no place that smelt like that could have been meant by God to be inhabited by man." In the morning they met some of F Force and were appalled: "stamped with the misery that was too awful to look at . . . skeletons with purplish skins, teeth that looked huge in shrunken faces and haunted eyes." Within three weeks they were to be in the same condition.[33]

When the soldiers of Lieutenant Coast's party left Tarsao at two in the afternoon they took five hours to walk six miles up and down a deeply rutted track through the forest. On the way they passed a clear stream on the banks of which was a beautifully situated Japanese camp that had a saw mill worked by British carpenters. The road was dry after that, but still steep. At seven o'clock they reached Tonsha Spring Camp, where the spring water was icy cold and crystal clear and where Lieutenant Coast accidentally got into the enclosure behind the Japanese cookhouse. A Korean private rushed up screeching at him and hit him in the face as hard as he could: this was apparently the usual method of telling a prisoner: "I believe you have lost your honourable way—the path is just over there, and I deeply regret that this enclosure is out of bounds." [34]

Before sunrise next day they were off again to walk the ten miles to Kanu, where they camped in tents in a field of lalang grass and found two majors who said that the Japanese had left them there with a handful of tools and a handful of men and told them to build a hospital, having assumed from the majors' dark blue arm-bands that they were doctors. Certainly the two were making a cheerful attempt to build a bamboo shack of some kind. At Kanu Mr Braddon's group stopped—the rest went on, never to be seen again for the most part, but the men detailed to stay in that mud-filled saucer and be bellowed at by First Star Private Kanemoto spent two weeks clearing a piece of jungle about a hundred yards by fifty and discovering that bamboo will not fall even when completely severed—the creepers hold it upright. They found it painful to walk on the needle-sharp spikes littering the ground and complicated to pull stems nine inches thick and forty feet long and full of water clear of the undergrowth. They built huts and they all got malaria. At the end of the fortnight they moved into a draughty wet tent in a small swamp a quarter of a mile away and there they stayed.[35]

Lieutenant Coast's party went on to Hintok, situated at the foot of a big tree-covered mountain, where the camp, surrounded by a bamboo palisade, possessed several unusual features. It had been a camp for Australians, who had built a complete water system of bamboo pipes that operated a shower system. They had made sixteen-foot-deep latrines that were actually clean. They included among their number an excellent bugler whose calls, blown on a silver bugle that raised echoes from the mountains, sounded magical. This was a particularly mountainous area: the next six or seven miles of railway had to be deeply blasted and steeply embanked. The next stopping-place was Kinsayok, over ten miles farther on, and during the march the men kept crossing the railway trace which was not always easy to see. The scenery was spectacular—limestone precipices hundreds of feet high, forest-filled valleys and a great hazy blue vista of mountains spreading for miles. The area also abounded in beautiful deep-grass-green butterflies. It was of course at Hintok that the "pack of cards" bridge was built.

Kinsayok turned out to be a very large camp, with excellent bathing in a clear stream and barges on the river where one could buy eggs, though one paid a lot more for them than at Chungkai. But the trouble at Kinsayok was the foul old huts that the prisoners were expected to use. They crawled with bed bugs, so that a man who sat for half a minute on the edge of the slats wearing shorts would get several bites on the thighs. The idea of trying to sleep there was dismissed at once, and the men slept on the ground in the open. Even there they got bitten, though not so badly, and, as if in partial compensation, experienced a tropical night so perfect that Lieutenant Coast was able to read his diary, written in pencil and very small, by the light of the great sunlike moon.[36]

In the morning they apathetically covered the next ten miles to Rin Tin, which they reached about four in the afternoon. Stories that Rin Tin was a plague spot had filtered through, and they found out why: it was a camp of ghosts, smelling of death and decay and "something worse," and eerily silent—no birds sang, no tree rustled. The atmosphere was ominously evil. The camp stood on a hill completely enclosed by a ring of tall trees; the huts were bare of slats but full of large lizards, bugs, lice, and huge fat flies. In a sad little oval clearing, already well overgrown, they found the burial ground with its two hundred and thirty-one graves, fast turning back to jungle. What had happened was that the camp, opened only three months before, had become so disease-ridden that the Japanese had closed it down except for parties passing through, and the soldiers' one idea on seeing it was to get away again as fast as possible.

They left Rin Tin before daylight and set off through jungle so dense that the trees met over their heads. In the misty light of early morning they heard the rather sad whistling of the tailless gibbons known as "Wak Waks" who inhabited that area and the forest further on: this was to be their morning music for a long time. The ground on which they walked was thick with wet leaves, with here and there "giant speckled fungi like huge brown arum lilies" growing three feet tall, here and there carpets of little mauve orchids, and blackened old trees with cascades of orchids, "white or apricot or mauve, pouring in sprays two feet long" down their trunks.[37]

At the next camp, Hindato, they found, to their surprise, clean tents and a sympathetic group of Japanese cooks who prepared a hot drink of nectar-like sugar-water for them. From Hindato they went on over dusty roads to Brankasi, another ten miles, and then to their objective, Takanun, past hills several hundred feet high and one in three steep, gashed with huge gullies and crested with trees. Takanun had three camps set apart from the town, which was a fairly large place with shops and houses and a metalled road leading to the wolfram mines near by. The camps, the river, the road and the railway all lay in a long narrow valley. On the river bank, shaded by a row of large trees, was the Japanese accommodation, neat new wooden-floored tents with matting in them, a small wooden house for the Commandant, and, further along, a quite big Siamese house, in a garden, with several canoes kept under the building. Half way up the bank was the Japanese cookhouse. Then came a piece of level ground, about an acre, where the men would dig over the ground and plant vegetables, and then the prisoners' area, also about an acre, roughly square, sloping, open and dusty. Here some twelve hundred men were provided with badly worn tents that would accommodate just over half of them. For the rest there was nothing. But for everything that was bad at this camp, it was worse in the other two, and that included the Japanese guards in charge. Lieutenant Ino at Takanun was known to have a better camp than anyone else wherever he went. He gave the men a day to settle in, and in that twenty-four hours they put up what seemed to them must be the most primitive dwellings that human beings had lived in for centuries. Twelve officers lived in tents designed for two. Later there were as many as eighteen. There was a deep pool edged with sand near by in the river, which was perfect for swimming and bathing and for washing clothes.[38]

It was here that the monsoon broke, and here that the full force of disease struck. From Takanun through the comparatively short distance up to Nikki and the Three Pagodas Pass it was the same kind of landscape—mountains covered with heavy jungle and forest, all of it monsoon country, all of it disease country, all of it lonely, desolate and menacing, and all of it, day after endless day, providing the same pattern of existence.

4

Every morning began with réveille blown shrilly on a whistle at six o'clock, its sound rousing the men from their fitful sleep. In the pitch darkness they lay listening to the rain on the canvas about twelve inches from their noses, wondering if it was a drizzle or a downpour. The ends of the beds and blankets were soaking because the tents leaked. One of the men, having slept on the matches to try to keep them dry, struck one and lit the lamp, which was made from a milk tin containing coconut oil and gave out a feeble, dim light by which the men, sitting up resignedly, took off their comparatively dry sleeping shorts and groped under the slats for their soaked working clothes. "We sit on the edge of the bed slowly combing our hair—God knows why, for nothing like that matters now," then they washed their faces in water drained off from the tent flaps into old tins kept outside. "In ten seconds that's over." Next came the dangerously slippery trek over to the cookhouse to fetch the breakfast of "pap" porridge and rice rissoles, for which journey they put bits of towels or gas-capes over their shoulders before stepping cautiously out into the downpour. The cookhouse was run by an officer assisted by a private, the hardest worked pair in the camp, who slept on a bamboo shelf fixed up under a sloping tree-branch. The shelf was thatched over with long grass and in this uncertain shelter they might perhaps keep two-thirds of their bodies dry. They lit fires, prepared and cooked the food entirely in the open.

The men paraded at first light and lined up in fives while the officers checked the numbers. In the grey-green misty drizzle they waited for the Japanese engineers to arrive in their cheap raincoats, bringing with them an elderly sergeant with a squint who carried a board and a stub of pencil and went around briskly detailing the working parties for bridging, cutting, embanking, timber moving or whatever. They set off for the site in a shambling walk and, when they arrived, put their belongings under logs to avoid the worst of the rain and set to work at once, as always in a state of nervous strain. The sudden shout from a guard was "one of the usual introductions to a bloody good clip over the ear or some specially dirty job to do." At widely spaced intervals came short breaks in which they drank "some hot concoction jokingly referred to as tea," asking permission: "Nippon—small yasumé O.K.? Cha?" (Short break for tea, please, all right?) Two soldiers did the brewing-up, working on strict rotation and never questioned by the Japanese who accepted this as an established Army custom; it was a coveted job.

There were the lunch intervals, spent on the work sites, the regular flurries of trouble and sudden sickness, and the way in which time dragged on: "at five-thirty the last hour of the day commences, and oh God, how slowly it always seems to go!" But at last came the order to pack up and check tools, and the men, swaying as they walked, went slowly back to camp to have a bathe in the river and eat their rice and stew at seven-thirty. Then they went into the huts and lay on the sleeping-platforms, or to the tents and lay on the so-called beds, watching the rain trickling down the canvas. When the water started to come in at a leaky seam they ran one finger down the canvas to make the trickle follow it so that it would not drip directly above their heads. It was quite dark by half past eight: that was the daily routine of their lives, day after day, week after week.[39]

As they lay in the dripping darkness, many men thought of vanished, modest pleasures—a newspaper full of fish and chips, a long hot bath with scented soap, a room of one's own to go to. Through their endurance alone the men of the Royal Norfolk Regiment had "worthily served the Britannia of their badge." [40]

5

Then, incredibly, on October 17, 1943, it was finished. The two ends, nosing towards each other through swamp and rock and jungle, over water and mud, actually met. Where they met the Japanese authorities, perhaps inspired by stories and films showing the pioneer days of the transcontinental railroads of America, laid a copper rail pegged with a gold spike. The first trains went chugging and rattling the length of the line, flag-bedecked locomotives pulling bunting-streamered trucks with attap roofs (the prisoners derisively called them "flying kampongs") in which, as Mr Audric heard, Japanese officers, wearing their long swords, sat "proudly, if uncomfortably." [41] (It is interesting to note that the Japanese, priding themselves on their modernity in weapons of war, clung to the swords. A study of the Samurai makes it clear that "the extreme reverence in which the ancient Samurai held their swords" persuaded Japanese officers "as late as the Second World War" to carry them, even going so far as "to lug these weapons with their heavy scabbards into battle" where they were particularly incongruous in hand-to-hand fighting with bayoneted rifles.[42])

Then came a curious incident. The Japanese commandants now announced a day's holiday and suggested that a religious service should be held to commemorate the completion of the railway. After consultation among themselves, the senior British officers agreed provided that they might organise it as they wished, without interference. The Japanese consented at once and expressed a wish to attend the service, which took place at the cemetery, at the foot of "the huge wooden cross by the bamboo trellis gate." The prisoners were paraded and drawn up on three sides of a square and, after a wait during which the British padre stood turning the pages of his hymn book, the Japanese arrived, the officers wearing their best dark green uniforms with their clumsy-looking top-boots and "ridiculously long Samurai swords." One Australian present was immensely impressed by the comparatively impeccable British turn-out: "half starved and in rags, they came to it like a crack regiment on parade," making a marked impression on the Japanese. The service was brief—a hymn and several prayers—and then the Japanese colonel stood on a stool and read out a speech in Japanese from "a vast scroll held before him." Wreaths of jungle flowers, made by the prisoners, were placed at the foot of the cross. The Japanese colonel stepped forward and saluted.[43]

Some observers thought this a fairly decent gesture. Lieutenant Coast did not. He and his companions thought it an insult and a mockery and he says that they were ordered to have the service. The Japanese officers present, "those close-cropped hog-like Asiatic equivalents of the Prussians," and the Japanese and Korean rank and file with their "expressionless, slab-like brute faces" who had "relentlessly helped them," were directly responsible for the three hundred dead in that cemetery alone "and for countless hundreds below." He observed the uneasy way in which the Japanese kept glancing round them: they seemed to know exactly what was in every British mind. Back in camp afterwards the men heard another speech, interpreted this time: it reminded them that they had started work on the railway in Chungkai, had gone on to Wan Po where they had blasted a cutting and built a great bridge, had then come up to Takanun where they had completed the sector allotted to them "in a satisfactory manner." For a month it had been difficult to get vegetable rations "owing to the bad road." Some of the prisoners had been ill, and some had died, but all the same they must acknowledge that they had "always been fairly and justly treated by the Imperial Japanese Army." To carry out any further task which might be given them "it is now your stern duty," the speech concluded, "to improve your health."

Lieutenant Coast summed up by saying that any comment on such a hypocritical speech was superfluous.[44]

Mr Braddon looked at the wreckage of men whose stern duty it now was to improve their health. Their bones stood out sharply through their loose purple-brown skins, their feet were torn with bamboo thorns, their legs had ulcers, their thighbones were covered in raw red patches, their arms were like sticks and their heads seemed shrunken. That remnant was all that was left of F Force and H Force.[45]

CHAPTER XI

A Bottomless Gulf

I

THE effect of the climate of Malaya and Siam is gradual, even though anyone arriving there is at once aware of the overpowering heat and intense humidity. Both drain the strength of vigorous people and produce slowed reactions, both physical and mental, unless special care is taken to guard against this. Central Siam is very hot indeed. It is also very wet, so the steamy country swarms with insects, particularly ants and mosquitoes. In the morning and evening it turns chilly and travellers shiver. Many a story has taken as its subject a European going to hell in the tropics, giving a picture of the heavily drinking planter and his wife wilting under the combined assaults of heat, rain, isolation, wild animals, and insubordinate natives, so much so that Britons who have lived in Malaya have become very touchy on the subject, insisting that the "whisky-swilling planter" is a nasty myth dreamed up by ignorant outsiders. Whether true or not, there is no doubt that the fictional characters have all been well-fed and well-housed, outwardly deferred to, in touch with home and, when driven to despair, within reach of a ship and with money for the passage. The prisoners on the Kwai would have envied the lot of these unhappy planters.

People say that it is possible to get used to anything, in time, but the less toughened and experienced men on the Kwai never did get used to the conditions of their life. After it was all over, they probably thought it just as well: at least they never became hardened to the point of indifference. Their instinctive kindliness comes out in all accounts: sudden acts of generosity, or of consideration, occurred frequently and unexpectedly. But life was hard.

The railway administration based itself at Kanchanaburi, the old walled town and market centre of its province, from which supplies were sent in progressively diminishing amounts upstream to the other camps. The line bridged the river at Tamarkand, where the width of the water varied according to the season from one hundred to five hundred yards, and went on over low land that flooded every year past Chungkai and Wun Lun, from where it climbed to a modest plateau at Bankao and reached the high cliffs at Wan Po where the river curves through limestone gorges. The ground goes on rising from there, first through solid jungle and then through more open country with stunted trees and scrub until it comes to the pass, described as a low saddle about a thousand feet above sea level, after which the route gradually drops down to the northern starting point of the line at Thanbyuzayat.[1]

There are three seasons in Siam: November to February (dry and comparatively cool and pleasant), February to May (dry and hot), and June to October (wet and hot). The building of the railway took a year and therefore spanned all three, starting with the most favourable, which was unfortunate for all concerned.[2]

Captain Burton felt that one of the worst things about the jungle had nothing to do with animals or insects but was the all-pervading smell, created by the damp heat. The heavy rains and day temperatures in the high nineties turned the jungle into a great forcing-house full of the wet sweet smell of rotting vegetation—like the smell of cabbage with peppery and musty ingredients added. The insects, of course, greatly added to the discomfort and disease: red ants bit the men continually, leeches fastened themselves to their damp skins and started jungle sores which turned into skin ulcers that never healed and flies settled in clouds on everything, spreading dysentery. There were also the mosquitoes, the worst scourge of all for they carried malaria, both the type called benign and the cerebral malignant, which drove men raving mad and against which they could do nothing.[3]

When storms came, they were of colossal force. The wind lashed through the trees, sending low black clouds scudding across the sky. Lightning flashed and sizzled in the treetops, rain fell more torrentially than the prisoners would have believed possible.[4] These storms died away as fast as they sprang up, leaving astonishingly fresh skies and, often, perfect tropical nights, velvety, spangled, and calm. Everything was larger than life: a week or two of dry weather left the roads inches deep in soft dust and the temperature 106 degrees in the shade.

The monsoon was a different matter, starting with seven days of regular afternoon duststorms that turned into a two-hour downpour at about four o'clock. All that time it grew hotter and more sultry. Then the monsoon rains began and went on for weeks, day in, day out, sometimes pouring, sometimes drizzling, but never stopping. Everything one touched oozed mud. Within two days every trodden surface was a morass, the roads developed deeper and deeper ruts and ridges of thick glutinous mud. Moving about in camp was a slithery, hazardous business, involving many falls, so that a man returning to hut or tent found a couple of inches of filthy mud on his boots and an inch of it coated on the seat of his shorts.[5] Men going barefoot, as they often had to do, tore their feet on the bamboo spikes that they could no longer see. They worked in the rain, they ate in the rain, and the mud that was everywhere even got into the food.[6] They came back in the rain to leaking tents and soaked bedding, where their kit, carefully placed that morning in a dry spot under the uncertain protection of a bit of sticky ground sheet or gas-cape, was by now at least partially wet. There was no chance for anything ever to get really dry.[7] And when the monsoon ended at last, it left behind great pools of stagnant water. Then the sun came out in all its scorching and pitiless heat and the beautiful nights returned with soft skies full of brilliant stars.[8] Such days increased the general load of misery: such nights underlined it.

The prisoners' clothes, the uniforms in which they had surrendered, sooner or later fell to pieces. A number of men managed to keep a more or less presentable pair of shorts which were worn only on special occasions (such as the Memorial Service), but for everyday wear practically everyone was dressed, if one can call it that, in the single garment known as a Jap Happy, which was really just a loincloth. A rectangular piece of cheap cotton with a tape at one end, it was tied around the waist with the cloth at the back, and this was then brought forward between the legs and tucked into the tape at the waist so that a small flap hung over the front, and that was that.

On the journey north along the course of the river, the average soldier's total equipment was probably the Jap Happy and a pair of patched shorts, a pair of boots that let the water in, and an old hat, together with a mess tin and spoon (or what the Australians called their "eating-irons"[9]), a water bottle with an unsatisfactory old cork, a ground sheet that had long since lost its proofing and was now not only leaky and sticky but smelly, a couple of sacks or an old blanket for bedding, and perhaps a share in a mosquito-net or a bit of one. Many had much less.[10]

The officers might be as badly off as the men, or they might have an old valise to carry their stuff in; one small haversack that went up the Kwai is still doing its duty, carrying the books of the owner's schoolboy son.[11] The officers might have a knife, an old wide-brimmed hat, one good and one bad shirt; one good and one bad pair of shorts; there might, too, be an old pair of darned grey socks. When the socks wore out there were never any more. When the boots wore out, men went barefoot unless the Japanese made an issue of cheap rubber boots which they sometimes did, or somebody made a pair of clumsy wooden sandals known as "clompers." [12] In every camp, sooner or later, someone made clompers, and very helpful they were. Apart from these few garments, and the identity discs that somehow or other no one ever lost, nothing was normally worn. There were however odd and touching variants. On St George's Day the prisoners who were Northumberlands managed to find white and red jungle flowers to stick in their hats because their regimental tradition puts up red and white roses on that day.[13] But taken as a whole, in their patchy rags inadequately covering their bones (every man had lost anything up to a third of his normal weight) and skin pitted with bites and sores and burnt by the sun, no army was ever more uniform.

2

Climate is closely linked to food, and food to disease. Inevitably food, or the lack of it, was a constant preoccupation among the prisoners. Their diet was basically rice. Major Peacock calculated that each of them had about eight hundred pounds of it over three and a half years, which works out at approximately nineteen pounds a month or a fraction over half a pound a day.[14] There were very tiny amounts of salted fish, pork, or buffalo: Mr Peters says that the Bedfordshires had one pig every third day for about fifteen hundred men.[15] There were a few vegetables including tapioca root, Chinese cabbage, sweet potatoes and pumpkins. From time to time duck eggs, peanuts, and pig oil were obtainable from the natives. There was little sugar, and the tea was weak, one tablespoonful often providing drinks for thirty men. The prisoners did the cooking. For most of them the only cooking they knew was the delightful experience of letting the sausages fall into the fire on picnics, yet, after intervals during which they learnt how to use the available food to the best advantage, they grew highly skilled. They developed such refinements as a kind of porridge made from polished rice husks and a sort of bread from ground rice and soya beans, prepared with the aid of improvised grindstones. The rice set aside for the prisoners was mostly of poor quality, broken-grained and proportionately low in value. The Dutch prisoners, most of whom were not new to the Far East, were very good at finding herbs and plants that they said contained vitamins; the Australians were particularly successful when it came to finding extra meat, especially buffalo, with which to supplement the diet.

It has already been said that whenever a party of prisoners stayed any length of time in one place they would start a vegetable garden which often resulted in quite a flourishing crop. They also kept hens and ducks if they got the chance. They traded the little money and some of the few valuables they had with Siamese or Chinese vendors who appeared daily at all but the most remote camps. Eggs, fish, fruit—particularly papayas, limes, tangerines and bananas that were either small and golden or large and purple—were among the foods they were able to buy. At Chungkai, where there were a lot of natives, these traders set up stalls, one of which was called Selfridge's by the troops because everything on it was labelled and priced in English. At Wun Lun they found curry sold by the ladle and a kind of macaroni-egg-onion dish called Ma Mee by the plateful, also a kind of sticky white jelly that the soldiers appropriately called "glop." They could buy Ma Mee at most markets, also little Siamese pancakes eaten with sugar and lime.

But there were never enough of these things, and there were long stretches of weeks and months in the more isolated camps higher up the river when the only food available was the everlasting rice, boiled into pap porridge with or without soya beans or fried and served as "nasi goreng" (the Malay name which was of course converted to "Nazi Goering" by the troops). They had grey wet stodgy rice with a few peanuts in it and, in the evenings, the notorious Jungle Stew and rice: a diet neatly described by Lieutenant Coast as a ghastly programme.[16] He also reported that in one Dutch camp in Burma during a lean period twenty-six dogs went into the pot. Men in all areas went out into the jungle at night to try to catch roosting jungle-fowl. There was a regular menu for fat, thin, cooked or curried rats.[17] At other times men found themselves eating snakes, vultures, iguanas and lizards. Mr Braddon, for the information of what he calls the shrinking reader, said that dog tastes like rather coarse beef, cat like rabbit, only better, snake like gritty chicken mixed with fish, and snails like bits of tyre, though he admitted these last were "Changi-style."[18] The men brought in what looked like edible plants from the jungle, and here the Dutch

Eurasians were invaluable in educating the rest as to what was poison-
ous and what was safe.

The prisoner-cooks were often ingenious and made bold experi-
ments. One of them invented a Christmas pudding of boiled rice fermented with limes, bananas and palm sugar and then steamed. Captain
Gordon found it not quite like anything he had tasted before—but
delicious.[19] They mixed lime juice and palm sugar with home-brewed
alcohol to provide drinks for "cocktail parties"; [20] the Siamese version
of vodka, a liquid called lao, was treated with sugar, lime and eggs, and
was then milder and nicer than a White Lady.[21] Of course such drinks
as these were rare treats; far more common was the river water poured
through disinfectant during the cholera scares so that it tasted like the
chlorinated water of a swimming pool. Sometimes there were a few
tins of condensed milk to be had, or a pot of Marmite. One cook
whipped up a blend of bananas, duck eggs and lime juice and poured
it over a bowl of rice—"a tasty dish." [22]

But there was never enough. The men were always hungry and so,
as Sergeant Harrison discovered at Hintok, were the Japanese who
received poor rations and were just as hungry as the rest.[23] Mr Audric
found that everywhere food supplies were often irregular: the river
in flood held up the barges, the roads (where they existed) were all too
frequently impassable. The Japanese were often unable to keep the
rations up to the ungenerous amount authorised by their own High
Command, though opinions vary about how hard they tried. And they
invariably appropriated any Red Cross food parcels or medical supplies, few as there were of these that got through.[24] The men tried to
steal these and often succeeded. Mr Braddon, swollen and dropsical
with beri-beri, stole a bottle of Vitamin B tablets from a Japanese
officer's haversack, ate the lot during the night, and two days later
retreated for a lengthy stay in the camp latrines while the accumulated
liquid poured out of him, leaving him after two further days weighing
eighty-one pounds and delighted.[25]

Every now and then something occurred to add variety to their
lives. There was for instance the Japanese fear of a wild baboon that
danced and screamed in the trees. The guards took the extraordinary
step of giving rifles to some prisoners and telling them to shoot it. For
several days the baboon was carefully missed while a small deer and
a few birds found their way into the cooking pots. Near Hintok the men
discovered an enormous area full of wild tobacco plants, which kept
them in smokes for months.[26] This was important because, after food,

tobacco was the prisoners' main preoccupation. From start to finish those who smoked with any regularity spent a lot of time and effort in finding cigarettes, the heavier smokers working the hardest at it, and they took hair-raising risks to buy tobacco, or to steal it from the Japanese. In lean times they substituted anything that faintly resembled it —tea leaves, rope, dried hibiscus leaves—and traded all kinds of valuables for it, clothes or presentation watches, and even the most precious souvenirs of home.[27]

3

All accounts underline the Japanese fear of wild animals, and emphasize how very few were seen. Some prisoners were actually disappointed at spending all this time in tiger country without seeing one. Several people reported seeing a tiger's pug marks but never saw one of those glorious creatures in its natural surroundings. There were rumours from time to time of guards being carried off by them, but as a guard was occasionally killed by a prisoner these stories may have been part of the essential cover-up. One officer above Rin Tin saw a panther.[28] There were monkeys in plenty, mostly baboons and gibbons, but these were more often heard than seen. There were, rarely, snakes. One officer killed a brown snake with a bamboo stick, discovering afterwards to his delight that it was an eleven foot eight inch hamadryad, which was promptly made into steaks in the cookhouse.[29] We have already seen how, if a man could find a small dead snake, he could introduce it into the stores and create a bogus panic during which a little profitable thieving might take place. Sometimes scorpions and lizards were seen, and everywhere along the river there were frogs. The croaking of the frogs during the rains made so much noise that the men sometimes had to shout in order to make themselves heard. There were plenty of birds, including mynahs, and beautiful flights of white egrets that skimmed up the river at sundown.[30] And there was the Phantom Dog.

The Phantom Dog went right up the Kwai and back, possibly several times, the whole length of the line. It had many different masters, sometimes more than one in separate places at the same time. It was exactly what its name implies, an imaginary dog (and of course a wonderfully shaggy one) about which the prisoners put on superbly convincing acts which greatly puzzled the guards, calling it to heel, offering it food, making it sit up and beg—all the correct dog stuff.

It helped morale considerably and was found to have survived the war, for it "reappeared" in Rangoon and Singapore among prisoners waiting for repatriation after the Japanese surrender.[31]

But of all animal life, that of which the prisoners were most aware —more than of the elephants, the buffalo or the sought-after deer, more than of the noisy monkeys or the dreaded snake—was the multi-million-strong force of insects and all the disease and discomfort that they brought. The noisiest were the most harmless—the cicadas and grasshoppers. But there were all the others too—flies, ants, midges, mosquitoes, lice, bugs. In clouds, in swarms, in armies, day and night without pause.

4

"The causes of death and sickness," writes Major Peacock simply, "were starvation, climate, hardship, accidents, occasionally personal violence, neglect, poor physique, despair, neurosis, and disease."[32] The diseases included: malaria in all its forms, recurrent fevers, dysentery, cholera, scurvy, pellagra, beri-beri, sleeping sickness, hookworm, ringworm, jungle ulcers and abscesses and general toxemia. The fatal casualties of all troops concerned totalled more than a third. Nearly every prisoner had some sickness, many had several bouts, and because of the poor diet every man lost weight (and consequently resistance) to an alarming degree. They were always crowded together, so that contagion was inescapable. Washing was difficult, as water was short, and in some areas bathing in the river was allowed only rarely. The dirt encouraged further swarms of flies, as it was hard to keep eating utensils clean and in the damp heat remnants of previous meals quickly went bad. Prisoners became vermin-ridden, an ordeal in itself. The river-water held the fearful risk of cholera unless every drop was boiled. Resistance was low so that the will to live was low too: sick prisoners often "infinitely preferred to lie down and die," for "death was so much easier."[33] Most of the troops were young, when appetites are heartiest.

Minor injuries and illnesses had a much more severe effect than they would have had in a less extreme climate among better-nourished people. For example, everyone sooner or later stubbed a toe against one of the bamboo stumps that stuck up through the floors of the huts and along the paths, and this minor injury could cripple a man for days.[34] Everyone got ulcers. These were excruciatingly painful and yet they started from so ordinary a beginning, a scratch one hardly noticed at the time. But the bamboo scratch went deeper than it seemed and next day showed the slight beginning of a sore. The sore would be fingered absent-mindedly, and the following morning there would appear an open ulcer half an inch across. This was never enough to report sick with, though the medical orderly might provide a wad of disinfectant held in place by a strip of rag. The next day the ulcer would be double that size and two days later half as big again: an open sore with a sup-purating red and yellow centre, like a carbuncle, that made standing up and walking acutely painful. Too much exertion produced a hole as big as a tennis ball and might even lead to eventual amputation.[35] The ulcers had to be scooped, which was agonising, and they smelt re-volting, thus adding to the wretchedness of the hospital huts and turning the stomachs of the men who tried to dress them.

The Japanese were callous towards their own sick so it was hardly to be expected that they would treat the enemy any better. One courteous and civilised lieutenant who acted as interpreter was con-stantly unable to produce any quinine but lent Mr Braddon two books, *Bushido or Japanese Chivalry* and *The Japanese Art of Arranging Flow-ers*.[36] In their frantic hurry to finish the railway, the Japanese tried to make the sick prisoners work. When they belatedly realised that the severely ill could not work, they simply cut down their rations, on the grounds that the sooner they died the better and there was little enough to go round.

One can only get a faint idea of what the prisoners experienced as they went in and out of the hospital huts, but for the squeamish this is more than enough. The few doctors among them worked heroically in impossible conditions. They had, for instance, no means of treating diphtheria. When it occurred they had to let it run its course, the "treatment" being simply to keep the patient lying flat on his back for two or three weeks, moving as little as possible and seeing no visitors, so that the strain on the heart would be reduced to a minimum and the poison could work itself out of the system. If there was any to spare, the patient had serum from a recovered patient. The men lying on the bamboo slats were plagued by lice so that they lay scratching, cursing and sweating; they were plagued also by bed bugs that when squashed smelt of bad burnt almonds. Unable to relax, unable to leave the sleep-ing platforms to relieve themselves, they sank into helpless misery.[37]

But the most dreaded disease of all was cholera. Starting up-country, it worked its way down the river: it "ran among us like a crazy woman, striking here and there in a fickle, erratic, chartless pattern," according to Sergeant Harrison.[38] Since everybody had dysentery, it was particularly difficult to diagnose cholera, which shares some of the same symptoms, and many men suffered periods of dreadful anxiety when the diagnosis was in doubt. Cholera was one illness the Japanese took seriously: knowing how quick, horrible and fatal it was, everyone feared it and all sorts of precautions were taken. The river was put out of bounds, food was covered with leaves, and, hungry as they were, the men were persuaded to throw away any scrap of food a fly had settled on. Spoons and knives were dipped in boiling water before meals, and drinking water was strained through disinfectant.[39] Some vaccine came to the camps, but not enough: there was about enough saline to treat one man in ten. The bodies of cholera victims were usually burned, a horrid process during which the corpses moved as the burning muscles contracted, but among the Tamil people it was the custom to bury them. Cholera struck the Tamils with peculiar violence. Great numbers of them were wiped out, and it was up to the nearest white survivors to go and dispose of their dead in quicklime pits. This was a frightening and horrible task which the guards enforced upon the prisoners.[40]

Incredibly, amid the chaotic conditions of life on the Kwai, surgical operations were carried out. They were mostly amputations, performed, as often as not, with a sterilized saw which was then sterilized again before being sent back to cut up a joint of meat in the cookhouse. Lieutenant Crawford had to help with an amputation once and only just avoided passing out under the combined assaults of weakness, nausea, and whiffs of chloroform.[41] Sergeant Harrison, however, underwent an emergency appendectomy which was a complete success,[42] and Major Peacock later set up a highly competent dental practice in which he treated Japanese as well as British and Australians. He quickly realised that if he accepted Japanese patients he could obtain anaesthetics and medical supplies that could be used for the prisoners' benefit. There were a few—never enough—dentists on the Kwai: they double-distilled rice spirit to produce alcohol, squeezed clove flower buds to produce oil of cloves, and used kapok for cotton wool.[43] If there was no dental drill, and usually there was not, a substitute was made out of a small hammer and a .303 bullet sharpened to a fine point, the hammer being tapped upon the bullet to flake or chip away the decayed enamel, "a jarring business." [44] There were, of course, no drugs to relieve the pain.

The prisoners, half-starved, filthy with parasites and disease and badly frightened of worse to come, worked till they dropped. The Japanese were cruel masters. It is necessary to stress again the fundamental difference in attitude, going right back to the medieval period. European knights saw no shame in capture under honourable conditions, indeed it could sometimes enhance their reputation, as Richard I found "when he blundered into the custody of the German Emperor Henry VI" during his journey back from the Third Crusade. Any captured European knight expected to be treated with courtesy and chivalry, and his vassals raised his ransom as a matter of course, the captor relying on this as one of the fringe benefits of the time. The Japanese knight who obeyed the Samurai code, however, was taught that capture or surrender were contemptible. They were taught to prefer death to dishonour, self-inflicted death if need be, as if taken alive "they could only anticipate brutal treatment." [45]

Mr Audric found that the working parties struggled under "the most appalling conditions of hardship and brutality." Beatings were frequent and often excessive.[46] Mr Peters said that for a minor offence there was a slap on the face, for something more serious a man was stood out in the sun, and a beating was more serious still "though happily none of our Battalion suffered this punishment." [47] At first a few of the more quick-tempered or resilient prisoners struck back, but "the reprisals were so savage that they found it better to submit, although this was often very difficult." [48] The safest thing to do, as they found out through trial and error, was to stand as still as possible, with the chin pulled well in, and try to take the blow without flinching—if they could do that there might be only the one. It was also a good idea to remove glasses and false teeth. The Japanese appear to have been quite unpredictable in their reactions, a blaze of anger was quite frequently followed by a relatively humane comment or the gift of a cigarette, and what would cause a towering rage one day would produce an indifferent shrug the next. Those who had direct dealings with them, wrote Major Peacock, "found them interesting, neurotic, imponderable, and frequently crazy." [49]

Captain Gordon agreed with this. He also pointed out that during the years of their military success and its slow decline the Japanese violated every civilised code, murdering their prisoners at first hand by bayoneting, shooting, drowning, beating or decapitation, and at second hand by denial of medical care, torture, starvation, and work beyond the limit of human endurance. He refers to the overall statistics, the four per cent death rate among prisoners held by the Germans and Italians as compared with the twenty-seven per cent scored by the Japanese, adding that on the Kwai the percentage was much higher. He summed up the railway as "that human rubbish-heap" where the Japanese cared nothing for human life. Just how cheap they held it is illustrated in the true story of one Japanese engineer who carefully explained to two prisoners how to make a dynamite charge and while they were still working on it set off the charge and blew them to pieces.[50]

There were plenty of chilling incidents elsewhere. There was, for instance, one guard at Changi, known as the Ice Cream Man because he always wore a white coat (he got to know of this in time and then the Australians called him Mr Peters and the British called him Mr Lyons which amounted to the same thing) who beat six or seven prisoners unconscious every day for not saluting him with the proper greeting.[51] There were also the tortures of the Kempei-Tai (the secret police) when they suspected that someone had a secret radio, but it was on the Kwai that health and morale were lowest and that punishments seemed worst.

Sergeant Harrison commented that the prisoners managed to carry loads, lift weights and perform feats of endurance that would never have been possible if they had not been quite literally forced into doing them. Each day was "a nightmare of slavery and heat" at the end of which they were always sure to return to camp "bone-weary, bruised, blood-smeared, and dreading the next day." Quite often a prisoner was hit or beaten for no better reason than that the Japanese guard concerned had been slapped or kicked by his superior officer and wanted to restore "face." Some would hit out with any object to hand, but others carried their "trade mark" with them: a pick handle, a bamboo rod, a length of fencing wire or barbed wire nailed to a stick. One guard carried a saw, with which he would strike, invariably at the head and face, with the flat of it "in his more benevolent moments," but "when irritated he would use the blunt edge, or, if highly offended, the cutting edge." On one occasion a Japanese guard knocked an Australian prisoner unconscious for not bowing deeply enough when passing, and when a complaint was made, the Japanese commandant, regardless of the fact that the Australian still lay in front of him on the ground, stated calmly, "No one has been struck." [52] Another guard, when an English soldier collapsed and fell down the embankment where they were shooting rubble, pulled the lever and let a ton of stones fall on the prisoner, burying him. Some of the other prisoners whose morale was at its lowest were heard to murmur: "Half his luck," though others more stoutly commented: "Your turn'll come." [53]

Punishment for work considered too slow normally included placing a man to face the sun and making him hold a rock or crowbar above his head at arm's length. This was also used for "setting an example." Face-slapping was constant, but this was standard practice in the Japanese Army. A Lieutenant Kumi, explaining to Sergeant Harrison: "Nippon slaps, but Nippon also get slapped," told him how, when he was doing his training, he made a mistake when sending a signal to a group of men on top of a mountain. As a punishment he had had to run up the mountain, where every man of the group slapped him, and then run down again to be slapped by his officer. He said that this was perfectly fair because "in war, my mistake costs their life." [54] A Japanese lance-corporal told Major Peacock that he had been beaten for not cleaning his boots properly. The boots, it was explained to him, were really the Emperor's boots and after being beaten he had to take them in his mouth like a dog and crawl fifty yards fifty times before bowing and apologising to every other recruit in turn, saying that he was sorry not to have taken better care of the Emperor's boots. [55]

It may have helped the prisoners to know that everybody got much the same treatment, including the Japanese soldiers themselves. Perhaps it was this spirit that made Sergeant Harrison say that if he ever had to fight in a war again he would like his fellow Australians around him, and a Japanese battalion on his left and a Japanese battalion on his right: "then perhaps even I might stand firm and give some cheek." [56] No wonder Miss Stevie Smith, in a conversation with a soldier, quoted him as saying: *

> My soldier from the wars returning said: "Crumbs, what with the Japs, the jungle, the animals and the Beds and Herts (that was his regiment), crumbs, it was indeed a circus."

5

It is interesting in the light of these accounts to find a few comments written by a Japanese. Mr Mamoru Shigemitsu, who was Foreign Minister from April 1943 to the end of the war, has a section on prisoners of war in his book, *Japan and Her Destiny*. He wrote that it was "terrible to think" that after the war "many wrongful acts involving inhumanity were brought to light"; that "no one could be more concerned

* Stevie Smith, *The Holiday*, London, 1949, p. 55.

than a diplomat that our treatment of prisoners and enemy aliens should leave no cause for complaint"; that he was "filled with anguish" at the disclosures made to him. He pointed out that "everything was under the control of the Army" so that "no one else could interfere," yet he did approach the Emperor, telling him that the Army Chiefs had said that "treatment was in accordance with the laws but that they had no objection to making careful investigation." The Emperor replied that "if there was any truth in the reports, it was a serious breach of duty and reflected shame on Japan." Deeply concerned, he issued an order instructing the Army "to put the matter right." Mr Shigemitsu said that it was within his knowledge that the order was duly issued and "had an excellent effect."

He also wrote that he received many letters asking why enemy prisoners "guilty of inhuman conduct" in burning people and their homes in air raids should "receive favoured treatment"—he does not specify what kind. And, in commenting on the war crimes trials, he said that these "reflected the characteristics of each nation," that "some indeed were medieval in their outlook" and that heavy sentences were pronounced on the basis of "written statements by prisoners and detained persons, which were accepted as they stood without further question, no opportunity of cross-examination being afforded."

He does refer to a number of examples of arrested guards and officers being favourably commented on by former prisoners who had considered them relatively kindly. All the same the idea of a court cross-examination of those responsible opens up a fascinating, if profitless, field of speculation.[57]

One thinks of H Force, for example: the three thousand men who came up from Changi in 1943 and spent the shortest but most horrific time of all the prisoners on the Kwai. Captain Burton was in H Force and said that they were faced with the worst of it. Compared to them the rest seemed hardened veterans who had learned how to survive.[58] Their casualty figures were not as "ghastly" as those of F Force, which had six out of ten, but were "not far behind." [59] Between these prisoners struggling to cling to life on the river and Mr Shigemitsu wrestling with his code and his scruples in his office, there stretches a bottomless gulf.

CHAPTER XII

The Question of Language

I

ONE of the most interesting aspects of the whole subject of this commentary is the problem of language.

An additional complication was added to all troop movements, large or small, by the apparent inability of the Japanese guards to count correctly. Time was wasted before starting a journey, before settling into camp, even before the daily issue of tools at the work sites, while groups of prisoners were counted and re-counted, each process resulting in a different total, with plenty of accompanying irritation for all concerned. Sooner or later the prisoners had to count their own men, and they had to learn to do it in Japanese.

Sergeant Harrison was taught to count "ichi, ni, san, chi" (one, two, three, four) and so on, but on several occasions he was slapped for no apparent reason after saying the word "chi"; in time he found out that "chi" also means death and that many Japanese believed it unlucky. The acceptable alternative was "yong." [1] This was one of many linguistic hazards.

The Japanese employed Koreans as guards as the war went on and the Japanese themselves were needed for combat duty. The Koreans proved even more capricious. Some Koreans were guileless and simpleminded. Some were plain brutal. Others, anxious for their own safety, tried to outdo the Japanese in every way they could in order to win their favour. The Koreans also brought a different language and therefore further problems of communication.

When communication is essential, however, a way will be found, however difficult. Consider the problem for a moment. Suppose you are a Japanese soldier, possibly a very ordinary, not particularly articulate one. Suddenly you are put in charge of a group of prisoners. To be sure, they are scum, the lowest of the low, mere cattle to be herded and worked, and they have absolutely no grasp of the principles of "right thinking." But the Emperor has put you in charge of them and, for the satisfaction of the Emperor, the honour of the Imperial Japanese Army of which you are a part, and the glory and success that are destined to crown the South-East Asia Co-Prosperity Sphere, your duties have to be properly carried out. So you must give them orders. They are fools, of course, but they cannot be held too culpable for not speaking Japanese: after all, you cannot speak English. So where do you begin?

Look now at the other side of the coin. Suppose you are a British soldier, also a very ordinary one. Through no fault of your own, you have fallen into the hands of these ape-like creatures, whose sole object appears to be to work you to death, as horses used to be worked by cruel and unscrupulous drivers. They also seem perfectly unpredictable, you never know what will prove, if not satisfactory at least acceptable, nor what will provoke them to a wild display of fury and the consequent ill-treatment. So you need to have some idea of what they are saying to you. They are shockers, of course, but be fair. You speak no Japanese —why should you? They speak no English—a deplorable oversight, but there it is. So where do you begin?

Out of this necessity, one of the strangest examples of lingua franca ever developed evolved between these two utterly different peoples. The Japanese seem to have based their part on two guiding principles: firstly using a few Japanese words the purport of which was unmistakable, of which perhaps the most frequently used was "Kura"—"the rudest," Colonel van der Post has written, "of the many rude ways in Japanese of saying: 'Come here, you!' ";[2] and secondly using a few English words, pronounced as best they could—usually with a vowel added at the end—of which the most frequently used was the notorious and self-explanatory "Speedo, speedo." On this modest foundation arose a really quite impressive linguistic edifice, though it developed slowly at first. Here are a few progressively selected examples.

First an absolutely vital one: "Benjo-ka, O.K.?" (Please may I go to the lavatory?) was followed by Japanese commands and criticisms, such as "speedo," "kirray" (salute), "bugerro" (fool), "damme damme" (no good), "mishi" (rice lunch, especially at midday on the job), and then extended to more complex instructions and comments such as: "All men go campu," "one man one," "Engrishu soldier no goodera," and "campu damme damme, worku finish all men bang bang" (camp very bad, when the work is finished you will all be shot). Major Peacock's name gave some trouble, but whereas most Japanese called him "Peacocko," one interpreter introduced him to Sergeant Yotanné as "Pekoe"; as this would not do, the Major drew a sketch of a peacock, with its tail spread, in the dust of the earth floor, and Yotanné, delighted, exclaimed "Kujacku!" which is Japanese for peacock. From then on he called Major Peacock "Kujacku shosa"—"shosa" means major.[3] "Shoko" means officer, "gunso" means sergeant. A young Japanese officer asked Sergeant Harrison: "You shoko-ka?" At the reply: "No, gunso," the officer went on: "All men worku?" They clearly weren't as they were playing cards at the time; a fellow Australian quick-wittedly said: "Hei. All men number one joto workers. Nippon presento yasumé." (Because we are such good workers Nippon has given us a holiday.) And the officer "accepted this outrageous statement with a pleased smile and a hiss of "Ah, so-ka." [4]

One charming anecdote of Sergeant Harrison's concerns a One Star Private named Morimoto who was talking about the Emperor's family to a man called Bill Stafford, a former rubber planter who had been a very fine skier before the war. Mr Stafford, a long, bony man in tattered shorts, with a "scruffy, unshaven face" and ringworm and tinea sores all over his skin, had been sheltering from the sun in one of the graves the party was digging. He said casually, "Ah, yes, Prince Chichibu. A charming fellow, simply charming." Morimoto gazed at him and "his eyes grew like saucers in his round, simple face," as he answered in an awed voice, "You speaku Chichibu-san-ka?" to which Mr Stafford was inspired to reply: "Hei. Prince Chichibu and I zoom zoom Switzerland." As a result, for the rest of the day "Bill was treated as an honoured guest and sat smirking under the shade of a tree while Morimoto brought him bananas and iced tea and while we commoners sweated and dug graves." [5]

In due course the conversational point was reached where Major Peacock was able to understand a guard called Hadimoto in the following "appalling mixture of pidgin English, Malay and Japanese which we used for communication":

Hadimoto speakie Engeris sojer no O.K.—Hadimoto speakie master Engeris sojer O.K. Hadimoto pintu sojer no O.K. Master speakie sojer no worko—sojer no worko muchee trouble Hadimoto Nippon shoko. Very good Hadimoto speakie master alla O.K.

This, as Major Peacock and others were soon to understand, meant: "Hadimoto should not speak to soldiers but speak to the English officer. Hadimoto should not hit English soldiers or the officer will tell them not to work, then Hadimoto will be in trouble with the Japanese officer. If Hadimoto behaves himself the officer will tell the soldiers to behave." [6]

This curious language was purely oral, consequently no two men use precisely the same spellings. For example Captain Burton refers to the Japanese guards on the march coming along the column and shouting: "All men stopka. Yasumé—campo very goodega." [7] Lieutenant Coast wrotes "yasmé," Sergeant Harrison writes "campu," Major Peacock writes "good-t na." To take another example, Colonel van der Post represents the Japanese pronunciation of the name "Lawrence" as "Rorensu" and, in a famous line, quotes the Japanese officer Hara as asking him: "Do you know Fazeru Kurisumasu (Father Christmas)?" [8]

And in a remarkable conversation between Major Peacock and Sergeant-Major Hibiju the following exchange occurs. The Sergeant-Major suffered from frequent hangovers, but it was a polite and convenient fiction between him and the Major that he had an attack of malaria each morning instead of two bottles of Thai whisky every evening, so each day opened with courteous inquiries from the Major about Hibiju's malaria. One morning Hibiju, with a damp towel round his head like Sydney Carton, murmured: "I sick man, malaria no good-t na. Big sick." He waved his hand feebly and then put it back on his forehead apparently struck by a sudden thought and said: "Peacocko, Takanun go. O.K. speedo go."

The Major said: "Me, do you mean? When go?"

The reply was: "Speedo."

"Now do you mean?" asked the Major.

The reply this time was: "Speedo, speedo—ricey five day, five day come back, bring dollar."

The Major decided that this meant he had to collect pay from somewhere, Takanun probably. He said: "But look here, I can't go now, I must have half an hour to get some kit."

Hibiju became irritable. Tightening the towel on his head he screamed: "Speedo, speedo, pom pom starto." [9]

A "pom pom" was a motor-boat, and the result of all this was a trip up the river lasting several days during which the Major enjoyed good meals and the company of the friendly Chang family and from which he returned with the pay and a lot of pairs of thin blue cotton shorts which wore out in a fortnight; but at least it was delightful for them to put on something new and clean. [10]

There was also Three Star Private Omitz who explained his frequent bursts of filthy temper by saying somewhat disarmingly: "Major, you think I very bad man. I no bad. I kickly wex." After puzzling over this Major Peacock, in an inspired flash, realised that he meant "quickly vexed," and recommended him to count twenty (in Japanese) next time he felt his temper getting the better of him.[11]

Occasionally the Major, as a veteran of World War I, found his own language becoming exotically complicated by a throwback to earlier linguistic customs, as when he shouted at a drunken Japanese: "Hashimoto, you're drunk, beaucoup zig-zag." To this lapse into 1914-18 slang Hashimoto with a mournful shake of his head replied, understandably in the circumstances, "Major no bloody good-t na no flend." [12]

It is faintly surprising to hear the word "bloody" emerging in that context. Apparently the Japanese have no swear words in their language and those who understood the English swear words disapproved of them. They had plenty of opportunity to disapprove, prisoner of war language being, as Lieutenant Coast pointed out, the foulest in the world. But the Japanese and Koreans who had little or no English somehow managed to pick up just these expressions, and they would thoughtlessly bring out some quite juicy examples while talking with prisoners.[13] The universal bad language became so common that in time it took on almost an affectionate tone: years later a former subaltern murmured one of the more overworked expletives reflectively in the middle of a perfectly ordinary speech, and went on in the same gentle voice: "They used to say that a lot on the railway—rather nice, really."

As if by a sort of reciprocal arrangement, the prisoners incorporated Japanese words or the pidgin phrases into their own conversations. Sergeant Harrison records two agreeable instances of this. One exchange took place when he went to the dentist and had the hammer and bullet treatment; at the end of this he ironically thanked the dentist with "Arigato, Captain-san," to which the dentist, "a tall English officer," answered in a pleasant tone: "And balls to you too, Sergeant." The other incident concerned an Australian called Con Chandler who had trouble with a heavy sack of peas that fell and winded him. Fighting for breath, he let out a stream of bad language, suggesting what the blank Japanese blank Empire could blank well do with the blank peas. All this commotion brought the guards running up, but as this sort of thing appealed to their sense of humour all they did was to tell Mr Chandler he was "a baby soldier" (a young and inexperienced one), and give him a tap on the head "chidingly" for his language and a Kinchi cigarette "to soothe his wounded pride." Coming up a few minutes later, Sergeant Harrison asked him: "Nippon presento baby soldier cigarette-ka?" to which he was hardly surprised to receive the answer: "You can get stuffed." [14]

The word "presento" was very useful: it could mean "That was a present to me," or "May I have that?" or "Will you give me that?" The cheap Japanese cigarettes were referred to by the troops as "Tojo presentos."

The use of the pidgin could occasionally lead to unexpected difficulties. In one of the camp revues there was a scene that got everybody in trouble because it showed a prisoner who had come home and forgotten what ordinary life was like. Wanting to "wash his hands" he picked some leaves off the "aspidistra," put them in his pocket and left the room. Then he asked for a banana by using the Malay word "pisang" which caused his "wife" to pass him, "reluctantly," the empty fruit bowl. The way the words were used made the audience roar with laughter and this infuriated the Japanese. Such words as "Kurrah!" "Buggairo," or "Benjo speedo!" were part of the daily vocabulary of prisoners and guards alike, but probably the Japanese were afraid that they were being laughed at. Whatever the reason, the piece was stopped with a curt "Pinish-ga!" [15]

"Once," recorded Sergeant Harrison, "a Japanese officer was told there was a 'short' in a vehicle's electrical system. 'Make all shorts longer!' he ordered." [16]

Coming back to basic essentials, one can apparently go a long way towards surmounting the language barrier in the Far East by using the phrases: O.K. (good); No O.K. (bad); and O.K.-ka? (all right?).

But perhaps the most delightful example of all is that of the reconnaissance aircraft, referred to by prisoners and the friendly guards as "Come look see go back speakie planes." [17]

It was not always plain sailing even when one had an interpreter to mediate between English and Japanese. Captain Gilchrist had an interview with Major-General Hamada at Chumpin on the day General MacArthur landed in Japan, and the interview was conducted through an interpreter, who suddenly caused Captain Gilchrist to do a double-take as he said without preamble: "The carp, very fine fish."

Captain Gilchrist nodded mechanically, then exclaimed *What?* and there was a pause before General Hamada spoke again; the interpreter explained: "In Japan, we the Japanese admire the carp, the honourable fish."

"You mean the carp, the fish? We are talking about a fish, you are sure?" Captain Gilchrist felt faint but pursuing.

"Yes," said the interpreter, "we agree, we the Japanese, the carp, the fish. The General, he speak the carp, the fish, the maximum."

Once again the floor seemed to slide from under Captain Gilchrist's feet. "My God, the carp, the maximum?"

Here General Hamada spoke again and the interpreter said: "Yes, the *old* maximum. The General speak the carp, the fish, the *old* maximum."

Captain Gilchrist murmured: "This is the end, the fish, the carp, the maximum . . ."

The interpreter set it right. "I commit faulty mistake. The General he speak the maxim."

"The carp, the fish. O.K., General, carry on." One can hear Captain Gilchrist's sigh of relief. It wasn't making much sense yet, but at least it was not completely crazy.

The General spoke again and the interpreter flourished up to his triumphant conclusion. "We the Japanese, we admire the carp, the honourable fish, because when caught for market, placed on block, the carp, the fish, he no longer struggle or bounce, he lie, he remain quiet, he submit, the carp, the fish."

Captain Gilchrist wrote afterwards: "I rather liked the way the persistent old General made his point at last, and I must say he stuck to it pretty well, the carp, the fish." [18] This too would be considered an example of "a very Japanese thought."

2

Like all closely knit groups of people the prisoners developed a jargon of their own, much of it incorporating general World War II slang (which was heavily flavoured by that most spectacular of armed services, the RAF), though a few examples are confined to the Singapore prisoners in general and the Kwai prisoners in particular.

Another example refers to perhaps the most dangerous thing that could happen: to become owner, or part-owner, of a canary. Those who did, and were discovered, were beheaded. A canary up the Kwai was a secret radio receiver. [19]

The prisoners referred to the camp hospital, or to part of it, as the

Death House, and to the detention or punishment room as the No Good House. Everything and everyone had nicknames and this included the guards. Some of the names were unprintable while others revealed a highly imaginative quality: the Undertaker, the Black Prince, the Mad Mongrel, Battlegong, Blue Sox, Tiger Skin, the Horse Doctor (who was a disagreeable Japanese medical officer), the Rat, the Frog, and Nattering Norman who was a cretin-like Japanese who could never stop mumbling.[20] One's personal group was one's "Kongsi"; the Malay expression "Tid'apa" was used to convey a shrug, a "can't be helped"; Siamese tobacco, which was "fierce," was called "Hags' Bush" or "Sikhs' Beard." The Dutch were frequently referred to as the "Gotverdommers."

One universal word was "doover," meaning a fried rissole or other fried rice mixture or "anything that wasn't rice or stew." Although Lieutenant Coast says that no one seems clear as to the origin of this word,[21] it has been suggested * that it is a corruption of "do for" in the sense "It'll do for today." In serving meals, those hoping for a second helping would queue up again, forming the "Leggie Queue" (from the word "lagi," Malay for "more"), and in the Officers' Battalion at one point there was a "Leggie Leggie Queue," for second left-overs. Quite a few officers would appear at every meal silently standing in this queue, eating their first helping as they waited, and watching the food containers to estimate their chances of picking up a few more scraps.[22] From this came the practice at times of taking regular turns for anything extra, hence the expression "the leggie number."

The Senior Officer's hut was known in every camp as The Imperial War Museum or "Snakes and Ladders." This odd expression developed from the universal use of the word "ladder" which had extended as follows. The saying: "Pull the ladder up, Jack, I'm all right" was compressed into "Ladders up!" which meant the same thing and was spoken in the same contexts. From that, "My ladder's up" meant: "I'm all right, I've got a cushy job." "Has he got a good ladder?" meant: "Has he found himself an easy job yet?" Everyone, of course, said "You've had it" when they meant "You've missed it," just as people did in England, and among the prisoners this usage, wildly developed, greatly puzzled the Dutchmen present, as well it might.[23]

* By Robert Druce.

3

Very little of all this was ever written down, except by prisoners who, like Lieutenant Coast, kept a diary. Even rarer are examples of English written by the Japanese. One quite celebrated example, however, is the following leaflet which was dropped in hundreds on the British troops before the surrender of Singapore. It was headed "Admonition," and reads as follows.

I have the honour of presenting you this admonition of peace from the standpoint of Nippon Samurai spirit.

Nippon Army, Navy and Air-Force have conquered the Phillippine Islands and Hong Kong and annihilated the British Extreme-Oriental Fleet in the Southern Sea. The command of the Pacific Ocean and the Indian Sea as well as the aviation power on the Western and Southern Asian Continent is now under the control of Nippon Force; India has risen in rebellion; Thai and Malay have been subjected to Nippon without having made any remarkable resistance. The war has been almost settled already and Malaya is under the Nippon's power.

Since the 18th century, Singapore has been the starting point of the development of your country and the important junction of the civilisations of West and East. Our Army cannot suffer, as well as you, to see this district be burnt to ashes by the war. Traditionally when Nippon is at war, when she takes her arms, she is always based upon the loyalty of breaking wrong and helping right and she does not and never aim at the conquest of other nations nor the extension of her territories. The war course of this time is, as you are well informed, originated from this loyalty.

We want to establish a new order and a zone of mutual prosperity in the East-Orient. You cannot deny at the bottom of your impartial heart that it is divine will and humanity to give happiness to the millions of the East-Orientals mourning under the exploitation and persecution. Consequently, the Nippon Army, basing upon this great loyalty, attack without reserve those who resist against them, but not only the innocent people but also the surrenderer to them will be treated kindly according to the Samuraism.

When I imagine the state of mind of you who have so well done your duty, isolated without any rescue and now surrounded by our Army, how much more could I not sincerely sympathize you. That is why I dare to advise you to make peace and to give you a friendly hand to co-operate for the settlement of the Oriental Peace. Many tens of thousands of wives and children of your officers and soldiers are heartily waiting in their native land for the coming home of their husbands and fathers and many hundred thousands of innocent people are also passionately wishing to evade the calamity of war.

I expect you do considerate upon the eternal honour of the British tradition and you be persuaded by my admonition. Upon my words we don't kill you, treat you as officers and soldiers if you come to us. But if you resist against us we will give you swords.

This document is a far cry from the language of persuasion developed since the war by the ad-men. Clearly compiled with the aid of a modestly-sized dictionary by somebody who thought the longer word the more impressive ("the British Extreme-Oriental Fleet" conjures up an almost irresistibly comic picture, a sort of mad amalgam of Lieutenant Pinkerton and The Mikado), it is a peculiar mixture of fact, half-truth, wishful thinking and downright lies, plus various phrases almost impossible to unravel. The writer has made only two spelling mistakes ("Phillippines" and "settlement") and his sentences are smoothly constructed. It was true that Hong Kong, Malaya, Siam and most of the Philippines were conquered or occupied, that Japan had command of the Pacific by sea and air and certainly wanted to establish a new order, as the use of Hitler's words implies. It was also true that the Siamese and the Malays had not for the most part put up much resistance. It obviously did seem to the Japanese, at that moment, that the war had been almost settled already. Millions of "East-Orientals" had indeed been exploited and persecuted, over a long period, and were tired of it. The soldiers' families (in most cases) did want them back, and "many hundred thousands of innocent people" were "passionately wishing to evade the calamity of war."

But Japan did not control the Indian Ocean, then or at any other time, and India had not (perhaps surprisingly) risen in rebellion. If Japan did "not and never aim at the conquest of other nations" then the Japanese had a peculiar way of showing it. All very well to say that the British troops wanted to go home, but what made anybody think that if they surrendered they would be instantly packed off to England in the first available ships? Too much need not be made of Japan's "breaking wrong and helping right" or promises of correct and kindly treatment "according to the Samuraism," as every nation goes to war with God on its side and faith in its own code. The whole of this "admonition" has a curiously simple, almost friendly tone: the word "honour" at beginning and end, the courteously phrased tributes to the beaten enemy "who have so well done your duty," and the stern short closing sentence (although the British were going to get the swords any way, as it turned out), all run counter to the popular opinion of the British generals at the time, who dismissed the Japanese as "gangsters." These sentences may be dishonest, reflecting an alien code, arousing heated feelings, but they are not the words of a gangster mentality. (Of course, the generals may have been hastily constructing suitable bits of propaganda, so one need not make too much of it.) The Japanese seem to have observed Churchill's own policy in his declaration of war which was meticulously phrased and of which he said disarmingly: "After all, when you have to kill a man it costs nothing to be polite." [24]

Another example of written English produced by a Japanese is the Order issued to all senior officer prisoners by the Japanese Commandant in mid-1943. Major Peacock was given a copy at Tarsao. The English in this one is much faultier. Describing it as the quaintest order he was ever presented with, he kept it as a souvenir.[25] It was typed on very flimsy paper, and one copy reads as follows, mistakes and all.

INSTRUCTIONS GIVEN TO P.O.W.S ON MY ASSUMING COMMAND
I have the pleasure to lead you on the charge of last stretch of Railway Construction Warden with the appointment of present post.

In examination of various reports, as well as the reult of Partial Camp inspection of the present conditions, am pleased to find that you are in general keeping discipline and working diligently, At the same time regret to find seriousness in health matter.

It is evident that there are various causes for inevitable for this end, but to my opinion due mainly to the fact for absence of firm belief as Japanese "health follows will" and "Cease only when enemy is completely annialated"

Those who fails to reach objective in charge by lack of health and or spirit, is considered in Japanese Army as most shameful deed "Devotion till death is good, yet still we have the spirit "Devotion to Imperial Cause even to the 7th turn in incarnation. The spirit that cannot come void by death

You are in act of charge in colleague with Imperial Japanese Army.

You are expected to charge to the last stage of this work with good spirit by taking good care of your own health

Besides you are to remember that your welfare is guarranteed only by obedience to the order of Imperial Japanese Army

Imperial Japanese Army, will not be unfair to those who are honest and obey them, but protect such. You are to understand this fundamental Japanese spirit and carry out the task given you with perfect ease of mind under protection of Imperial Japanese Army.

Given in Kanchanaburi June 26th, 1943

COL SIJUO NAKAMURA
Commander of P.O.W.s Camp Thailand

This is a most illuminating document. The translator has made several spelling mistakes ("reult," "annialated," "guarranteed") and he appears to have thought the inverted comma could be used like a French accent, the full stop too perhaps. But he battles away with the unfamiliar phraseology, sprinting ahead gaily when a section can be repeated and conveying the well-known Japanese euphemism in the words "seriousness in health matter," which meant that prisoners could and did fall ill and drop dead right and left in the most inconvenient way. Through his carefully built paragraphs one sees Colonel Nakamura emerge as a conscientious officer, anxious to do well on assuming command, honestly believing that to serve Japan was a privilege and that the prisoners should have no trouble in persuading themselves that they had changed sides and were working for the Japanese cause. Also, in his opinion, one had only to be good in order to be healthy: an interesting link with the Christian idea that illness is sin, though in this case no account was taken of such details as malnutrition, disease, and despair. To such a man, the prisoners' state of mind was incomprehensible. Yet it is possible to see Colonel Nakamura as a man rather than a monster —a curiously naïve man, it is true, to have dictated and distributed such a letter. There is a Shakespearean flourish, too, in that phrase

"Given in Kanchanaburi": almost one would have expected him to refer to "our cousin of England."

There was nothing Shakespearean about the post cards issued to the prisoners to send home: these were bleak in the extreme. Printed in advance, headed IMPERIAL JAPANESE ARMY, they contained half a dozen lines which the senders could leave in or cross out, with one or two blank spaces where a few words could be inserted. Sometimes they had a space for the date. Some began: "I am interned in (blank)." Some, more pathetically, started: "Your mails and (blank) are received with thanks." Hardly any letters got through to the prisoners. On the very rare occasions when a bag of letters did come—the twenty-five word messages allowed through the Red Cross—there was an emotional scene in which those men who had received mail took it off to read quietly and often through tears, while those who had none retired equally quietly to struggle with their thoughts. Letters were shared around: Mr Braddon had one from his sister that created a wonderfully warm impression. It had taken sixteen months to reach him, and was very simple: "Dear Russ, Mum's puddings are still as lumpy as ever. Oodles of love from us all. Pat." He and his friends took ten minutes to read it.[26]

Some of their post cards carried the words "My health is excellent"; others kindly provided a choice: "My health is (good, usual, poor)." Every card had the line: "I am ill in hospital." It was pathetic to see prisoners who were ill delete the phrases about being in poor health or in hospital in order to spare their families additional anxiety. The cards also said: "I am working for pay/I am not working." Some said: "I am paid monthly salary." The endings were either: "My best regards to (blank), yours ever" or "Please see that (blank) is taken care, My love to you." There was a space for the signature.

These scrappy little cards took months to get to their destination and some never did that—one plane carrying such mail crashed in England and a heap of burnt cards was discovered in the wreckage, a few fragments of them still decipherable enough to send on. It must be emphasised that in any case there were only one or two issues of these cards over the three and a half years. The men's families cannot be blamed for feeling that their husbands, brothers, and sons had dropped out of human ken; certainly in England at the time they were hardly ever mentioned except in their own homes.

4

Not too surprisingly, the Far East sector of World War II inspired little poetry, compared for example with that written about the Air Force or the North African campaigns, both subjects being great stimulators of some extraordinarily uneven verse. Some prison-camp poems have found their way into the anthologies, but these were usually written in German prison-camps. The researcher, hopefully rummaging, will find a few poems that convey something of the atmosphere of the war in Asia, and the prisoners in particular, though not all were written with that area specifically in mind, let alone with these men. One poem, "Jasper, Marble and Khaki Drill" by Reginald Levy, is set in India among newly-arrived troops but still seems to have something to say concerning the men of Singapore, Malaya and Siam. It pictures the "incongruous fate" of the soldiers in their "khaki commonplace" among the brilliant colours, gaudy sunsets and strange music of the East, and ends with a thought that struck painfully into the consciousness of every prisoner who set eyes on a Siamese temple.

> *Mile End Road*
> *And Norwich, Camberwell, Glasgow and Brum*
> *Rubbernecking the Taj Mahal (bestowed*
> *By a prince on an unwilling people)*
> *Wishing it were our own church steeple.*[27]

There are several lines in "Poem after Victory" by John R. Townsend that are also appropriate. The theme of this poem is the weary acceptance by those still alive of the emotions they could not allow themselves to feel during the fighting: pity, grief, pain. The soul, "black and stagnant," just now "receiving and giving nothing," has to re-learn its gentler emotions. One finds the lines:

> *Now for some time will the prisoned words be calling*
> *Or the waves of feeling beat on the walls of the brain:*
> *For the storm is over . . .*

and the key phrases portray "the worn uncertain survivors" and the task of "counting his dead in the morning." [28]

In the same collection appears a poem called "Armistice" by John Lehmann. This could equally well have been called "Homecoming," as that is exactly what it represents: death has gone, hopes can be cherished once more, weapons discarded, one can dance and drink toasts, Birnam Wood has marched to ransom Dunsinane—and, with "sirens booming through the harbour air/And all the applauding windows opened wide," the words "like suns" of "reunion and reprieve," rung out on the "garland bells," blaze out for "the lost traveller, with sun-bleached hair/Dazed on the gangway." Left behind is "the ill dream" of the "divided graves, desert or jungle":

> *And the great axle of doom that seemed to run*
> *Backwards for ever to the unlucky dead*
> *Palpable over them as tank or gun,*
> *Dissolves in mist . . .*[29]

It is curious how words that seem fitting to the prisoners are mostly from poems about victory, as though that were no less bitter.

CHAPTER XIII

It Goes On For Ever

I

ONCE the railway was finished, the pressure on the prisoners eased a little. All of them agree that the remainder of their period of captivity was comparatively pleasant—that is to say the railway marked the worst and nothing was quite so dreadful after that. It is rather like being the man whose toothache is a fraction less painful but whose legs are still broken. For those, like Major Peacock and Lieutenant Coast and Mr Braddon, who remained in Siam, there was not only more leisure but more room. A number of fairly fit prisoners, among them Sergeant Harrison, were sent to Japan to work in the mines; many more, among them Captain Burton, had their time on the railway cut short by illness, and were sent back to Singapore. Of these, many were too far gone by the time they were put on the south-bound trains, and died on the way. Others, mercifully, reached Singapore alive, and their condition and appearance provided a dreadful shock for the soldiers in Changi who had been there all along and had heard little about the railway and what it had meant during the intervening months.

"How," asked Lieutenant Coast, "amid disease, slave labour and the perpetual monsoon rain, did we keep our sanity?" [1]

At times there was no doubt about it, morale sank to the lowest depths. All accounts mention this. For one thing there was plenty of inter-rank resentment. The senior officers, forced to mediate between the Japanese and the prisoners, felt they carried an unfairly heavy burden; the NCOs believed that they would get what blame there was any way; the private soldiers knew that private soldiers always carry the full heat of the day; while the young subalterns were certain that their position, poised uncomfortably among the rest, was the least enviable. A finicking insistence on military protocol by some of the older men, particularly by the English as opposed to the Australians, caused resentment. There

251

were international biases too, the common enough prejudice of Pommie* against Aussie and both joining to execrate the Dutch.

Apart from these feelings, there were personal struggles with temptation: men stole valuables from companions to sell for food or tobacco, helped themselves to more than their fair share of what food there was (as shown in the Leggie Queue), took the attitude of "Damn you, Jack, I'm all right!" over matters large and small. Many tried to exaggerate a mild illness or minor injury to get an extra day or two in bed instead of out on the job. Some, though these were few, did this continually, living in the camp hospitals for months at a time, and quite often dying there too, from sheer inanition. Long periods of successful feigning of illness often led to real physical or mental collapse and it is clear that these dodgers were left more heavily marked than those who worked and survived. In many cases, of course, deaths occurred because men had simply lost the will to live. A few contrived painful and desperate accidents for themselves so that they could be sent back to base camp or to Singapore.

There were a few genuine villains, some of them ex-convicts, who were dealt with by their own fellows, sometimes quite summarily. These men were very different from the forthright genuine merchant-adventurers who cheerfully scrounged on behalf of everybody.[2] There were fluctuating periods of low morale when deep depressions swept over practically everyone. But most of the men were young and resilient; most of them wanted to live to see better days; most of them never wavered in their fundamental belief that they were on the winning side and that they only had to hang on long enough to see the light at the end of the dark valley. Those who were older, like Major Peacock, might have had less resilience but in its place they had developed a balanced philosophy of life that kept them going.

One thing at least that could have been a real problem was spared them. There were all these thousands of men, and there were no women. Because of the poor diet, the hard work, and the perpetual disease, sex ceased to exist. It could have been a considerable source of difficulty, but it never was to heterosexuals or homosexuals alike. What did exist, taking the place of ordinary sexual feeling, was a sort of brotherly love—a man would be concerned about his friends, would share with them what he had, would draw comfort from their company. The viewpoint that people have when they are working together on an absorbing

* Australian slang for Englishman, the precise equivalent of "Limey."

project was what really sustained these men, and, since the project was fundamentally the matter of survival, it was absorbing indeed.

An occasional clean-up, inadequate though it had to be in the usual camp conditions, helped morale. If the officers or the sergeant-major or some other NCO suggested that "some interior economy [Army words for cleaning barracks] was necessary," then everyone would join in, taking the bamboo slats off the sleeping platforms and passing them through the flames of one of the camp fires to get rid of lice and bugs, washing bits of fabric after a fashion, scraping the earth floors: all to good effect.[3] It was good to bathe and swim in the river, too, and to have the rare treat of a haircut or beard trim.

However, laughter was the greatest help and the occasional quite incongruous incident dramatically raised morale. Singapore was not the only place where there were houses of ill fame patronised by the Japanese soldiers, and several accounts mention occasions when a Japanese guard would leave the pair of prisoners he had charge of at the door, handing them his rifle for safekeeping. They would sit on the steps and wait for the guard to return. One truck driver prisoner, on one of these visits, was offered two hundred dollars for the guard's rifle by an enterprising Siamese, and of course accepted the money. The guard eventually came back and the driver suggested that he must have left his rifle behind in the house, though naturally the subsequent search revealed nothing. The guard was in a panic about what would happen to him when he reported the lost rifle, and the driver began to feel sorry for him, as he was not particularly vicious, so he suggested: "You go to your Nippon Quarter Master, Nippon, and you keep him talkie-talkie five minutes. I get rifle." The guard, willing to try anything, and apparently too dim-witted to wonder where the driver could possibly get a rifle from, agreed at once, and the driver took him along to the Japanese Quarter Master's Store, and watched him go in. When he came out a few minutes later, he saw a rifle on the seat of the truck. The driver had taken it out of the Armoury and no one was any the wiser. The overjoyed guard thanked the driver effusively, and that evening brought him six tins of condensed milk and sixty dollars in cash. There was another quick-witted driver who sold two tyres off his lorry for a hundred and fifty dollars each while the guard had gone into the jungle to have a benjo and managed to get away with it by pretending to go for a benjo himself, coming back to the truck and putting on a bewildered act at the inexplicable disappearance of the tyres.[4] What the Army knew about "the gentle art of flogging" was brought to a high pitch of delicate efficiency throughout the years of captivity and cheered many people.

Amusement could even be extracted from the Japanese habit of taking a stick to anything that would not go, including machinery. Seeing one Japanese thrashing the radiator of a stalled truck, an Australian prisoner, poker-faced while his companions were choking with laughter, suggested that he was using the wrong kind of stick and would do better with bamboo. The laughter was even harder to bite back when the Japanese solemnly followed this advice.[5]

Some of the linguistic exchanges helped morale, too, as did the Phantom Dog. There were also incidents that proved amusing to look back on even though they were not always funny at the time. On one of the long marches up the river a group of four or five young officers decided to drop out and get some sleep. They were all "fed up with being told it was only one more mile" and they lay down beside the railway track. The area at that point was scrubby, the trees had been cut back and the place was infested with sand-flies. To keep the flies at least partially off they thought of covering themselves with a cloth and the first to come to light as they scrabbled wearily in their kit was a Union Jack that one of them was carrying. They spread this over them and lay in a more or less neat row under its colourful breadth. In the early morning they were awakened by "guttural shouts from the other side of the track" and saw several Japanese who, hardly surprisingly, had assumed that they were cholera victims laid out for burial and did not intend to investigate more closely. The cherry on the trifle of this story is the fact that two of the people who slept under the flag that night were much later to find themselves in positions of some eminence in two of England's most distinguished public schools.[6]

2

What else kept the morale going on the Kwai?

The radio did. All accounts emphasise that the men took tremendous risks to smuggle the forbidden "canaries" along the river so that the soldiers were seldom completely deprived of the fragments of news. The spare parts, batteries, and carefully dismembered sets were smuggled in with skill and daring, carried with outward coolness past Japanese guards, sent forward in lorry-loads of Japanese supplies where they were packed under sacks of rice as the Scarlet Pimpernel's aristos were hidden under the cabbages, even tucked away inside the kit of Japanese colonels. On the road or in the camps they were shifted daily so that only a couple of men at a time knew where they were, in order to reduce the hazard of disclosure under torture. There were alarms at times, and the Japanese military police, the dreaded Kempei-Tai, sometimes came in and took the place apart. It sometimes happened that they found the radio and then there were beheadings. But mostly they did not. The scraps of news picked out of the air at such risk did a great deal to boost morale in all the camps. The men knew that Britain was still in the fight—more, things were going better. They heard that Italy and France had been invaded, that Italy had collapsed and Germany had surrendered, but of course many details did not reach them. For instance they did not hear about the interesting Japanese custom described here by Mr Walter Lord:

> On a table in the centre [at top level military and naval conferences] there was always a box of Sakura cigarettes, some cheese, and that great symbol of their victories—a bottle of Johnny Walker Red Label whisky "liberated" from Singapore.[7]

They did not hear either about the brave and lonely fight that Yamashita put up in the Philippines, when his men lived in caves and ate rats while MacArthur's troops redeemed their General's pledge, "I shall return." But this was still a long way off.

Trading with Siamese and Chinese who brought their supplies up the river in barges and sampans and passed on scraps of news and sometimes medical necessities along with the food they sold also helped to keep the men's spirits up. Fishing was a constant form of pleasure, very useful too in supplementing the meagre rations. Mr Peters said that the river swarmed with fish and did not appear to have been fished in previously: a few fish "were persuaded to leave the river with the aid of a little dynamite." [8] There were books: about a third of the prisoners had brought a book or two with them, salvaged from the wreck of Singapore, and these were eagerly devoured, sometimes being read aloud. Captain Burton came to know Agatha Christie's *Mystery of the Blue Train* very well indeed.[9] Mr Braddon had his copy of Shaw's *Prefaces* confiscated,[10] but retained his sanity by (of all things) learning by heart much of Hitler's *Mein Kampf*, though he said that the best book he came across was A. A. Milne's *Winnie-the-Pooh*. His friends were slightly contemptuous at first, but his frequent roars of laughter at

Pooh's poems and Eeyore's acid comments were infectious and in the
end they all read it and loved it. It is touching to think how much the
gentle enchantment of the Surrey pinewoods and lines like "the more
it *snows,* tiddley-pom" helped even men who, like Mr Braddon, had
never seen England.[11]

Poetry-reading groups were formed and other study groups got
going. The men took these courses seriously and their interest in the
subjects they had taken up often continued once the war was over.
Lectures were organised as they had been in Singapore, where anyone
was welcome to speak; no matter how boring the speaker or the topic,
the lecture was greedily listened to. Some of the unlikely subjects that
came up were the growing of apples and roses, the keeping of pets,
touring in the Lake District, climbing in Norway, messing about in
boats, the three Louis—XIV, XV, XVI, the scientific approach to golf,
how to design a house (there were plenty of lively ideas about this
one), and even the odd instalment of that endless Army serial, military
tactics or gunnery. In this last category, if the speaker happened to be
a senior officer, it was noted with wry amusement that he was still going
by the book and propounding theories that would have helped his
hearers avoid the more glaring strategical errors of World War I.[12]

Discussion groups sprang up everywhere and were well liked if
they dealt with serious subjects like religion or politics and were led
by someone who had gained the respect and affection of his fellows.
Captain Gordon was approached by an Australian sergeant who told
him: "We feel we've seen the absolute worst there is—right? Now we
believe there's got to be something better." [13]

This particular group discussed ideas, beliefs, prejudices, faith and
doubt. It grew steadily larger and freely aired all kinds of opinions
about the better world the men wanted to live in after the war. Talking
about it made it seem more real and gave many men the will to live to
see it; it also made them readier to help one another. As far as their
national prejudices went these were over-simple, as usual, so that the
Australians were said to be obscene about everything, the British flippant about everything, the Dutch solemn about everything. But in discussion these feelings were released and this helped to build up mutual
respect and friendliness.[14]

Debating teams were organised and toured the huts, disputing on
topics assigned to them. Two favourites were: "Has twentieth century
man lost the ability to entertain himself?" and "Resolved: that old age
pensions should begin at twenty-one." When the debaters grew tired

of a set speech they changed sides and "presented the opposite point of view with gusto." [15]

A light-hearted variant on the debates and discussions was the quiz game—spelling, general knowledge, twenty questions or anything anyone could think of. One youthful major described himself as "Stupidity Corner" because he never got a right answer, but he came into his own on one occasion when his question was: What could one buy in England before the war for exactly £750? Lovingly and precisely "Stupidity Corner" described a particular Aston Martin, down to the last detail, to a delighted audience. [16]

One prisoner possessed a tattered copy of the cricketers' bible—*Wisden*—and every evening for many weeks about a dozen men sat round a rough bamboo table discussing the game (or was it a religion?) for hours on end. They were so serious and intent that Major Peacock thought at first they were planning to escape. They talked about teams, real and hypothetical, alive and dead, and worked out a survivors' team, happily spending hours drawing up the club rules, setting down future fixtures, and designing a blazer badge with a river and elephants on it. The Major thought that the great cricketers would have been pleased to know how their beloved game helped to restore morale and sanity. [17]

The card players were a race apart. This tends to be so anywhere, regardless of circumstances. It is well known that, during all critical campaigns, trench warfare in Flanders, the London blitz, the run-up to D-Day, card players have doggedly carried on with their shuffling, cutting, dealing, playing, oblivious to bomb and shell or anything else going on around them. It was no different on the Kwai.

3

Something else that was a great help in keeping the men going was the opportunity to work creatively. Those who made "clompers" or repaired clothes or nursed the sick or did the cooking or pulled out teeth or, like Voltaire's Candide, cultivated the garden, were usually happier and less distraught than their fellow prisoners. But apart from these skills there also appeared some expressions of pure art. One or two prisoners were genuinely talented artists, notably one young man who later became very famous as a cartoonist and illustrator who practised patiently for hours. His patience was rewarded when in 1946 his first book was published. It was a group of drawings made during his war service. [18] All sorts of amateurs tried their hand, some for the first time. They could hardly have chosen a worse moment to begin, for materials were scarce and the atmosphere hostile, but they improvised with admirable resourcefulness. The jungle was full of wood, a lot of it beautiful in colour and texture, so men who had been able to keep their pocket-knives could take up carving. (When they went back to Singapore they worked on perspex windscreens from crashed planes.) Those who wanted to draw used bamboo bark or odd pages torn out of notebooks, and on these they drew with stubs of pencil or bits of charcoal from the cooking fires. Those who wanted to paint pounded pieces of rock to powder, produced a kind of dye from plants, and blended these together with machine oil. For brushes they used shreds of rag on sticks. In time they set up an improvised art gallery at the end of one of the huts. This exhibition included carvings, sculptures, blueprints or line drawings of sailing-ships, portraits of other prisoners or relations—one man drew pictures of his children as he imagined they would look now. Some drew sketches of prison scenes or painted the surrounding landscape. Those who visited "the gallery" were quite often encouraged to take up some form of creative art themselves so that the therapy spread.[19]

There there was music, one of the most powerful healers of all. Some prisoners were fine musicians, others enthusiastic amateurs. Scratch collections of instruments, some of them cleverly improvised, were assembled in the various larger camps. Practice sessions were held and concerts given. It was notable that the Japanese guards and officers liked these concerts and attended them. As for the men, everyone went, even if it meant being carried there. Some of the programmes were ambitious: Lieutenant Coast reports one that included the Unfinished Symphony, Eine Kleine Nachtmusik, and four of the Enigma Variations. The music was propped up on wooden music-stands lit by tiny oil lamps. A typical collection of instruments would include one or two decent violins plus a few cheap Red Cross ones, a couple of clarinets and accordions, three or four trumpets or cornets, two guitars, and "a magnificent string-bass made from three-ply sugar-chest wood and cable wire" which of course could not be bowed but which "plucked well." [20]

Everyone loved the music. One night Captain Gordon saw a working-party trailing wearily into camp at Chungkai, bound for their evening meal. As soon as they heard the sound of music—the Unfinished Symphony on this occasion—they stopped and sat down. The rice could wait. As they listened, their faces relaxed and slowly came to life.[21]

Mr Peters said that the Japanese were "very perturbed" that the men continued to sing "at all times," but some nights there was community singing. There were all the old standbys like "Tipperary," "Loch Lomond" and "John Peel," as well as plenty of hymns, and, of course, bawdy barrack-room ballads—Lieutenant Coast refers to one called "I'm a Sailor You Can Tell by My Oriental Smell." [22] There was a lot of singing in the huts during the evenings especially if anybody had an accordion, mouth-organ, or tin whistle. One man (later he became a highly popular entertainer at the Berkeley Hotel) had a portable organ, and he would sit on a box in the centre of a hut and play his delightful boogie compositions that helped the men to forget their physical suffering for a while.[23] There was carol-singing at Christmas and the familiar old verses in that strange place had a particularly moving effect. A number of parodies of well known songs became popular, like "On the muddy, bloody banks of Kan'buri" and one of "The Mountains of Mourne" that Major Peacock himself wrote.[24] There was also much Gilbert and Sullivan ("a prisoner's lot is not a happy one").

From music such as this it is a short step to the stage, and plays, revues, pantomimes and skits were produced. The artists used liquid mud (which never ran short) to plaster on pieces of wood to make the scenery, boiled up leaves and bark to make paints and created drapery and costumes out of old green Japanese Army mosquito-nets which had to be hidden quickly if any high-ranking Japanese appeared to make a sudden inspection. There was a wardrobe master who took charge of the homemade clothes and scrounged many surprising items—sometimes something as unlikely in those surroundings as a pair of flannels or a blue scarf or a white shirt. A former film make-up man did the make-up which was also all home-produced.

The whole thing came to be highly professionally organised, particularly at Chungkai, where a Theatre Committee was set up to arrange the productions, starting with one-act plays like *The Dear Departed* and going on to a musical comedy which made the reputation of the committee and the producer. At rehearsals the producer sat on a stool marked with his name in the best Hollywood tradition, and his clothes were just as outlandish as those of the whipcord-breeches boys: clompers, sunglasses, a pink Jap Happy, and a knitted dark blue cap. Addressed punctiliously as "Mr A.S.M." the Assistant Stage Manager sat beside him on a smaller stool after hanging up the call board on a bamboo thorn. For three weeks at a stretch they would have several rehearsals a day and on the night the actors were called for seven as the curtain went up (*sic*) at eight-thirty. One of the musicals included lovely old songs like "My Friend Elizabeth" and "Wonder Bar." There was an all-dancing show. There were Dutch shows, one of which included a "lotus dance" and imported native acrobats. There was the topical show, *Thai-Diddle-Diddle,* in which everybody got into trouble over the pidgin English scene [25] and there were straight plays like *Night Must Fall, Major Barbara, Doctor Clitterhouse.* There were pantomimes and the stage effects were often brilliant: Major Peacock said that he had seen much less effective décors in the West End.[26]

In addition to these corporate efforts, there were plenty of individual ones. Men arranged birthday parties for their friends, managing to produce a "cake" or a cup or two of extra drinks; at Christmas they gave little homemade cards and gifts and on special days the prisoners sang or played their regimental songs. Men who in civilian life had been Masons contrived some semblance of the Masonic regalia and held meetings.[27] Old jokes and catch-phrases went the length of the line from Changi to the Three Pagodas and back, including the ubiquitous "Taxi!" and Mr Harry Smith's lugubrious "You'll never get off the Island." Morale was at its lowest during the building of the railway, but it is notable that it did not just level off but actually picked up during the endless twenty-two months that followed. Of course the moonshiners helped there: a fearsome brew was concocted from thin rice porridge fermented with sugar, strained, and fermented for a fortnight with added sugar and bits of fruit, at the end of which time a liquid appeared which might taste like anything from raw cider to lighter fuel. Luckily it only took a little to make a man cheerful and not enough could be made at once to be really dangerous, though no doubt it would have been deadly if taken in quantity.[28]

The raised morale showed itself in a curious episode which was repeated more than once for it is recorded in several accounts from different places, where the prisoners saw train loads of wounded Japanese, in a horrible state of neglect, waiting in railway sidings on their way south from the Burma front. Without hesitation the prisoners gave them water, receiving in return whispers of "arigato" from the surprised, but grateful, enemy troops. Captain Gordon said that it made him realise for the first time what the parable of the Good Samaritan was really about.[29] Major Peacock felt proud that someone had felt and behaved so generously.[30]

4

There were now two main groups of prisoners: those who remained in Siam and those who did not.

The ones who stayed up-country now had time to fish—a pleasant way to spend an evening even for those who never caught anything—to swim and to play a little football or water-polo in the intervals of making roads to replace those washed away by the monsoon, repairing huts and caring for the sick men, of whom there were still a great number.[31] The worst cases were sent south, but by February 1944 there was a steady movement of troops coming down the line to Chungkai, and it was soon clear that the camps were being evacuated one by one. By the end of February they were cleared as far down as Takanun, where Major Peacock had gone to collect pay ("speedo, speedo, pom pom starto"), and the prisoners began their move from there on March 1, the morning after a tremendous storm. They all noticed how much more room there was in the trains going down than there had been coming up. One train left Takanun at nine-thirty in the morning and arrived at Chungkai at about midnight. The prisoners were glad to be making the trip in daylight as it gave them a chance to have a good look at the work they had done; as the string of trucks dragged itself slowly along the ups and downs of the first sixty miles they had ample opportunity.[32] The fertile vegetation had sprung up fast and already the look of the landscape had altered a good deal. Lieutenant Coast counted thirteen abandoned trucks that had rolled down the embankments on his side of the line. Brankasi was now a locomotive repair depot and a huge transport camp. The most impressive part of the line, nearly ten miles of a real mountain railway hewn and blasted from the stone switchback, was near Hintok. Soon after that the train, moving at a regular thirty to forty miles an hour, on lines that felt really solid, made comparatively short work of the rest of the journey down to Chungkai, which at that moment, with nearly ten thousand people in it, was chaotically full.

The camp was a mile and a quarter in circumference, had a bamboo fence all round, and a cleared path just inside this fence where the men walked for exercise. There were three main sections: the hospital, about ten huts each over a hundred yards long, packed with the severely sick men, the Blue (sick men), and the Red (fit men). They were allowed to bathe in the river at set times. The canteen, though the quality was low and the prices high, displayed an astonishing selection of foods, including fried or boiled eggs, omelettes, fruit cakes and tarts, ginger or coffee fudge, sugar discs, some particularly good shortbread, curry, stew, soup, bananas (other fruit was scarce), and Dutch "sambals," a Javanese dish made in many flavours but always hot or spicy. All available ingredients like peanuts, eggs, fish, chilis, and vegetables went into sambals and whether hot or not these were enormously popular.

Chungkai also had a railed-off square, shaded by mango trees, where remedial physical training was gently and patiently carried out to straighten bodies twisted and bent by disease and overwork. The results were often striking. Close by the barber and his assistants cut hair for five cents, and not far off was the football field where matches were held every night. There was also the theatre, where the big productions and some of the best concerts took place. Generally speaking Chungkai had the makings of a quite tolerable camp if one were not ill, but the hospital and the sick were ever-present and there were still daily funerals in the cemetery. This, the cemetery, was the most beautiful part of the camp. Rows of flowering bushes and trees, surrounded by hibiscus hedges blazed in glory. Apart from the twelve hundred graves there, and the disabled in the hospital sector (there were separate sections for bacillary and amoebic diseases, ulcers and amputations) it was obvious that every man in the Blue part would have been in hospital in normal conditions. The fit men collected water, wood, and fruit, and did exercises. Lieutenant Coast had some lessons in Malay in the intervals of working on hut-construction. Between the lessons he watched Malayan dancing and was given a fascinating detailed account of pearl fishing by a Eurasian called Lorenzo.[33] Chungkai was reckoned to be the best camp in Siam: if conditions were bad there, they would probably be worse anywhere else. When one came to realise that it was the largest and longest-established of the camps, nearest to a town, and that one could in time get used to the stale, unhealthy smell and the crowded, garbage-littered river, it did not seem so bad. When the men going north to Japan or south to Singapore as work or sick parties had left, there was room to lead a fairly quiet life.[34]

It surprised the soldiers arriving in Chungkai from camps further up-country to find that some of the inmates had been there since they were sent to Siam. Some were genuinely ill but others had simulated illness so long and successfully that they had actually become physically sick or mentally unbalanced. Since they had stayed in the huts and never got sunburned, they were called "the moon men" by the rest. There were very few moon men.[35]

The prisoners from up-country stayed in Chungkai throughout 1944.

They soon found out that among its other drawbacks the area flooded every year, sometimes twice a year, as was the case in 1944. Consequently they were set to work building dams, though the Japanese left this a bit late, not having seen the need for them until the water was within a foot and a half of the top of the main river bank and still rising. So the men had to work in shifts through the night and, not surprisingly considering the pace at which they worked, the topmost dam broke at one point so the second condition of the camp was worse than the first. The flood water was eventually contained, however, and when the level went down and stayed down, some of the officers managed to make a table and benches to eat their meals at. Such luxuries were hitherto unknown. Two armchairs which were put together at the same time and stuffed with sacking were relatively comfortable but soon produced some of the juiciest bed bugs in Siam.[36] Major Peacock made a kind of pillow from a piece of ground sheet stuffed with kapok, and said that if ever he had to be a prisoner again (which God forbid) the one thing he would want most of all would be a cushion.[37]

Life was monotonous apart from the periodic scares over the possible discovery of the forbidden radio sets, which still supplied fragments of news, most of it sounding better though still depressingly far away. The activities of the camp racketeers, whose biggest interest was in hooch, followed closely by the cashing of cheques through friendly outsiders—something which did not always work—also broke the tedium. In the second half of 1944 there were more jobs to be done and most of them were strenuous—working in the gardens, repairing old huts, building new ones, digging trenches, clearing bamboo from paths, and building a moat ten feet deep with an eighteen-foot-high outer bank all round the camp. As there was nowhere to escape to it was never made quite clear just what this moat was for. From time to time small parties were sent up the railway to do maintenance work. The days passed slightly more quickly than the prisoners had come to expect: of course it was easy to lose count of time. Gradually the officers were separated from the men until, in February 1945, after precisely three years in captivity, the officers were sent down to Kanchanaburi where they arrived on the nineteenth of the month. Anxious about possible Kempei-Tai searches, Lieutenant Coast buried his diary under a tree before leaving Chungkai.[38]

By all accounts Kanchanaburi was a bad camp, bare mud with no trees to shade it, away from the river, fenced by bamboo and barbed wire, with only one gate, and consisting, for the prisoners, of a single straight row of over a dozen long huts, the end of which was part store and part hospital. The water supply came from two wells known as the British and the Dutch, worked laboriously by hand, and the bathing place was a partitioned square criss-crossed by ditches. Every yard or so small bamboo platforms projected over these ditches, where two men could stand with a tin between them and get some sort of a wash. The huts were overcrowded, the cooking was done in the open, and work went on from nine till one and from three till six. About three thousand officers and nearly two hundred Other Ranks were lodged in less than thirty-five thousand square feet—that is about ten square feet to a man, a disagreeably high density. The camp commandant, a Japanese captain, was suspicious, brutal, and excessively keen on the hated formalities of saluting and bowing.

The work started with the virtual rebuilding of the entire camp, which took two months, during one part of which Major Peacock rather enjoyed making mud bricks: "the filthy mess we got ourselves into was rather pleasant." [39] After that came the digging out and cleaning of another moat and the repairing of the fences. Castor-oil bushes of two varieties and some flowers were planted. The floor of the camp had to be raised above flood level, and to do this the "levelling party" was formed, an organisation that was to become notorious. It continued to exist long after the original levelling was done and all accounts draw a picture of an excruciatingly monotonous job: officers carrying stretchers of earth or buckets of water and doing the camp fatigues, dressed in their mud-stained Jap Happy cloths and wooden clompers, "shambling about at the slow coolie walk in every direction." [40]

Major Peacock and a friend set up a tailoring business and made Jap Happies and converted old kitbags into shorts. They also invented a small roller from finely cut pieces of bamboo on which they could make up cigarettes.[41] The men played games—basketball or volleyball—in the evenings, and there was a small improvised theatre where hastily rehearsed productions were put on. It was now, when he decided to abandon tailoring, that Major Peacock set up as a dentist. Some groups were sent on errands, mainly to Tamarkand to fetch bamboos, a popular job because it took them away from the prison for a while, past ordinary people and dwellings, and by great clusters of flame trees with their orange-red flowers glowing brilliantly against the fragile, feather-like green leaves and the hot, deep blue sky. There were clumps of frangipani too and the men picked its scented white blooms and stuck them in their hat-bands.[42] They were able to swim at Tamarkand and, when the mangoes were ripe, to eat fruit.

Some men went down as far as Nakom Paton, where they found

the camp filled with sick and convalescent men. There was a separate enclosure for the sufferers from leprosy, and another for those who had gone insane. "I marvelled," said Captain Gordon, "that there were so few." [43]

And then the grapevine flashed the news that Germany had been defeated. It was hard to grasp at first.

5

What became of the rest of the men who had left Siam?

They all started out in the same way—by train to Singapore, where, like those coming down to Chungkai, they had at least more room to move than on the dreadful journey up, as well as the fortifying knowledge that they were (as they saw it, with some justification) coming out of the valley of death. Once in Singapore they were sorted out. Not regimentally—regimental units were generally split up from the time the railway parties started travelling north—but into two groups, those that were staying on the Island and those that were not. Sergeant Harrison's group, which was to go to Japan, had a few days in their old camp at River Valley Road, where they were welcomed by their old friends, the bugs and lice. In June they were moved to Changi, where practically all the Singapore prisoners had spent their time since the departure of the up-country parties. On July 1 they sailed for Japan, which they reached after a hideously uncomfortable journey. The old coffin-like ships had pitched and rolled through rough seas with the unfortunate men locked below decks in cramped and overheated conditions where they were left to stew in their own juice. In Japan these same men were set to work in the mines, and there they stayed for the last year. The work was dangerous and dull, the food was poor, but at least it was more bearable than Hellfire Pass. [44]

One group set out and never arrived. Mr Peters was among the thirteen hundred fittest men picked out in September 1944 to go to Japan, but a submarine attack on September 12 sent the old coffin-ship to the bottom after "five days of a hellish voyage." Mr Peters and an Australian stayed afloat for five days before being picked up by an American submarine whose crew could not do enough for them. They gave them, apparently, "everything except the submarine" and they were sent back home, feeling miraculously lucky, which indeed they were. [45]

Captain James was sent to Japan and his sea voyage lasted a month: it was just as awful as the rest. They docked at Moji where he thought the people and surroundings very drab and poor. With his white hair he was shouted at by the children in the streets: "Prisoner of war grandpapa!" Omori camp, seven and a half miles south of the Imperial Palace, had five wooden barrack blocks, each a hundred feet by twenty-four, with eight-by-four bed space for each of the five hundred and twenty men, who slept in double-deck bunks with an eight-foot passage down the middle. At each end were two twelve-by-ten cubicles for the officers. In the perishing cold of winter, the water froze in the three twenty-foot wash racks which only managed a faint trickle of water in the summer. The latrines were overflowing concrete pits swarming with white maggots. The food was vile, the morning roll call was at five in summer and six-thirty in winter, and the evening one at any time between six and ten according to the whim of the officer in charge.[46]

"It is a pity," wrote Captain James, after he found himself at four in the morning on August 30, 1945, a free man on board an American ship, "that their heroism contrasts so strangely with their atrocious behaviour to their captives." It was a generous statement. He had witnessed many horrors.[47]

6

Captain Burton's party, which included quite a number of Royal Norfolks, went to Syme Road camp, which had been prepared by the fittest survivors of F Force and H Force. It seemed like paradise after Siam: wooden huts, proper beds, electric light, showers. On arrival every man simply went to sleep on the floor, but in the morning they began the exhilarating process of getting themselves thoroughly clean. To have running water seemed miraculous. With the most scrupulous care they washed every part of their persons and every scrap of their kit, washing away the smell, of the purgatorial jungle from which they had escaped, with luck, for ever. All beards had to go and go they did, with the vermin in them. Shoes were polished and badges of rank were worn. Morale went up and never fell steeply again.

Those who saw something of Singapore, notably the truck drivers who commuted between the smaller camps and the big main camp at Changi, found it a lost, forgotten and rather eerie place. The men from the north at first goggled at the street lamps, but then they noticed how strangely quiet the whole place was: the streets were deserted, there were few shops open and those that were seemed to be dropping to pieces, their paint peeling and their awnings and shutters flapping. The framework of the city, however, was curiously unchanged since that day, a lifetime ago, when they had left it. The prisoners who had stayed on the Island all along were horrified at the sight of the railway survivors. One driver told Captain Burton that when the first batch arrived he had been frightened that they would die in the truck before he could land them safely at the camp. Within a few weeks, though, the newly arrived men had reached the low but viable level of health of those who had never left Changi.[48] The condition that took the longest to clear up was the variety of skin diseases.

The big project that everyone fit enough to work was engaged on was the airfield. The Japanese had decided to construct this in the opening months of 1943, and Captain Russell-Roberts was among the Changi men who started work on it in April of that year. It was a big undertaking—the main runway was three thousand yards long. The Japanese brought bulldozers to move stones, sand for the surface, as well as trucks that ran on rails. In parties of a hundred with an officer in charge of each, two thousand men went out to work in shifts, seven to two, two to nine.[49] The first shift left at dawn, reaching the area between Changi and the sea as the sky was going pink, and worked on the airstrip all day, gouging stone from the white hillside. The glare from the stone and the white surface of the airstrip tired them.[50]

The food situation improved. There was, for instance, an issue of soya beans. The Dutch officers evolved a method of producing a kind of cream cheese from these, using a wine-treading process which caused much amusement and resulted in a substance called "Tempi." [51] The men received regular pay and spent their Japanese Malay dollars on coconuts and pineapples in the camp canteen. They arranged a concert party for Christmas 1943 and this proved tremendously successful. Captain Burton wrote some sketches for it and Mr Ronald Searle painted the décor.[52]

News came from Changi to Syme Road via the truck drivers, who were sometimes able to smuggle in notes; some Australians built a radio set out of parts stolen from Japanese vehicles and found, when they came to operate it, that the scanty fragments of information passed on to them by their own Command were (as they had suspected) about a month out of date. Every camp had its canary, and when all the men were transferred to Changi in the spring of 1944, these came too and were used on a sort of rota, according to which camp the current CO had come from: if it were an Australian, all the British canaries were pirates and the Australian counted as official; if it were the Selarang CO, the Selarang canary was official and all the rest were pirates.[53] In the centre of Syme Road camp the officers ran a little café called the Flying Dutchman where they drank coffee made from toasted rice and ate rice biscuits, rice cakes and soya bean sandwiches; naturally it was enormously popular and a great morale booster.[54]

When they were transferred to the great stone jail and barrack complex of Changi at the north-east corner of the Island they were counted in by an inexpert performer with an abacus, given a long speech by the Japanese Officer Commanding, and then lodged in the jail, a three-story H-shaped concrete building with noisy iron stairs and metal grilles, three men to a cell the size of a small bathroom. It grew so stuffy at night that in time they were allowed to sleep in the courtyard. After a break in pattern during which some of the prisoners were moved to Selarang (where Colonel Prattley of the 5th Battalion was quartered), they moved finally into the attap huts and low concrete buildings that had been the jail employees' dwelling in peace time, and found it a decided improvement.[55]

Because there were seven thousand men in Changi at this time, in a jail planned for six hundred, many improvements were needed and the resourceful prisoners set about making them. They changed oil-burning boilers into wood-burning boilers, using tree-stumps out of the swamps for fuel; bored latrine-holes forty feet deep in every courtyard; made attap huts; planted gardens; constructed showers from stolen pieces of piping. They also made brooms and brushes, soap from palm oil and potash (a cake a fortnight for everyone), paper, artificial limbs, clompers, shoe soles from latex mixed with sand and urine, adhesive tape, mugs, spoons and food containers from green filing cabinets, and created an ashy sort of toothpaste. One final touch: they equipped every floor with an electric coil that would light cigarettes.[56]

Tailors patched shorts from green canvas tent flaps—Captain Burton had a pair with thirty-six patches.[57] Jewellers repaired spectacles and any watches that had not been traded for food, and one genius came up with an engraving machine that would stamp the words "Rolex Waterproof" on any watch so that it became worth many dollars on the black market. The 18th Division engineers designed and built a lychgate which thirty years later was set up and dedicated at Bassingbourn Barracks, Cambridgeshire. Plants that they cultivated grew as much as two inches a day and the green leaves were chopped up and boiled into a slimy green mass which had a revolting taste but was so rich in vitamins that it kept dysentery and beri-beri at bay.[58] Up in Siam they did this too—and fixed up steam ovens that were supposed to disinfect clothes and bedding, though the effect seemed rather to be that the eggs hatched all the faster. There were papermakers in Siam, clipping up straw with blunt scissors; "exquisite long-haired young men with enormous bamboo cigarette holders" did something mysterious to the straw that enabled them, on a good day, to produce about a gross of little pieces of very coarse and straw-like lavatory paper. Others in Siam made dyes from plants, the two principal colours being chocolate brown and a sickly khaki green which so appealed to one Japanese officer that he bought good white shirts in Bangkok in order to have them dyed this unbecoming colour.[59]

But to return to Changi. The Japanese, headed by their CO, Captain Takahashi, whom Captain Russell-Roberts described as a humanitarian with "a refreshingly cynical sense of humour," stayed in the background for much of the time.[60] The prisoners collected books for a camp library, put on concert parties in a makeshift theatre that they built and called the Coconut Grove, and resumed the discussion and lecture groups.[61] They carved on perspex and drew and painted on the homemade paper. Captain Russell-Roberts learned to type, having bought a typewriter from a fellow prisoner for four pounds of peanuts and a packet of "loathsome cheroots." [62] Mr Braddon finished learning *Mein Kampf* by heart and tried as a fresh mental exercise to remember the second movement of the Bruch Violin Concerto and the proof of Pythagoras' theorem: he drew triangles all over the airstrip with the point of his changkol and got arrested while doing it because the guard thought they were plans for a canary. Some men stole army jerseys from the Japanese, unwound the wool into balls and knitted socks, then sold them back to the Japanese for ten dollars a pair. Mr Searle produced a monthly magazine called *Exile.* One man began to teach himself medicine and he is now a doctor with excellent qualifications. Another man who had been in charge of the Westminster Theatre before the war produced plays. For Christmas 1944 they put on a pantomime—*Twinkletoes*. It contained tunes that the men came away humming and according to Mr Braddon there are few ex-inmates of Changi who cannot sing the words and tune of "Castles in the Air." The theatre was closed down early in 1945 because General Saito objected to the song "On Our Return" which was the final number of the latest musical.[63]

There were several marked differences now in the conditions of daily life. There was a change, during that last interminable year, in the Japanese attitude: weekends were observed, only morning work permitted, beatings and blows were few. In the wood-gathering and gardening areas a relatively peaceful and healthy, if monotonous, existence was possible, though the word "relatively" must be insisted upon for in normal conditions all the Changi prisoners would have been sent to convalescent hospitals for lengthy periods. Their vitality was low, they grew tired quickly, had dizzy spells and blackouts, and were thankful to be allowed to rest in the afternoons. On Saturday evenings they had entertainments, on Sundays they cleaned up, visited other parts of the jail, attended religious services, and, in the evening, took part in "the goldfish parade," the walk right round the inner perimeter of the camp, in which every one joined who could walk.[64]

Some, in parties of a hundred, were taken over the Causeway into Johore to dig tunnels and foxholes. This was nasty work but cheering as it made it quite clear that the Japanese were preparing for a possible invasion. For the work areas outside the wire the working-parties amused themselves by varying the "eyes right" orders in their own way: perhaps the nicest of these was: "Look at him," "You've seen him." [65]

The atmosphere was changing, in these last months of the war, but in spite of the improved conditions the men were depressed. The time dragged so slowly. There were only fragments of news. Where were the Allied armies, what were they doing, where was the hope of rescue? Had the rest of the world forgotten? Did anybody, anywhere, care? And if the captives woke one morning to find the Allies hammering at the gates, would they not be butchered by the Japanese in a last frenzied stand? Wild rumours circulated: the Japanese were hoping the prisoners would mutiny so that they could all be shot; they were going to put the prisoners in the front line when the Allied attack came; they were going to take all the prisoners back to Siam. There were still men ill and dying, still scares about the canaries, still men in the No Good House. It was hard to believe in liberation.

CHAPTER XIV

The Garland Bells

I

BUT there was no doubt about it: the end was coming. The signs were showing for all to see.

The first of these appeared in mid-1944 in Siam and at the end of 1944 in Singapore—tiny flakes of silver moving steadily across the sky in a pattern as formal as a dance. These were Allied aircraft carrying out bombing missions and dropping leaflets. More than anything else that had happened so far this sight heartened the prisoners after the long and hopeless silence. Up there were friends, messengers from the world outside, their presence a token that things were changing, rescue coming, there was room for hope after all. Small wonder that the prisoners rushed out into the open and waved and shouted like mad— and were promptly clouted back by the infuriated guards, who could read the message too.

The railway was bombed. Some of the bridges, put up at such cost in pain and blood, were damaged or destroyed. Ironically, some prisoners were killed. It did not take the rest of them long, however, to know when to expect the raids, even to take them for granted, sending reports of the damage by word of mouth up and down the line and spending more and more time in the slit trenches that served as shelters, hoping fervently that the Japanese would not make them build the railway all over again. Repair parties were sent out to patch up the track, but luckily the work did not amount to much.

Now the attitude of the guards started to change. Some of them became much kindlier, others more remote, staying away from the prisoners as long as they could. Personal violence became less frequent. When leaflets were dropped containing insulting pictures and stories about the Japanese, the Siamese roared with laughter and collected all they could find to show the guards, who appeared to take no notice. Only a short time before there would have been savage reprisals. The

Japanese kept on saying things like: "War finish one hundred years" and "Nippon number one," but they did not repeat them so often, nor with the earlier ring of confidence.

When the end did come, it took most prisoners by surprise. They had been accustomed for so long to taking one day at a time and never letting themselves look into the future, knowing very well how hard it would be to defeat the Japanese, that they found the fact of victory difficult to take in when finally it stared them in the face.

The end came in different places, but the basic pattern was much the same.

On August 15, 1945, exactly three and a half years to the day since Singapore fell, Sergeant Harrison and his friends heard rumours that the Japanese were crying in the streets and thought the end must be near. The final test would be whether the prisoners' food boxes were taken to be filled ready for work next day; for a while there was no indication, but then the words were spoken that could mean only one thing: "Tomorrow all men yasumé." For a moment the prisoners were almost paralyzed but then with a rush of feeling the long-hidden flags were brought out and "everyone suddenly burst out singing." When the Japanese did not come charging in to clear the room with their rifle butts they knew it was all right, that they would survive after all. The scene was unforgettable: men jumped insanely up and down, there was hugging and back-slapping, some sank to their knees, some wept, and a few walked outside alone in the evening to try to think about the miracle of their deliverance. They all stayed up all night.

A strange twilight period followed, during which the men played games, including many table tennis matches with their erstwhile guards. There was a church parade, where the padre reminded them that while for most men there are three fresh starts in life (baptism, first communion, and marriage), the prisoners now had the unusual privilege of a fourth. Many ex-prisoners (as they now technically were) developed temperatures and stomach upsets from an excess of nervous emotion. Food supplies were dropped by parachute and the Japanese hurriedly painted in huge letters on the camp roofs such information as PW CAMP NUMBER 21, 608 MEN, so that, according to one optimistic Australian, the rescuers would know "how many blondes to drop." Japanese civilians now came into the camps to do the fatigues, and the men lolled about watching them and threw them packets of cigarettes in a lordly, feudal way. They went all over the city collecting souvenirs: swords were especially popular, requisitioned with mock severity and a great flourishing of blank forms normally used to register diseases of an intimate kind.

What brought Sergeant Harrison back to normal was a visit to Hiroshima. "One does not rob a tomb."[1]

2

Captain Gordon, like Major Peacock, spent an uncomfortable few days watching the Japanese prepare strong defensive positions, in his case at the base of the foothills that overlooked a wide flat spread of paddy fields and the shore of the Gulf of Siam. The Japanese were jumpy and unpleasant, "the air crackled with tension." One mid-morning the guards abruptly disappeared—they just walked away up the road—so the prisoners sensibly downed tools and lay resting in the shade. When the guards returned drunk, some time later, and without explanation sent the men back to camp, the Japanese commandant summoned the senior British officer and spoke with him. Very soon word flashed from one end of the camp to the other. The men started to sing and the guards melted away. Accustomed to singing war songs to harden their nerves before battle, they apparently thought that the prisoners were preparing to slaughter them and so prudently vanished into the surrounding countryside. One of them, before going, bowed ceremoniously to Captain Gordon who, somewhat at a loss, smiled at him. The guard smiled uncertainly back and said: "Okayga?" "Okayga," replied Captain Gordon, still smiling. The guard, not waiting for anything else to be said, "streaked for the hills."

In all the camps feelings burst out freely. Flags, carefully hidden for years against this moment—one soldier had used his to line his sleeping-bag—were soon flying from the flagpoles. Liberty revues were produced in the camp theatres. The canaries came out of concealment and were put into operation at once—there was a big backlog of news. Within a day or two an American paratrooper came wandering by, having lost his way. He was the first visitor from the outside world and was given a delirious reception, surrounded by "a yelling crowd of skinny, bronzed, bearded, half-naked savages," seized joyfully and carried shoulder-high through the camp. For hours they bombarded him with questions about the war and he patiently told everything that had happened, describing the whole course of the war's events through the three and a half years that had passed: the Coral Sea and Midway . . .

the turn at Alamein . . . Stalingrad . . . the invasion of Italy . . . the slow push through Burma and the island-hopping in the Pacific . . . the Normandy beachheads . . . the liberation of Paris . . . Arnhem and the Bulge . . . Remagen . . . Berlin . . . the Tokyo fire raids . . . and the big new bomb that had been dropped at Hiroshima, wasn't it, and yes, Nagasaki . . . To the captives he was the living representative of the freedom they had dreamed of for so long.[2]

It was this hunger for news that made the WRNS * officers in Colombo run news reels non-stop for the men to watch while their ships were docked on the long voyage home. It seemed as if they could never have enough.[3]

The soldiers slowly realised that they had come through their ordeal. Not only that: they had brought out with them a personal philosophy of life. They had become aware that "there is more to life than bread and bacon, pounds and dollars, Cadillacs and Rolls-Royces." [4]

3

In Kanchanaburi, the radio batteries had packed up about the middle of June, so there had been no way of checking the truth of the rumours that started in early August. Siamese passing in buses began to shout: "War finish! You go home!" and bamboo-carrying parties came back into camp with stories of peasants in the fields waving to them and calling out "O.K.," but there was no sudden change in the behaviour of the guards. But then on August 16 rumours were stronger than ever. The men longed to believe them but could not imagine that the Japanese had given in already. Unable to eat or settle to anything, they spent the afternoon talking and talking, going the rounds of the camp from one group to another, saying the same things over and over again. Then at last, just before sunset, the commandant confirmed the fact, and the camp went mad.

"Well, really," Lieutenant Coast goes on, "*mad* was not the right word." It was more an undisciplined surge of emotion. A wild clamour of voices and laughter, people rushing about with tears in their eyes, shaking hands, grinning, swearing, and then, with relief, breaking into song. They quickly staged a concert which went on half the night and was full of silly clowning and the bluest of jokes which had them all roaring whether funny or not. No one could keep still for long and

* Women's Royal Naval Service.

though some snatched a few minutes' sleep they were all up again at dawn.

They still found it impossible to grasp the full truth. They were still in camp, living on rice, with filthy rags to wear and the same old bug-ridden slats to sleep on. The first thing to do was to try to change all that.

Presents poured in. The Japanese commandant weighed in first with six bottles of French brandy. The Siamese flooded the camp with food, the best that could be found in Kanchanaburi. The guards sat about dumbly watching the prisoners walking freely wherever they chose to go. Some officers were entertained to a superb Siamese meal at a tiny wooden café. On leaving they stood watching an exceptionally beautiful sunset—silver, grey and green.

There were many parties and various "excursions" were arranged. Some of the men, for instance, went up to Chungkai to find Lieutenant Coast's buried diary, which a painstaking search failed to discover. Though the last inmates had left for the south only six weeks before, it was obvious already that the jungle was rapidly reclaiming Chungkai.

Swiss Red Cross people came to Kanchanaburi, bringing supplies. The camp overflowed every evening with the traders' fruit. Lieutenant Coast spent twenty-one dollars on three tablets of real soap, and a paratroop captain who had left London only two weeks before paid them a visit: he answered all their questions, though when they asked him if they smelt and he immediately shouted back "No!" they were convinced he was just being polite. Then groups of Dutch Eurasians came down from the Burmese border. The Kanchanaburi men were horrified to see them: they arrived looking as though it was still the worst days of the railway, a sight hard to forget or forgive. The Japanese guards never came closer to being killed. However, it did not come to that. The Kanchanaburi soldiers enthusiastically took on the task of looking after these poor newcomers and found it both rewarding and healing.

In the midst of all this activity, the knowledge that the Japanese had originally planned to kill all their prisoners in the eventual retreat spread slowly. The war had ended abruptly enough to prevent this, but it is no wonder that Lieutenant Coast commented soberly: "We were very, very lucky to be alive." [5]

4

Major Peacock was pulling out teeth when the news broke. He had
been transferred, with a group of fellow-prisoners, just a few weeks
before the end to Nakhon Nayok, a camp situated the better part of
sixty miles north-east of Bangkok. The journey there was an acutely
uncomfortable stop-go process. It started in moonlight with a long
wait at the mosquito-ridden station. When the train steamed in at last
it was fully loaded, so the men had to hang on where they could. They
were drenched by a two-hour rainstorm and burnt by splinters that flew
from the wood-burning engine. They felt better when they got to
Nakom Paton, though, because they could see the considerable bomb
damage the Allies had done there. An air raid occurred during the
night. All next day they stayed sweltering in the sidings and in a nearby
patch of jungle, and at sunset boarded a different train which had several truckloads of wounded and sick Japanese attached to it, to whom
the prisoners without hesitation offered water. In the morning the party
had to cross the river on foot, as the bridge had been bombed and
could no longer support the weight of a train. The rest of that day was
spent in a cluster of coconut trees. The following day they moved on
to Bangkok, travelling on the roof of another train, where they were
grilled by the sun and soaked by the streaming rain. They tried not to
fall asleep as they had to duck under bridges and it was all too easy
to lose one's balance on the curved roofs.

Bangkok station, lit only by oil lamps and candles, full of the smoke
of bonfires, crowded with Japanese sick, wounded and dead, among
whom mingled a weird-looking mob of Siamese, presented a grotesque
spectacle. Eventually the prisoners were hustled into sampans, taken
downstream for a couple of hours, and then parked by a huge ruined
warehouse where they stayed for two days. A train took them on part
of the way but they had to walk the rest, a gruelling ordeal reminiscent
of the original "death march" up to Kanchanaburi. Everybody was
taxed to the limit of his endurance, men's feet bled freely as they
walked, and Major Peacock and his doctor companion drank nineteen
pints of liquid each, mostly water. Having marched thirty miles in
eleven hours with the thermometer reading over ninety, they entered
their camp just as a sudden icy rainstorm caught them with such force
that they fell to their knees. Staggering a few minutes later into the
huts, they collapsed into sleep.

In the morning the major and the doctor started work at once in the medical hut and they kept this work up till the end. There was plenty to do and they saw little of the guards, but all the same they grew depressed, and for the first time Major Peacock began to doubt his chances of survival.

He need not have worried. On the morning of August 14 the Major was hurrying to complete a dental extraction. There was very little chloroform and the patient was likely to come to before the operation was finished, so when a wild-eyed Dutchman rushed into the hut and tried to shake hands the Major naturally shoved him off impatiently; then, finishing the job, he turned and asked what the matter was. The Dutchman told him and he and his assistant rocked their unfortunate victim into a semi-conscious state and shouted in his ear the splendid words they had dreamed of for so long: "War finishee, alla men go home."

There was no spontaneous communal singing at Nakhon Nayok, but within an hour or so three flags were flying on three flagpoles (the Union Jack and the flags of Australia and the Netherlands), and some liquor came in. This was followed by a large consignment of meat from local sources. Paratroops arrived, supplies were dropped, and there was almost a fortnight of hopeful, speculative, confused existence before the men were brought out in the middle of a pitch dark night, piled into battered old lorries that broke down with maddening frequency, and driven the sixty miles to Bangkok Airport.[6]

5

Far away at the tip of the long peninsula, on the Island, among the Royal Norfolks and others crowded into Changi, the story was the same: rumours, speculation, excitement, stern self-reminders not to expect too much, then someone coming into a hut at night and whispering; a reply of: "My God! No, it can't be! Are you sure?" and then, during the next few days, the moving out of the Japanese guards and their replacement by the Kempei-Tai, once so dreaded but now behaving impeccably. Swiss Red Cross officials and then civilians appeared. Later the paratroops came in and the celebration of victory followed the same pattern as it had everywhere else. Captain Burton's party gave the first officers who reached them the best food they had, and were told bluntly how lousy it was: "If this is the best—God help you. I'd hate to see the worst." [7] Mr Braddon and some friends walked into Singapore town to watch Mountbatten drive up to the steps of the civic hall where the Japanese commander, Itagaki, handed over his sword. Mr Braddon then visited HMS *Sussex,* where he stayed two days, enjoying the Royal Navy's hospitality, which not only provided plenty to eat and drink but also baths and clean clothes. New troops came in on the transports that eventually were to take the bulk of the prisoners off. The few Americans got the full treatment from their government, one of them being flown straight back to Texas.[8] Mr Braddon went back to Changi in a jeep with eighteen other sightseers and joined in the dazed and happy muddle.

The prisoners there were trying to adjust to the new situation—eating lavishly, talking about the future, taking short trips all over the Island, collecting souvenirs, shopping, visiting the officers' club, gawking at anything and everything, and revelling in the simple freedoms of a walk at leisure, a view of the sea, the slow warm realisation of being at liberty. The 1,297 days were over.

6

Looked at dispassionately, the whole Singapore affair, the days of captivity and the campaign that went before them, provides an almost copybook example of how not to do things. Leaving out the years of indifference and neglect, and taking as a starting point the moment when Percival assumed command in Malaya, the British part in subsequent events could hardly have been more mismanaged. If proper defences had been constructed in those seven months . . . if the troops had been allowed to do realistic training in the sacred rubber plantations and jungle tracks . . . if there had been enough troops, equipment and transport . . . if there had been enough aircraft and they had been modern . . . if the aircraft could have protected the fleet . . . if there had been carriers . . . if the land attack could have been stopped in Malaya, let alone Johore . . . if the reinforcements had not been sent . . . if they had been sent in time to toughen up before the battle . . . if the three services had co-operated . . . if the civil governments had cooperated with the services . . . if the radio had worked . . . if the Singapore residents had taken the invasion threat seriously . . . if the Causeway had either been completely destroyed or worthily defended . . . if the searchlights had worked . . . if Percival had not believed himself outnumbered . . . if one of the commanding generals had taken a really forceful, positive attitude . . . if troops and civilians had been told the facts . . . if any one of these things had been different from what they were, the outcome might have been different. But as rigidly as in any classical tragedy, error piled on error to lead to an inevitable and catastrophic end, and the end also of unquestioned British influence in Asia.

It is hard to fault the Japanese for their conduct of the Malaya campaign, indeed, for the way they handled the full sweep of events for the first four months, when they captured territories stretching from Rangoon to Rabaul at the cost of fifteen thousand lives, four hundred aircraft and "a couple of dozen warships, none of them larger than a destroyer." [9] (Of course it was the very size and ease of these successes that made them fall victim to the "victory disease" that caused their eventual downfall.)

It was in the aftermath of these first successes that they went wrong. Obviously it was sensible to employ their prisoners to do any jobs that would assist her war effort (in Britain, many prisoners of war were usefully occupied on farms), but it was the height of folly not to realise that fit and well-fed men will work much better than half-starved, sick men, and that harsh treatment will sooner or later recoil sharply upon those who mete it out. The Japanese High Command was as short-sighted as the British High Command had been: never at any time did they seem to appreciate the difference between voicing pious sentiments in Tokyo and actually impressing their views on Sergeant Yo-tanné, Nattering Norman, or the Ice-Cream Man in Changi. And in the end, when all the cards were down, the victors could apparently think of nothing better to do than to hang a few obvious scapegoats, as if that would be of any use to the survivors or the dead, or help to an understanding of those who had said so often: "War finish one hundred years."

Something has to come out of all this on the credit side, and it seems to have come from the survivors themselves. They had certainly gone the long way round to prove it.

Former Captain Louis J. Caffrey, MC, of The Rifle Brigade, whose career in World War I had been an extraordinary mixture of the harrowing and the bizarre, and who was regarded by all who knew him as outstandingly courageous, took a view diametrically opposed to the traditional Japanese one. In August 1945 he had been listening to the celebrated late night broadcast by the Prime Minister, Clement Attlee, with its splendid opening sentences: "Japan has surrendered. The last of our enemies is laid low." "Well," remarked the sixty-seven-year-old Irishman with relish, "we're on the only list that matters—the list of survivors."

The men of the Lost Division who were still alive felt the same, bewildered as they were. The first weeks of wild, unrestrained joy were over, it was time to go home, and those who had been assigned to fetch them out were understandably apprehensive. Few details had filtered through to England, even though communications were now re-established, and the Allied servicemen whose orders were to go in to Singapore and Siam and bring out the "lost men" faced a situation of the greatest delicacy. They were naturally full of goodwill, but the more imaginative among them felt inadequate. They were fit, cheerful, well-fed, well-dressed, full of cocky energy, riding the crest of victory, and now they had to call on all their reserves of gentleness and tact in encountering their fellow-soldiers whose war experience had been so bitterly different. There were as many ways of approaching this problem as there were men tackling it. A rare one whose situation was enviable was the Dakota pilot who asked for a certain sergeant-major because he had to tell him: "Your son is here to fly you home." [10]

It was not necessary to overdo the gentleness and tact. These prisoners were not the human wreckage discovered in mid-Europe when the gates of the concentration camps were opened and the first job was that of sorting the living from the dead; where life is so nearly extinguished, little note can or need be taken of the manner of rescue, or of its accompanying words. But the Far East prisoners were not political. They had been fighting soldiers, so they faced their comrades-in-arms across a gulf that only time could bridge, if it could ever be bridged at all. They could not say: "What do they know about us?" but they could not avoid thinking it. Everyone did the best he could, usually with gifts —food, drink, cigarettes, medicine, vitamins, clothing, news, and kind words. To many, the best gift of all was a real bed, with a proper mattress and sheets and pillows, fresh and clean and three feet broad, and four feet away from its neighbours.

It was a slow business. RAPWI—the initials stood for "Rehabilitation of Allied Prisoners of War and Internees"—soon came to be referred to as the "Retain All Prisoners of War Indefinitely" organisation; [11] and yet probably the very slowness of the procedure was a help to these disoriented men. The best treatment was the nonchalant, unquestioning manner of the RAF pilots, most of whom looked impossibly young to have earned the medal ribbons they wore, and one of whom flew the party that included Major Peacock out of Bangkok. The whole thing was wonderfully casual, starting with the navigator's not turning up. The pilot was heard shouting to one of his crew: "Hi Stinker, where's my bloody navigator?" It was apparently concluded that he must have pushed off to pick up a bit in Bangkok. If that was the case he could "bloody well hitch-hike back to Rangoon—this crate's off." The aircraft left without him. It climbed and circled the famous Sapphire Shrine, and only now did the passengers make the unsettling discovery that there was no door on the machine. They pointed this out to one of the crew, who seemed mildly surprised. "Now, when did we have that bloody door, Jack?" He decided that the (blank) members of another flight must have taken it—certainly it had been there only the week before. "He leaned out in a speculative way, a hand on each door post, as though searching for it, frightening us earthbound clods to death." [12]

Often pilots on the Rangoon route flew along the Kwai so that their passengers could take a last look at the railway they had built. It was strange seeing it from the air. They tried to pick out the graves, but the jungle concealed them. Everyone who had been there left something of himself and the men, especially the more sensitive among them, realised this. The cumulative effects of three and a half years of anxiety and mental stress are hard to calculate. Most prisoners, Major Peacock thought, developed some eccentricity, but remained reasonably sane and sensible. One friend told him that if he ever got out of the war alive he would never again fear anyone or anything.

The Major knew that every survivor would believe to the end of his days that he had had a miraculous escape.[13] Lieutenant Coast, as we know, agreed with him: "We were very, very lucky to be alive." [14] The list of survivors is the only list that matters. Of course some took longer than others to return to a normal state. It took Captain Burton a long time: thirteen years after the war he found he had to walk out of a Canadian hotel when a Japanese trade delegation arrived in it; all the old hatreds flooded back.[15] Mr Braddon remained sceptical about there ever being true peace with Japan; her population crams the four islands, she still makes munitions, she still needs the oil, the tin, the rubber, she called the years of war with China "the China Incident." [16]

Yet Hiroshima cured Sergeant Harrison once and for all, and Lieutenant Coast was back in Siam in 1948 for quite a long stay. Captain Gordon became a minister, and both he and Sergeant Harrison have kept in touch with former fellow-prisoners. Many many have done so:

with some it was because their common ordeal created a special
bond, with others because nobody else seemed to be able to understand.
There is a reunion at the Royal Festival Hall every year, and until his
death in 1966 General Percival always went—and was given a great
welcome too.

But there is a scar on every man all the same. Particularly for those
who were among the youngest in captivity and spent (say) a twenty-
third birthday on the Kwai, they have left in the depths of that river
nearly four of the irrecoverable years of the golden youth they should
have known. Anyone looking for the graves now can find them in two
cemeteries that are three miles apart. Five thousand and sixty-one men
are buried in Kanchanaburi, of these 3,459 are from the United Kingdom. One thousand seven hundred and forty men are buried in Chungkai, of them 1,329 are from the United Kingdom. At Kanchanaburi,
where Colonel Nakamura issued his order, where the Levelling Party
was formed and where Major Peacock made mud bricks and practised dentistry, it is just over a mile from the cemetery to the river.
Chungkai cemetery can only be reached by boat, and is the original
burial ground started by the prisoners; most of those buried there died
in the "hospital" which the prisoners built. The two cemeteries are
beautifully kept, peaceful, bright with flowers and shaded by trees;
when the local boatmen know that a visitor is a former prisoner they
roar with laughter and admiringly say to him: "You still alive? You
iron man!" Every year there is a wreath-laying ceremony by the British,
Australian and Dutch ambassadors.[17] With what thoughts do they go
there now? Is it a chore, are they too young to have known what the
war was like? At Chungkai the inscription reads: "Their name liveth
for evermore." But is this true? Do people remember?

A number of men have revisited the scenes of their captivity. Captain Burton had a posting to Malaya and wanted to show his wife
round Changi. There was no difficulty about looking round the outside
but the superintendent would not let them in to see his old cell in the
jail as there was a security scare on and the jail was full of political
suspects. It naturally struck Captain Burton as ironic that he was not
allowed in where once he had so longed to get out.[18] Major Peacock
had, as befits the veteran, gone quietly home (with his son, who had
been flown out to meet him) and settled to work again, but twenty years
later he and his wife found that the ship on which they were taking
a trip was unexpectedly stopping for a few days in Bangkok. The Major
had always declared that he would only lay eyes on the River Kwai

again "by mistake," but, once in Bangkok, he could not resist the temptation to have another look for himself, and to show Mrs Peacock some of the places where he had been. Realising thankfully that the horrors had faded in his mind and that what remained clear were the odd, bizarre or even amusing incidents, he found it a fascinating pilgrimage and came home to write his book.[19]

The single track railway line still exists, and is used by the Thai State Railways, who have patched it up and put it in good order. It runs from Bampong up to a place called Saiyoke Waterfall, which, as far as one can judge, is not far from Kinsayok, the place with the lovely clear stream and the dreadful, bug-ridden huts. The line was bought after the war by the Siamese Government from the Allies for a payment of fifty million bahts, which works out at approximately £875,000.[20]

One of the most famous war memorial inscriptions in the Far East is the one at Kohima (where, incidentally, the 1st and 2nd Battalions The Royal Norfolk Regiment gained battle honours). It reads simply:

> When you go home
> Tell them of us and say
> For your tomorrow
> We gave our today.

"When you go home tell them of us and say . . ." Here the present-day reader comes to a full, uncomfortable stop. What can one say? What can one add? Did these men die in vain? Did the Japanese, whose dead are commemorated in similar memorials in similar places, one of the most impressive of which is the double obelisk "To the Fallen" on the beach at Kota Bahru, die for nothing? Can one accept the dedication of "those quiet stones" to all the fallen "by those shores and beneath those waters of the pale aquamarine China Sea, friend or foe"?[21] Is it possible that only the men who were there can truly understand?

7

One concentrates on the men who came back. Some of them, once it was all over, admitted that they would not have missed it for the world (Sergeant Harrison was one of these):[22] others behaved as though it was a bad dream from which they had awakened, they hoped, for ever. But outwardly they all took a commonsense view, simply noting that they put on enormous amounts of weight during the journey home, and that their families and friends did not therefore have to suffer seeing them at their worst.[23] Most of them were taken off by ship, and sailed away over the deep blue water the way that they had come a lifetime before. As Mr Braddon's ship went out, it passed another where Harry Smith stood leaning on the rail, looking melancholy as always; as one man they roared out the old catch-phrase, "You'll never get off the Island." In the distance they could see the tower of Changi jail, flying the Union Jack.[24]

Most of the British prisoners reached home in October. The *Ormonde* brought to Southampton what was left of the 5th Bedfords, including Lieutenant-Colonel Thomas and Regimental Sergeant-Major Dunham, though not all units of all the regiments concerned managed to travel together.[25] It did not matter all that much. What had happened was this.

Plans had necessarily been made to retake the territories conquered by Japan, and the Malaya plans stemmed from the successful reoccupation of Burma. This involved two projects: an assault on the Port Swettenham–Port Dickson area (Operation Zipper) for October 1945 and Singapore (Operation Mailfist) for December 1945. These were part of a large overall design that took as its centrepiece the invasion of Japan itself.[26]

Photographic reconnaissance was carried out for both these Operations in the spring of 1945, and in May the date for Zipper was advanced to August as Japan had by then become weaker than Admiral Mountbatten had originally expected. He started detailed planning on June 1, proposing to make the assault with the Fourteenth Army and nine escort carriers. Zipper was modified a good deal during the summer and then the Japanese surrender in August made the actual assault unnecessary. However as the ships and men concerned in the operation were already moving to their appointed stations it was quaintly decided to go ahead with Zipper as planned (minus, of course, the fighting) on the grounds that this would cause less trouble than cancelling the whole thing.[27]

Admiral Walker, flying his flag in the *Nelson,* arrived off Penang on August 28, and received on board a group of Japanese officers who promised free passage for his ships and gave details of all the minefields in the whole area. Admiral Power, flying his flag in the *Cleopatra,* arrived at Penang on September 1, and next day Rear-Admiral Uzumi signed the surrender of Penang on board the *Nelson* (the same day as the surrender ceremony on the USS *Missouri* in Tokyo Bay). The Royal Marines occupied Penang and Sabang and the *Cleopatra* sailed for Singapore, joining the occupation force in the Malacca Strait, and anchored off the Island on September 3, accompanied by HMIS *Bengal* and joined next day by the *Sussex,* the *Rotherham,* and the *Kedah.* On the evening of September 4 Lieutenant-General Itagaki came on board the *Sussex* to sign the surrender of Singapore and Johore.[28]

At eleven o'clock the next morning the reoccupation of Singapore began, led off by troops of the 5th Indian Division, while the *Rotherham* sailed round the Island to the Naval Base where her commander, Captain Biggs, assumed command at once and was shown round by the Japanese Chief of Staff. He quickly realised that there was no love lost between the Japanese Army and Navy, but was pleased to find that the Japanese readily and willingly supplied every facility he asked for. Former dockyard workers arrived, some of them bringing their British employers' silver, which they had kept hidden during the Japanese occupation. The Japanese helped out too, cutting the grass on the playing fields. About five hundred of them did this—by hand, with scissors.[29]

The full Zipper assault convoy now steamed up to the coast at Port Swettenham, where the first troops and vehicles came ashore on schedule early in the morning of September 9. They did not keep to the schedule, however: the sloping, swampy beaches and an offshore sand-bar drowned a number of vehicles and caused fearful traffic jams, but on succeeding days more carefully selected positions were occupied and fresh beachheads opened up. On September 12 a landing went perfectly except for one landing craft described as "over-enthusiastic" which "took the beach at twelve knots and disappeared into the jungle" coming out again a week later, "a small village having sprung up under its bows." By the end of September well over sixty thousand troops, seven thousand vehicles and twenty-five thousand tons of stores had been landed.[30]

Meanwhile the Japanese were being shipped out, but first they were deprived of their considerable loot—the civilians released from Syme Road were later given the pick of this. The British entered Kuala Lumpur unopposed on September 13, the day after Admiral Mountbatten presided at the official surrender ceremony in Singapore. The Municipal Buildings, carefully stage-set, made a dignified background for the formal uniforms of the chief participants and the more casual dress of the four hundred spectators, who included ex-prisoners as well as reporters. General Itagaki and Admiral Mountbatten signed eleven copies of the Instrument of Surrender.[31]

Everyone commented on the ex-prisoners' perfect demeanour. An Army nurse said that they were the most courteous and considerate people she had ever met.[32] One ship's captain confessed that two privates in the Argylls looked rather wistfully at the ship's cat and said that a fortnight before "it couldn't have got twenty yards along the upper deck with its fur still on." [33] Another was fascinated to see how quiet the men were at first, how they slowly came to life again and then wanted above all else to talk and talk, pouring it all out to appalled and absorbed listeners.[34] Another admitted that, though he had felt worried when he took them on board because they all had a strange staring look in their eyes and he feared they might be a problem, their behaviour had in fact been exemplary. Gruffly he concluded: "Glad to have had the privilege of bringing you home." [35]

It was a privilege for anybody to bring them home. But it was not as simple as all that. On the surface it seemed splendid—the ships came into home waters, then into harbour, all other ships sounding their sirens in salute. The familiar watery sunlight shone, all the windows opened and the garland bells rang and people waved, and the worn uncertain survivors, the lost travellers with the sun-bleached hair, long since having counted their dead in the morning, came slowly into the centre of the focus to meet their welcome and, let us be sure, an utter lack of understanding. It has taken a long time for some understanding to develop—this is shown by the fact that most of the books on the subject did not appear until the nineteen-sixties.

But for the moment, in October 1945, four years from setting out, they found it hard enough to believe that they were home, that the ill dream was over. Chance, fate, the hand of providence, whichever it was, had brought them back, among them those that remained of The Royal Norfolks, who had once again maintained that Regiment's reputation. General Horrocks was right. In Singapore and on the Kwai the fighting for sheer physical and moral survival had been fiercest, climatic conditions most vile and the odds against victory most daunting. So the Ninth Foot had been sure to be there.

8

Eighty years before, at the end of another war, the leader of the defeated side had paid tribute to his men in words that seem to fit the
men of the Singapore campaign very well:

> After four years of arduous service, marked by unsurpassed
> courage and fortitude . . . the brave survivors of so many hard-
> fought battles, who have remained steadfast to the last . . . will
> take with you the satisfaction that proceeds from the conscious-
> ness of duty faithfully performed.[36]

—And he had signed it: Robert E. Lee.

Notes

(Refer to Sources p. 299 for details.)

CHAPTER I

1. Leasor, pp. 29-30.
2. *Ibid.,* pp. 30-31.
3. Hough (FHD), pp. 20-22, 148-149, 167.
4. Hough (Z), p. 34.
5. *Ibid.,* p. 20.
6. *Ibid.,* p. 41.
7. Leasor, pp. 105-107.
8. *Ibid.,* p. 108; Swinson, p. 33.
9. Barber, p. 121; Morrison, p. 12.
10. Leasor, pp. 114-115.
11. Morrison, pp. 40-42.
12. Anderson, p. 345.
13. Braddon, p. 42.
14. *Ibid.,* p. 48.
15. Coward, p. 291.
16. Anderson, p. 345.
17. Spencer Chapman, p. 35.
18. Morrison, pp. 24, 25-26.
19. Mackenzie, p. 225.
20. Perelman, p. 350.
21. Fitzgerald, fp. 264.
22. Swinson, p. 35.
23. Barclay, pp. 116-117.
24. Parkinson, p. 113.
25. James, p. 185.
26. Russell-Roberts, p. 23.
27. McCormac, p. 3.
28. Russell-Roberts, p. 31.
29. Leasor, p. 109.
30. *Ibid.,* p. 128; Swinson, p. 38.
31. Churchill, I, p. 336.
32. Roskill, I, p. 555.
33. Bateson, p. 89; Kirby, I, p. 35.
34. Jones, pp. 122-123; 184-185.
35. *Ibid.,* p. 195.
36. Collier, pp. 67, 107.
37. Churchill, II, p. 236.
38. Parkinson, p. 113 *et seq.*
39. *Guardian* of 13/1/42
40. Churchill, II, pp. 350-351.
41. *Ibid.,* II, p. 511.
42. Collier, p. 63.
43. Churchill, II, pp. 525-526.
44. *Ibid.,* II, p. 526.
45. *Ibid.,* II, p. 396.
46. *Ibid.,* II, p. 396.
47. Bateson, p. 89.
48. Barber, p. 43; Swinson, p. 39.
49. Churchill, II, p. 544.
50. *Ibid.,* II, p. 446.
51. *Ibid.,* II, p. 551.
52. *Ibid.,* II, pp. 554-555.
53. Morrison, p. 43.
54. Swinson, p. 10.
55. Leasor, p. 151; Swinson, p. 18.
56. Russell-Roberts, p. 24.
57. Churchill, III, p. 157.
58. Gillison, pp. 39-42.
59. Lord, p. 50.
60. Jones, p. 212.
61. Parkinson, p. 113 *et seq.*
62. Percival.
63. Russell-Roberts, p. 266; Brereton.
64. Bateson, p. 46.
65. Collier, pp. 94-95.
66. Barber, pp. 21, 22.
67. Russell-Roberts, pp. 25-26.

68. Bateson, p. 82.
69. Barber, p. 44.
70. Morrison, pp. 15-16.
71. Braddon, pp. 36-37; 38; 44.
72. *Ibid.*, pp. 40-43.
73. Barber, p. 24.
74. James, p. 193.
75. Hough (Z), p. 75.
76. Leasor, p. 112.
77. Kirby, I, pp. 163, 51, 78, 181.
78. Gillison, p. 151.
79. Bateson, p. 25; Kirby, I, p. 92.
80. Hough (Z), pp. 103, 104, 107, 111, 115.
81. Peters, pp. 93-95.
82. Tuchman, p. 44.
83. Morison, III, p. 138.
84. Morrison, pp. 11, 12, 13.
85. Swinson, pp. 8, 18.

CHAPTER II

1. Long.
2. Bateson, pp. 19-20.
3. Thomas, pp. 51-52.
4. Lord, p. 63.
5. Collier, p. 114; Bateson, p. 19.
6. *The Times*, 17/11/41
7. Bateson, p. 82.
8. Hough (Z), pp. 111-112.
9. *Ibid.*, p. 112.
10. *The Times*, 19/11/41
11. Braddon, pp. 44-50.
12. James, p. 193.
13. *Ibid.*, pp. 195-196.
14. *Ibid.*, p. 197.
15. *Ibid.*, p. 198.
16. *Ibid.*, p. 199.
17. *Ibid.*, p. 200.
18. Gilchrist, p. 7.
19. *Ibid.*, p. 16.
20. *Ibid.*, p. 9.
21. *Ibid.*, p. 10.
22. *Ibid.*, p. 11.
23. *Ibid.*, p. 12.

24. *Ibid.*, p. 13.
25. *Ibid.*, p. 16.
26. Collier, pp. 110-111.
27. Mackenzie, p. 226.
28. Braddon, p. 34.
29. Bateson, p. 83.
30. *Ibid.*, p. 39.
31. Lord, p. 3.
32. Bateson, p. 25.
33. Parkinson, p. 115.
34. Barber, p. 48.
35. Collier, p. 136.
36. Kirby, I, pp. 175, 25.
37. Mackenzie, p. 244.
38. Braddon, p. 48.
39. Mackenzie, p. 188.
40. Gillison, pp. 204-205; Ross, p. 83; Bateson, p. 92.
41. Bateson, pp. 25-26; 142-143.
42. Braddon, p. 53.
43. *The Times*, 2/12/41
44. Morrison, III, p. 138.
45. Hough (Z), p. 113.
46. *The Times*, 3/12/41
47. Hough (Z), pp. 114-115.
48. *Ibid.*, pp. 116, 82.
49. *Ibid.*, pp. 118, 121.
50. *Ibid.*, p. 119.
51. Roskill, I, p. 561; Morison, III, pp. 156-157.
52. *The Times*, 5/12/41
53. Barber, p. 24.
54. Swinson, p. 48.
55. Gilchrist, pp. 18-19.
56. Kirby, I, pp. 174-175.
57. *The Times*, 6/12/41
58. Peters, p. 93.
59. Mackenzie, pp. 233-234.
60. Hough (Z), p. 123.
61. Collier, p. 139.
62. McCormac, p. 2.
63. Braddon, pp. 54-56.
64. Russell-Roberts, pp. 25-26.
65. Mackenzie, p. 234.
66. Barber, pp. 23-24, 25, 27.
67. Mackenzie, p. 226.
68. Bateson, pp. 80-81.

69. Mackenzie, p. 237.
70. Leasor, pp. 166-167.
71. Barber, pp. 28-30.
72. Morrison, pp. 47-48.
73. Barber, pp. 30-31.
74. Collier, p. 149.
75. Bateson, p. 49.
76. *Ibid.*, pp. 28-29; Collier, pp. 114-115.
77. Churchill, III, p. 477.

CHAPTER III

1. McCormac, p. 3.
2. Connell, p. 45.
3. Gilchrist, pp. 13, 14, 15.
4. McCormac, p. 4.
5. Morrison, p. 48.
6. Collier, pp. 114-115, 103.
7. Bateson, pp. 32, 33, 34.
8. Morrison, pp. 50-51.
9. Barber, pp. 39-40.
10. James, p. 205.
11. Peters, p. 93.
12. Bateson, pp. 83-84.
13. Mackenzie, pp. 189, 191.
14. Russell-Roberts, pp. 26, 27, 28.
15. Collier, p. 145.
16. Bateson, p. 98.
17. Barclay, pp. 118-119.
18. Bateson, p. 98; Mackenzie, p. 249.
19. Morrison, p. 49.
20. Barber, p. 37.
21. Bateson, p. 95; Hough (Z), p. 127; Morrison, p. 60.
22. Mackenzie, pp. 238-239.
23. Bateson, p. 98; James, p. 205.
24. Bateson, p. 98.
25. Collier, p. 145.
26. Russell-Roberts, p. 28.
27. Mackenzie, p. 245.
28. Braddon, p. 62.
29. Barber, pp. 46-47.
30. James, p. 205.
31. Hough (Z), pp. 129, 130, 131.
32. *Ibid.*, pp. 132, 135, 134.
33. Bateson, p. 84.
34. *Ibid.*, p. 48.
35. Morrison, p. 65.
36. Hough (Z), pp. 136, 139.
37. *Ibid.*, pp. 136, 138, 140.
38. *Ibid.*, pp. 141, 143; Morrison, p. 61.
39. Hough (Z), pp. 146, 148.
40. *Ibid.*, pp. 146, 149, 150, 151.
41. Barber, pp. 49, 50.
42. Bateson, p. 98; Mackenzie, p. 250.
43. Collier, p. 142.
44. Leasor, p. 168.
45. Collier, p. 143.
46. Morrison, p. 167.
47. Barber, pp. 50-51.
48. Churchill, III, p. 489.
49. *Ibid.*, p. 498.
50. Swinson, p. 67.
51. Mackenzie, p. 246.
52. *Ibid.*, p. 247.
53. Morrison, pp. 68-69.
54. Mackenzie, p. 242.
55. Morrison, p. 60.
56. Collier, p. 145.
57. Russell-Roberts, p. 28.
58. Mackenzie, p. 256.
59. Bateson, p. 49.
60. Collier, p. 162.
61. Kirby, I, pp. 206, 208.
62. Collier, pp. 164-165.
63. Mackenzie, pp. 259, 252.
64. *The Times*, 12/12/41
65. *Guardian*, 12/12/41
66. Churchill, III, p. 564.

CHAPTER IV

1. Leasor, p. 195.
2. *The Times*, 13/12/41
3. Swinson, pp. 78-79.
4. Barber, p. 55; Morrison, p. 69.

5. Connell, p. 57.
6. McCormac, p. 6.
7. Morrison, pp. 73-74.
8. *Ibid.,* p. 76.
9. Sutherland, p. 98.
10. Russell-Roberts, p. 30.
11. Morrison, pp. 99-100.
12. Swinson, pp. 80-81.
13. Barber, p. 57.
14. Morrison, p. 98.
15. Swinson, pp. 81-82.
16. *Guardian,* 16/12/41
17. *The Times,* 16/12/41
18. Morrison, p. 70.
19. *The Times,* 20/12/41
20. *Ibid.,* 17/12/41
21. Gilchrist, pp. 208-212.
22. Bateson, pp. 84-85; Collier, p. 152; Mackenzie, pp. 201-202.
23. Barber, p. 58.
24. *The Times,* 19/12/41
25. *Guardian,* 19/12/41 and 20/12/41
26. Russell-Roberts, p. 33.
27. Bateson, p. 85; Mackenzie, p. 206.
28. Gilchrist, p. 14.
29. Mackenzie, p. 263.
30. Bateson, pp. 49-50.
31. Mackenzie, p. 264 *et seq.*
32. *The Times,* 23/12/41
33. *Guardian,* 23/12/41
34. *Ibid.,* 24/12/41
35. Barber, p. 63.
36. Mackenzie, p. 268.
37. *Ibid.,* pp. 211-212.
38. Collier, p. 155; Bateson, p. 86.
39. Bateson, p. 86.
40. *Guardian,* 26/12/41
41. Braddon, p. 63.
42. Swinson, p. 86.
43. Barber, pp. 62-63.
44. *Ibid.,* pp. 65-66.
45. Bateson, pp. 99, 100, 101.
46. Swinson, p. 82.
47. Russell-Roberts, p. 34.
48. Mackenzie, pp. 270, 275-276.

CHAPTER V

1. Spencer Chapman, p. 35.
2. Bateson, pp. 103-104.
3. Russell-Roberts, pp. 34-35.
4. Peters, p. 93.
5. Connell, p. 58.
6. Mackenzie, p. 276.
7. Barber, pp. 67-69.
8. *The Times,* 30/12/41
9. Morrison, p. 101.
10. *The Times,* 6 & 7/1/42
11. Russell-Roberts, p. 35.
12. *The Times,* 31/12/41
13. *Guardian,* 31/12/41
14. *The Times,* 1/1/42
15. Mackenzie, pp. 278-279.
16. Russell-Roberts, pp. 36-37.
17. Mackenzie, pp. 272-273.
18. Russell-Roberts, pp. 38, 40.
19. Mackenzie, p. 320.
20. Brereton.
21. *Guardian,* 1 & 2/1/42
22. McCormac, p. 8.
23. Sutherland, p. 98.
24. Collier, p. 172.
25. *The Times,* 7/1/42
26. *Guardian,* 7/1/42
27. Barber, p. 71.
28. McCormac, p. 8.
29. Barber, pp. 72, 73, 71.
30. Russell-Roberts, p. 41.
31. Collier, pp. 173-174.
32. Mackenzie, pp. 324, 327, 329.
33. Collier, p. 175.
34. Sutherland, p. 105.
35. Barber, pp. 77, 78.
36. Swinson, pp. 93, 92.
37. Barber, p. 79.
38. Russell-Roberts, p. 42.
39. Kirby, I, p. 284.
40. Morrison, pp. 108, 109, 110.
41. *Guardian,* 9/1/42
42. Russell-Roberts, pp. 43-44.
43. Morrison, p. 111.
44. *The Times,* 10/1/42
45. *Guardian,* 10/1/42

46. Morrison, pp. 113, 114, 115, 116.
47. Braddon, pp. 64-65.
48. *Ibid.,* p. 67.
49. Barber, pp. 81-82, 83.
50. Swinson, pp. 96, 97, 98.
51. Spencer Chapman, p. 35.
52. Mackenzie, p. 269.
53. Brereton.

CHAPTER VI

1. Horrocks, p. 117.
2. Carew, p. 118.
3. Brereton.
4. Leasor, p. 18.
5. Mackenzie, p. 337.
6. *Ibid.,* p. 340.
7. Coast, p. 31.
8. Mackenzie, p. 343.
9. Morrison, p. 119.
10. Braddon, p. 67.
11. *Ibid.,* pp. 68, 69.
12. Russell-Roberts, p. 45.
13. Mackenzie, p. 343.
14. Russell-Roberts, p. 47.
15. *The Times,* 14/1/42
16. Bateson, p. 182.
17. Swinson, p. 102.
18. Braddon, pp. 71-72.
19. Churchill, IV, p. 55.
20. *Guardian,* 17/1/42
21. Barber, pp. 83-87 *passim.*
22. Mackenzie, pp. 343-344.
23. *Guardian,* 19/1/42
24. Swinson, p. 93.
25. Churchill, IV, pp. 56, 58-59.
26. Swinson, p. 109.
27. *Guardian,* 13/1/42
28. *The Times,* 20 & 21/1/42
29. Barber, pp. 89-93 *passim.*
30. Braddon, pp. 75-100 *passim.*
31. Russell-Roberts, p. 47.
32. Morrison, p. 125.
33. Mackenzie, pp. 351, 352.
34. Russell-Roberts, pp. 58-59.

35. Mackenzie, p. 352.
36. *Ibid.,* pp. 354-356.
37. Russell-Roberts, pp. 60-61.
38. *Ibid.,* pp. 62, 63, 64.
39. Barber, pp. 93, 94, 95.
40. Churchill, IV, pp. 56, 58, 61.
41. Peters, p. 93.
42. Swinson, p. 117.
43. Barclay, pp. 127, 165.
44. De Guingand, pp. 56, 59.
45. Mackenzie, p. 371.
46. Russell-Roberts, pp. 264, 265-266.
47. *Ibid.,* pp. 65-66.
48. *Ibid.,* pp. 67, 69.
49. *Ibid.,* pp. 77-78.
50. *Ibid.,* p. 83.
51. Kirby, I, pp. 328-329.
52. Peters, p. 93.
53. Churchill, IV, p. 68.
54. McCormac, p. 8.
55. Barber, pp. 102, 104, 106-107.
56. McCormac, p. 12.
57. Barber, p. 108.
58. Russell-Roberts, p. 84.
59. Mackenzie, pp. 372-373, 362, 368.
60. Russell-Roberts, pp. 90, 93-94, 96-97.
61. James, p. 216.
62. Sutherland, p. 100.
63. Morrison, p. 143.

CHAPTER VII

1. James, p. 217.
2. Morrison, p. 133.
3. Russell-Roberts, pp. 100, 102-105, 108.
4. James, pp. 217, 218, 220.
5. Morrison, p. 143.
6. Barber, p. 114.
7. Morrison, pp. 147-148.
8. *Ibid.,* pp. 146-147.
9. Barclay, p. 123.
10. Bateson, p. 112.

11. Barber, p. 118.
12. Collier, p. 190.
13. Bateson, p. 112.
14. Peters, p. 94.
15. Mackenzie, p. 382.
16. Churchill, IV, pp. 91-92.
17. De Guingand, p. 56.
18. Burton, p. 27.
19. Barber, p. 121.
20. Morrison, pp. 149-152.
21. Barber, p. 124.
22. Morrison, pp. 152-153.
23. Barber, p. 122.
24. Leasor, p. 225.
25. Swinson, p. 126.
26. Morrison, pp. 154, 155, 157, 159, 160.
27. Barber, pp. 128-129.
28. Swinson, p. 117.
29. Leasor, p. 225.
30. *Guardian,* 3/2/42
31. Barber, pp. 118-119; Swinson, p. 128.
32. Morrison, p. 166.
33. Barber, pp. 136-138.
34. Morrison, pp. 171-172, 173.
35. Barber, pp. 140-141.
36. Swinson, p. 131.
37. Morrison, p. 175.
38. Barber, pp. 146-147; Swinson, p. 131.
39. Barber, p. 149.
40. James, pp. 222-223.
41. Swinson, p. 132.
42. Morrison, p. 175.
43. Mackenzie, p. 385.
44. Morrison, p. 176.
45. Barber, p. 150.
46. Churchill, IV, p. 93.
47. Mackenzie, pp. 384-385, 386.
48. Barber, pp. 151-153.
49. Swinson, pp. 135-136.
50. James, pp. 223-224.
51. *Guardian,* 9/2/42
52. Barber, p. 181.
53. *Ibid.,* pp. 155-156.
54. James, p. 225.

55. Russell-Roberts, p. 121.
56. Morrison, pp. 178, 179, 180.
57. Coast, Ch. 3, *passim.*
58. *Guardian,* 10/2/42
59. Mackenzie, pp. 390-391.
60. Churchill, IV, pp. 93-94.
61. Swinson, p. 135.
62. Morrison, pp. 180, 183.
63. Leasor, p. 243.
64. Mackenzie, p. 399; Morrison, pp. 184-185.

CHAPTER VIII

1. *The Times,* 14/2/42
2. Mackenzie, p. 390.
3. Sutherland, pp. 98-105.
4. Mackenzie, p. 393.
5. Barber, pp. 184-185, 161, 164, 167, 169-170, 172, 163; Swinson, p. 139.
6. *Ibid.,* pp. 175-176; 138.
7. Swinson, pp. 139-140.
8. Barber, pp. 182, 183.
9. *The Times,* 12/2/42
10. *Guardian,* 12/2/42
11. Russell-Roberts, p. 124.
12. Barber, p. 188.
13. Mackenzie, p. 398.
14. Swinson, p. 124.
15. Barber, pp. 190, 193.
16. *Ibid.,* pp. 195-196.
17. Churchill, IV, p. 95.
18. Barber, p. 257.
19. *Ibid.,* p. 198.
20. *Ibid.,* p. 199.
21. *Ibid.,* pp. 200-202.
22. James, p. 229.
23. Leasor, p. 243.
24. James, p. 231.
25. Mackenzie, p. 399.
26. Peters, p. 95.
27. Burton, p. 38.
28. Barber, pp. 206-207.
29. James, p. 231.
30. Churchill, IV, pp. 96-97.

31. *Ibid.,* p. 96.
32. Mackenzie, pp. 399, 360.
33. Churchill, IV, pp. 99, 97, 96.
34. Russell-Roberts, p. 126.
35. Mackenzie, p. 400.
36. Swinson, p. 140.
37. Mackenzie, p. 397.
38. Barber, p. 213.
39. *Ibid.,* pp. 214-215.
40. James, p. 232.
41. Barber, pp. 218-219, 222.
42. James, p. 248.
43. Russell-Roberts, p. 127.
44. Sutherland, p. 104.
45. Russell-Roberts, p. 128.
46. Churchill, IV, p. 99.
47. Barber, p. 223; Swinson, p. 145.
48. Swinson, pp. 145-146.
49. James, p. 249.
50. Swinson, p. 146.
51. Barber, pp. 224-225; Swinson, p. 148.
52. Leasor, p. 252.
53. Barber, pp. 227-228; Swinson, p. 149; newspaper reports.
54. *Guardian,* 16, 18, and 20/2/42
55. Churchill, IV, p. 100.
56. Barber, pp. 229, 236-237, 233, 232, 234.
57. *Ibid.,* p. 36; Russell-Roberts, p. 135.
58. Russell-Roberts, pp. 128, 130-131.
59. Burton, p. 39.
60. Barber, p. 231.
61. Leasor, p. 259.
62. Craig, p. 304.
63. Mackenzie, p. 401.
64. Tsuji, p. 185.
65. Leasor, p. 259.

CHAPTER IX

1. *The Times,* 16/2/42
2. Russell-Roberts, p. 138.
3. *Ibid.,* pp. 135-136.
4. Barber, pp. 241-242.
5. *Ibid.,* p. 243.
6. Masters, pp. 155-156.
7. Van der Post (SS), p. 35.
8. Barber, pp. 244-246, 248.
9. *Ibid.,* p. 249.
10. Russell-Roberts, p. 137.
11. Carew, p. 119.
12. Barber, p. 252.
13. *Ibid.,* p. 263.
14. *Ibid.,* p. 259.
15. Coast, p. 13.
16. Burton, p. 44.
17. Peacock, p. 7.
18. Morrison, p. 130.
19. Coast, p. 14.
20. Burton, p. 46.
21. Harrison, p. 138.
22. Burton, p. 57.
23. Coast, p. 40.
24. *Ibid.,* p. 29.
25. Harrison, pp. 141-142.
26. Braddon, p. 172.
27. *Ibid.,* p. 171.
28. *Ibid.,* pp. 177-178.
29. Burton, p. 66.
30. Coast, p. 15.
31. Gordon, p. 21.
32. Braddon, p. 178.
33. Gordon, p. 64.
34. Braddon, p. 179.
35. Gordon, p. 21.
36. McCormac, *passim.*
37. Crawford, *passim.*
38. Fisher, pp. 85-86.
39. Audric, p. 118; Braddon, p. 223; Harrison, p. 206.
40. Peacock, pp. 14-15.
41. Coast, pp. 64-65.
42. Harrison, p. 154.
43. Peacock, p. 147.
44. Harrison, pp. 153-154.
45. Gordon, p. 71.
46. Harrison, p. 147.
47. Coast, p. 100.
48. Peacock, p. 134.
49. Braddon, p. 184.

50. Burton, p. 74.
51. Coast, p. 60.
52. Peacock, p. 134; Braddon, p. 184.
53. Gordon, p. 70.
54. Burton, p. 75.
55. Peters, pp. 96-99.
56. Harrison, p. 150.
57. Peters, pp. 96-99.
58. Braddon, p. 187.
59. Burton, pp. 83-90.
60. Coast, p. 103.

CHAPTER X

1. Harrison, p. 154.
2. Audric, p. 116.
3. Peacock, p. 47.
4. Harrison, p. 161.
5. *Ibid.*, p. 161.
6. Peacock, p. 48.
7. Braddon, p. 205.
8. Peacock, p. 48.
9. Coast, p. 74.
10. Harrison, p. 193.
11. Gordon, pp. 82-83.
12. Harrison, p. 192.
13. *Ibid.*, p. 192.
14. Coast, p. 75.
15. Braddon, p. 204.
16. Harrison, p. 161.
17. Burton, p. 107.
18. Coast, p. 74.
19. Harrison, p. 160.
20. Audric, p. 119.
21. Gordon, pp. 82-83.
22. Coast, pp. 86-87.
23. *Ibid.*, pp. 93-94.
24. Audric, p. 119.
25. Coast, p. 95.
26. *Ibid.*, p. 96.
27. Braddon, p. 194.
28. Audric, p. 119.
29. Coast, p. 98.
30. Braddon, p. 194.
31. Coast, p. 99.

32. Braddon, pp. 194-196.
33. *Ibid.*, pp. 197-198.
34. Coast, p. 103.
35. Braddon, pp. 198-200, 203.
36. Coast, p. 105.
37. *Ibid.*, pp. 106-107.
38. *Ibid.*, pp. 108, 110-111.
39. *Ibid.*, pp. 113-118.
40. Sellwood, p. 93.
41. Audric, p. 120.
42. Varley, p. 26.
43. Audric, p. 120.
44. Coast, pp. 145-146.
45. Braddon, pp. 223-224.

CHAPTER XI

1. Fisher, pp. 88-89.
2. *Ibid.*, p. 89.
3. Burton, p. 100.
4. Coast, p. 98.
5. *Ibid.*, p. 112.
6. Harrison, p. 169.
7. Coast, p. 112.
8. Gordon, p. 76.
9. Braddon, p. 202.
10. Coast, p. 94.
11. Brereton.
12. Coast, p. 94.
13. Peacock, pp. 130-131.
14. *Ibid.*, p. 283.
15. Peters, pp. 96-99.
16. Coast, p. 136.
17. *Ibid.*, pp. 150-151.
18. Braddon, p. 266.
19. Gordon, p. 179.
20. *Ibid.*, p. 181.
21. Coast, p. 245.
22. Gordon, pp. 198-199.
23. Harrison, p. 195.
24. Audric, p. 115.
25. Braddon, pp. 216-217.
26. Harrison, p. 196.
27. *Ibid.*, pp. 136-137.
28. Coast, p. 107.
29. *Ibid.*, pp. 202-203.

30. *Ibid.*, p. 90.
31. Peacock, pp. 104-105, 274.
32. *Ibid.*, p. 282.
33. Crawford, p. 80.
34. Peacock, p. 285.
35. Coast, pp. 118-119.
36. Braddon, pp. 215, 207.
37. Coast, pp. 83-84.
38. Harrison, p. 170.
39. Crawford, pp. 64, 79.
40. Coast, pp. 119-120.
41. Crawford, pp. 179-184.
42. Harrison, p. 180.
43. Peacock, Ch. 20, *passim*.
44. Harrison, p. 134.
45. Varley, pp. 32-33.
46. Peters, pp. 96-99.
47. Audric, p. 118.
48. *Ibid.*, p. 115.
49. Peacock, pp. 172, 61.
50. Gordon, pp. 62, 81.
51. Braddon, p. 264.
52. Harrison, pp. 109, 143, 162.
53. Braddon, p. 206.
54. Harrison, p. 155.
55. Peacock, p. 72.
56. Harrison, p. 279.
57. Shigemitsu, pp. 343-349.
58. Peacock, pp. 134-135.
59. Burton, p. 77.

CHAPTER XII

1. Harrison, p. 143.
2. Van der Post (SS), p. 10.
3. Peacock, p. 30.
4. Harrison, pp. 152-153.
5. *Ibid.*, p. 110.
6. Peacock, p. 76.
7. Burton, p. 96.
8. Van der Post, p. 19.
9. Peacock, p. 139.
10. *Ibid.*, p. 169.
11. *Ibid.*, p. 179.
12. *Ibid.*, p. 199.
13. Coast, p. 225.

14. Harrison, pp. 135, 139.
15. Coast, pp. 181-182.
16. Harrison, p. 202.
17. Peacock, p. 246.
18. Gilchrist, pp. 225-226.
19. Peacock, p. 185.
20. Coast, p. 140.
21. *Ibid.*, p. 158.
22. *Ibid.*, p. 136.
23. *Ibid.*, p. 225.
24. Churchill, III, p. 480.
25. Peacock, p. 190.
26. Braddon, pp. 242-243.
27. Gardner, p. 163.
28. *Ibid.*, pp. 190-191.
29. *Ibid.*, pp. 188-189.

CHAPTER XIII

1. Coast, p. 123.
2. Peacock, p. 58.
3. *Ibid.*, p. 136.
4. Coast, pp. 152-153.
5. Burton, pp. 111-112.
6. Brereton.
7. Lord, p. 7.
8. Peters, pp. 96-99.
9. Burton, p. 125.
10. Braddon, p. 190.
11. *Ibid.*, p. 175.
12. Gordon, p. 199; Coast, p. 124.
13. Gordon, p. 129.
14. *Ibid.*, pp. 146-149.
15. *Ibid.*, p. 199.
16. Coast, pp. 124-125.
17. Peacock, p. 223.
18. Searle, p. 40 (Drawings).
19. Gordon, p. 155.
20. Coast, pp. 183, 178.
21. Gordon, p. 161.
22. Coast, p. 137.
23. Braddon, pp. 239-240.
24. Peacock, p. 213.
25. Coast, Ch. 22, *passim*.
26. Peacock, p. 224.

27. Mrs D. Shimeild.
28. Peacock, p. 215.
29. Gordon, p. 216.
30. Peacock, p. 252.
31. Coast, p. 163.
32. *Ibid.*, pp. 167-168.
33. *Ibid.*, pp. 169-171.
34. *Ibid.*, p. 199.
35. Peacock, p. 219.
36. Coast, p. 203.
37. Peacock, p. 229.
38. Coast, p. 209.
39. Peacock, p. 239.
40. Coast, p. 213.
41. Peacock, p. 240.
42. Coast, p. 214.
43. Gordon, p. 189.
44. Harrison, p. 207.
45. Peters, pp. 96-99.
46. James, pp. 260, 263, 265-266.
47. *Ibid.*, p. 301.
48. Burton, p. 140.
49. Russell-Roberts, pp. 208-209.
50. Braddon, p. 248.
51. Burton, p. 144.
52. *Ibid.*, pp. 146-147.
53. Braddon, pp. 249-250.
54. Burton, p. 149.
55. *Ibid.*, p. 157.
56. Braddon, pp. 244-247.
57. Burton, p. 164.
58. *Ibid.*, pp. 163-164; Braddon, p. 247.
59. Coast, pp. 221-222.
60. Russell-Roberts, p. 210.
61. Burton, p. 157.
62. Russell-Roberts, p. 178.
63. Braddon, pp. 252-255, 271.
64. Burton, p. 161.
65. *Ibid.*, p. 158; Braddon, p. 280.

CHAPTER XIV

1. Harrison, pp. 251-255, 258, 266-267.
2. Gordon, pp. 222-225, 227.
3. Mrs H. Yexley.
4. Gordon, p. 128.
5. Coast, pp. 228-229, 231, 235-236, 237-238, 240, 247.
6. Peacock, pp. 249-262, 265-269.
7. Burton, p. 177.
8. Braddon, p. 282.
9. Winton, p. 22.
10. Peacock, p. 271.
11. Braddon, p. 282.
12. Peacock, pp. 271-272.
13. *Ibid.*, pp. 285, 288.
14. Coast, p. 247.
15. Burton, p. 180.
16. Braddon, pp. 283, 286.
17. Audric, pp. 112-114.
18. Burton, p. 180.
19. Peacock, Preface.
20. Audric, pp. 113-114.
21. Mackenzie, pp. 240-241.
22. Harrison, p. 280.
23. Peacock, p. 281.
24. Braddon, p. 283.
25. Peters, p. 99.
26. Winton, p. 197.
27. *Ibid.*, p. 212.
28. *Ibid.*, pp. 370-372.
29. *Ibid.*, pp. 372-373.
30. *Ibid.*, pp. 375-376.
31. *Ibid.*, pp. 374, 377, 379.
32. Peacock, p. 275.
33. Winton, p. 357.
34. *Ibid.*, pp. 357, 367.
35. Peacock, p. 275.
36. Catton, p. 455.

Sources

ANDERSON, PATRICK: "Singapore," from *Places* (New York 1957), also conversations.

ARKUSH, DAVID: conversations.

AUDRIC, JOHN: *Siam: Kingdom of the Saffron Robe* (London 1969, New York 1970)

BARBER, NOEL: *Sinister Twilight* (London and New York 1968, London [P] 1970)

BARCLAY, C. N.: *On Their Shoulders: British Generalship in the Lean Years 1939-1942* (London 1964)

BATESON, CHARLES: *The War with Japan* (Sydney 1968)

BLACKWATER, C. F.: *Gods Without Reason* (London 1948)

BOULLE, PIERRE: *The Bridge on the River Kwai* (London and New York 1954)

————: *The Source of the River Kwai* (London 1957)

BRADDON, RUSSELL: *The Naked Island* (London 1952, [P] 1968)

BRERETON, C. J.: conversations.

BURTON, REGINALD: *The Road to Three Pagodas* (London 1963)

CAREW, TIM: *The History of the Royal Norfolk Regiment* (London 1967)

CHURCHILL, WINSTON S.: *The History of the Second World War:* Volume II, *Their Finest Hour,* Volume III, *The Grand Alliance,* Volume IV, *The Hinge of Fate* (London and New York 1951)

COAST, JOHN: *Railroad of Death* (London 1946)

COLLIER, BASIL: *The War in the Far East* (London and New York 1969)

CONNELL, JOHN: *Wavell: Supreme Commander* (London 1969)

CRAIG, WILLIAM: *The Fall of Japan* (New York 1967, London 1968, [P] 1970)

CRAWFORD, HEW T. M.: *The Long Green Tunnel* (London 1967)

DE GUINGAND, FRANCIS: *Generals at War* (London 1964)

FISHER, CHARLES A.: "The Thailand-Burma Railway" (article in *Economic Geography,* 1947)

FITZGERALD, C. P.: *A Concise History of East Asia* (London and New York 1966)

* Wherever a paperback edition is mentioned this is the edition that the author has referred to.

GILCHRIST, ANDREW: *Bangkok Top Secret* (London 1970)

GORDON, ERNEST: *Miracle on the River Kwai* (London 1963, [P] 1970)

Guardian: files of *Manchester Guardian*, 1941-1942.

HARRISON, KENNETH: *The Brave Japanese* (Adelaide 1967)

HORROCKS, SIR BRIAN: Foreword to Carew's *History* (see above).

HOUGH, RICHARD: *The Fleet That Had to Die* (London and New York 1958) (reference in the Notes "Hough FHD")

————: *The Hunting of Force Z* (London 1963, [P]. 1970) (reference in the notes "Hough Z")

JAMES, DAVID H.: *The Rise and Fall of the Japanese Empire* (London 1951)

JONES, F. C.: *Japan's New Order in East Asia* (London 1954)

KIRBY, S. WOODBURN: *The War Against Japan:* Volume I (London 1957, New York 1961)

LEASOR, JAMES: *Singapore: The Battle That Changed the World* (London 1968)

LONG, GAVIN: Foreword to Bateson's *War with Japan* (see above).

LORD, WALTER: *Incredible Victory: the Battle of Midway* (New York 1968)

MC CORMAC, CHARLES: *You'll Die in Singapore* (London 1956)

MACKENZIE, COMPTON: *Eastern Epic:* Volume I, *Defence* (London 1951)

MORISON, S. E.: *History of United States Naval Operations in World War Two*, Volume III: *The Rising Sun in the Pacific* (Boston 1952)

MORRISON, IAN: *Malayan Postcript* (London 1942)

PARKINSON, ROGER: *The Origins of World War Two* (London and New York 1970)

PEACOCK, BASIL: *Prisoners on the Kwai* (London 1966)

————: *Peacock's Tales* (London 1970)

PERCIVAL, ALICIA C.: conversations.

PETERS, G. W. N.: *The Bedfordshire and Hertfordshire Regiment* (London and New York 1970)

POTTER, JOHN DEANE: *A Soldier Must Hang* (London 1963)

RIVETT, ROHAN D.: *Behind Bamboo* (London 1946)

ROSKILL, S. W.: *The War at Sea*, Volume I (London 1956)

ROSS, J. M. S.: *The Royal New Zealand Air Force* (Wellington 1955)

RUSSELL-ROBERTS, DENIS: *Spotlight on Singapore* (London 1965)

SEARLE, RONALD: *Forty Drawings* (Cambridge 1946)

SELLWOOD, A. V.: *The Saturday Night Soldiers* (London 1966)

SHIGEMITSU, MAMORU: *Japan and Her Destiny* (London 1958)

SPENCER CHAPMAN, F. N.: *The Jungle Is Neutral* (London 1949)

SUTHERLAND, DOUGLAS: *The Argyll and Sutherland Highlanders* (London and New York 1969)

SWINSON, ARTHUR: *Defeat in Malaya* (London and New York 1970)

THOMAS, DAVID: *The Battle of the Java Sea* (London 1968, New York 1969, [P] 1971)

The Times: files 1941-1942.

TSUJI, MASANOBU: *Singapore: The Japanese Version* (London 1962)

VAN DER POST, LAURENS: *The Seed and the Sower* (London and New York 1963) (reference in the Notes "Van der Post SS")

————: *The Night of the Full Moon* (London 1970)

WINTON, JOHN: *The Forgotten Fleet* (London 1969, New York 1970)

Other Works Not Directly on the Subject but Referred to:

CATTON, BRUCE: *Never Call Retreat* (London and New York 1967)

COWARD, NÖEL: *Present Indicative* (London 1940)

GARDNER, BRIAN: *The Terrible Rain: the War Poets 1939-1945* (London 1966)

MASTERS, JOHN: *The Road Past Mandalay* (London and New York 1961)

PERELMAN, S. J.: *The Most of S. J. Perelman* (New York 1958, London 1959)

TUCHMAN, BARBARA W.: *The Zimmermann Telegram* (New York 1958, London [P] 1967)

VARLEY, H. PAUL and MORRIS, IVAN and NOBUKO: *The Samurai* (London 1970, New York 1971)

Index